Sex and

Sex and Politics

The Family and Morality in the Thatcher Years

Martin Durham

MACMILLAN

First published 1991

Published by
MACMILLAN EDUCATION LTD
Houndmills, Basingstoke, Hampshire RG21 2XS
and London
Companies and representatives
throughout the world

Edited and typeset by Povey/Edmondson
Okehampton and Rochdale, England

Printed in Hong Kong

British Library Cataloguing in Publication Data
Durham, Martin
Sex and Politics: the family and morality in the Thatcher years
1. Great Britain. Government. Policies. Influence of pressure
groups.
I. Title
328.41078
ISBN 0–333–49848–8 (hardcover)
ISBN 0–333–49849–6 (paperback)

For my parents

Contents

Acknowledgements

This book has long been in germination, during which many people have helped me in my research. Firstly, I would like to acknowledge the help of the campaigning organisations who kindly provided me with material or allowed me to attend their events. My thanks to the National Viewers' and Listeners' Association (especially John Beyer), Family and Youth Concern, LIFE, SPUC (especially Anni Batten), CARE, the Conservative Family Campaign, the Community Standards Association, the Order of Christian Unity, the National Council for Christian Standards in Society, the Labour Life Group, the Human Life Council, Rescue, the Association of Lawyers for the Defence of the Unborn, Feminists Against Eugenics, the National Campaign for the Family, the Bristol Family Life Association, Prolifers for Peace, the British Housewives' League and the Christian Affirmation Campaign. I am especially grateful to Graham Webster-Gardiner, Valerie Riches, Phyllis Bowman and Keith Davies for granting me interviews and to Jim Kennedy, John Carmody, Jim Gallagher, J. Alan Smith, Rita Lomax, Paul Lennon, Molly Overs and James Hayes for discussing their work with me. My thanks also to my editors, Dilys Jones, Steven Kennedy, Keith Povey and Victoria Yogman.

I am also indebted to Diane Munday, the Haringey Lesbian and Gay Unit, William McIlroy, the Family Planning Association, Colin Francome, and Sunetra Puri and Jesus Amadeo of the International Planned Parenthood Federation, all of whom were generous in response to my request for access to research materials, to Sean Gabb, for answering my questions on Conservatives Against Sex Censorship and to Harry Phibbs for allowing me to attend a meeting of the Federation of Conservative Students. I am similarly grateful to the British Newspaper Library, Hornsey Public Library, Warwick University Library, Birmingham Central Library, University of Birmingham Library and Wolverhampton Polytechnic Library.

Numerous people have helped me over the years, by unearthing material, by offering encouragement and even, in one case, by the gift of a beautifully-written schedule for completing the book when finishing seemed impossible. I cannot record all my debts but my grateful thanks to Cornelia Usborne, Lucy Bland, Andy Bell, Nigel Ashford, David Edgar, Andrew Sanders, Bob Willis, Joan Isaac, Susan Reinhold, Ann Stewart, Steve Gill, Jill Kirby, Wendy Thomas, Jon Bernardes, Jagtinder Sidhu, Wayne Parker, Mark Hanson, Mike Cunningham, Jenny Rice, Frank Sharman, Jeremy Crook, Jim Denham and many others.

Finally, without the support of Wolverhampton Polytechnic, both financially and through its admirable secretarial staff, this book would have had to germinate even longer. To all those who have helped my research over the years, not least the many students who have had to hear me lecture on the subject, I take responsibility for any weaknesses in the study which follows if they share responsibility for any merits.

MARTIN DURHAM

Introduction

This is a book about sex and politics. It is a study of the Thatcher government, the pressure groups concerned with questions of family and morality and the issues they have brought to the fore. The debates which it examines – ranging from abortion to sex education – have received considerable media attention and raise important issues. Yet, while much has been written in the area, there has long been a need for a more substantive account. Material has lain scattered in press reports, parliamentary minutes and the publications of campaigning organisations. Relatively little study has been made of the campaigning bodies while discussions of the Thatcher government often tend to neglect issues of family and morality altogether. The work that follows has both an empirical and an analytical purpose. In part, it is a study of the activities of moral crusading organisations in recent years. In attempting this, one of our main concerns has been to set out, in as accurate and balanced a way as possible, how moral campaigners see the issues and the arguments they make. But it is also intended to challenge previous interpretations of the relationship between Thatcherism, sexual morality and moral crusading organisations.

The latter part of the seventies saw the rise in both Britain and the United States of new forms of conservative politics. The American New Right, which has been the subject of a considerable amount of discussion, was made up of a number of components, of which one of the most important and certainly the most publicised was Jerry Falwell's Moral Majority. Arguing that American society was endangered by abortion, pornography, feminism and homosexuality, the largely born-again Christian forces of the Moral Majority and similar organisations played a prominent role in the coalition that brought Ronald Reagan to power at the beginning of the eighties. Coinciding as this did with the rise of the New Right in

Britain and the electoral victory of Margaret Thatcher in 1979, it was almost inevitable that commentators would see British events through an American lens.

Margaret Thatcher's rhetoric of Victorian values and traditional morality invited the suggestion that Conservatism in Britain too was turning to moral majority politics. The forceful presence of a campaigning lobby against sexual permissiveness, associated above all with Mary Whitehouse, likewise tempted commentators to see these forces, often fervently Christian in character, as a British variant on the politically-aligned 'moral right' of the United States. Finally, the important part that opposition to abortion has played in American conservativism has encouraged an assumption that the 'pro-life' movement is part of the political right. Commentators have taken the anti-abortion movement to be the same as the organisations campaigning for 'family values', have drawn an equals sign between both movements and Thatcherism and, above all, have argued that the Thatcher government and the British New Right is engaged in a campaign to enforce traditional moral values in the family and people's sexual lives. It is the contention of this study that none of these is the case.

The construction of our account has presented a number of problems. It is not focused solely on the Thatcher government or the New Right or the constellation of organisations which cam-paign around moral issues. Instead it is concerned with the relationship between all of them. Difficult choices have had to be made about what to include and what to exclude and none of the terms that could structure these choices is fully satisfactory. While the organisations we are examining have been called moral crusades they are not concerned with all the issues that come under the heading of morality. While the notion of the politics of the family captures much of what follows, there are important areas of family life that are not included. Finally, while much of this work is concerned with sexual relationships, that too needs qualification, as our discussion of opposition to abortion and embryo research will make clear. Our choice in the end has been made in the light of what issues the moral crusades themselves have concentrated on during the Thatcher years.

The opening chapter is intended to set the scene for the discussion that follows and will trace the emergence of the modern moral lobby, the rise of Thatcherism and the developments that each seek to oppose. The subsequent discussion of the key debates during the Thatcher government can best be organised into two categories. The earlier chapters are concerned with issues clustered around the regulation of human reproduction. The first of these looks at the most important of the campaigns, that against abortion. What has the anti-abortion movement achieved in recent years, why has it extended its campaigning to other issues and where does it see its campaign going? In a subsequent chapter we take up the movement's other main concern and the most important new issue to emerge on the moral lobby's agenda, embryo research. Between the two chapters, however, we will look at an issue that had achieved comparable attention earlier in the eighties only to suffer eclipse more recently – the provision of contraception to girls under the age of sixteen and the efforts of Victoria Gillick to insist on parental consent as a precondition.

In the following chapters we will be examining two issues concerned with the representation of sexuality, firstly obscenity, the issue which, along with abortion, takes up the largest portion of moral lobby energies, and then sex education, including the inception of Clause 28, the section of the 1988 Local Government Act forbidding the 'promotion' of homosexuality by local councils. Having discussed these key areas of sexual politics during the Thatcher years, we will then be in a position to examine the argument that the government has been pursuing an agenda to restore a traditionalist sexual order. This will entail some general discussion of the different moments at which the government has expressed concern over the moral state of the country but will also include an examination of the dispute over a crucial touchstone for sexual values – the government's AIDS education campaign. Having examined both the moral campaigns and the government, in the final section of the study we will turn our attention to the way different components of the New Right have responded to the issues and what stance the moral lobby takes towards the Thatcher government and the right.

It is impossible within the confines of a single book to examine all that the moral lobby has said and done since the election of Margaret Thatcher. Each chapter, of necessity, has had to be selective in the ground it covers, and because much of our focus is on Parliament and government, the work of moral campaigners in other areas has had to be given only passing reference.

Furthermore, some issues have received little or even no attention. Campaigners, for instance, are often strongly hostile to euthanasia and were highly active in the successful fight to defeat the government's attempt in 1986 to end the restrictions on Sunday trading. I have chosen not to explore these areas, because this study is particularly concerned with issues of sexual morality. Other questions – single-parent families and divorce – are coming onto the political agenda and, as such, are referred to in the book. But, while moral campaigners do have strong views on these issues, they have not, so far, succeeded in making them campaigning issues of the same intensity and prominence as the topics I have focused on. How the national political debate develops on these two issues will shed a new light on (and, it is hoped, confirm) the arguments put forward in the chapters that follow. But the moral issues on which campaigners have expended the most energies in recent years will make up the greater part of our focus. Through these case-studies, along with the more general discussion later, we can best test and challenge the view that Thatcherism and the British moral lobby are this country's equivalent to America's Moral Majority.

The resignation in late 1990 of Margaret Thatcher and her replacement by former Chancellor of the Exchequer John Major is likely to result in a temporary eclipse of 'pro-family' issues. Having played almost no part in the debates with which we are concerned, Major will not take the party in a moralist direction. But the issues will not go away any more than the moral crusades and the Tory backbenchers that raise them. Conservatism in the nineties will not escape the debates over abortion, single parenthood, sex education and other issues which we discuss in the pages that follow. How it responds will owe not a little to the priorities and policies of the previous government but the distinctive rhetoric of Margaret Thatcher will no longer frame the issues. For some, both supporters and opponents of the party, a myth may well emerge, that the end of the Thatcher government represented the end of a determined campaign to restore traditional moral values. That this is a mythical reading of Thatcherism in power needs to be argued now not only to make sense of the eighties but in order to understand the nineties.

1 The Permissive Society and the Moral Lobby

In article after article in recent years, the family in modern Britain has been described as in crisis. Rising divorce rates, one-parent families, abortion, homosexuality, pornography – all have been cited as indices of a nation facing social collapse. Moral campaigners have called for the restoration of traditional values while prominent politicians, not least Margaret Thatcher, have decried the effects of the permissive society. Issues of family and morality have taken on a high national profile as parliamentarians debate abortion and embryo research and newspaper headlines announce the latest controversy about sex education or what can be shown on television. In subsequent chapters we will be examining the battles over such issues since Margaret Thatcher's election to office. But our account cannot start in 1979. Instead, we must look to an earlier period if we are to trace the roots of the modern moral lobby and the developments which it opposes.

Despite their supposedly private nature, sex and the family have long been part of British politics. The moral crusades we are studying and the issues they raise have a long history and there are important continuities, in particular, between the modern moral lobby and the social purity movement of the late nineteenth century, when campaigners were particularly active, above all around prostitution and the age of consent.[1] The organisations they set up were strongly influenced by Christianity in their concern for sexual morality and the centrality of the family. But campaigners were also concerned at the general direction of society, and saw sexual disorders as symbolic of a crisis in the nation itself. Thus for one campaigner, writing in 1885, immorality had undermined Rome and now threatened to undermine Britain, while, for another

5

campaigner of the period, impurity, in threatening the family, also threatened the disintegration of the State.[2] In their concern for sexual morality, the family and the state of the nation, they anticipated much of what is argued by their modern descendants. But the earlier movement, while it persisted into the twentieth century, and even gained some legislative success, progressively weakened in importance and by the fifties had almost ceased to exist.[3] New issues would emerge and it would take the events of the following decade to create a new movement. For both the moral crusades and the developments they seek to reverse, the crucial decade is the sixties.[4]

The very forces which had eaten away at the roots of the earlier organisations were crucial to the changes later campaigners would oppose. The decline of organised religion, the erosion of those sections of the middle class most identified with what we might call 'Victorian values' and the fall in the size of families, with all that entailed for beliefs about women's role, each contributed to putting into question how sex and the family were seen. Already in the earlier part of the century changing assumptions were to lead to the Church of England adjusting its stance on birth control. Developments after the Second World War would put even greater strain on scriptural precepts, pushing sections of the Churches to give ground in other areas and encouraging the argument that what once had been seen as sin should now be judged in terms of motive and context. The rise of a consumer society and the improvement in living standards inevitably changed both expectations and forms of leisure. Films, books and magazines which emphasised sexual themes became more easily available and what had begun as an expansion of artistic freedom, with the successful court defence in 1960 of D. H. Lawrence's *Lady Chatterley's Lover*, rapidly became overtaken by the rise of a commercial sex industry with its 'soft' and not so soft pornography. Advertising too became increasingly sexualised. And, perhaps above all, there was the ubiquitous television set, bringing into millions of homes argument over religion and 'the new morality', the work of controversial dramatists and satirical attacks on authority figures.

Against this background, an array of pressure groups, ranging from the Divorce Law Reform Union to the Abortion Law Reform Association, found the political situation propitious to their concerns. Both parties after the war had embraced the view that consensus around full employment, state welfare and a mixed economy would secure economic success and popular support and, from the late fifties, major strands of opinion were attracted to the idea that an affluent and more fluid society needed a more liberalised approach to moral issues. On the right, 'Progressive Tories' were often favourable to moral reform while, in the Labour Party, 'revisionists' such as Anthony Crosland and Roy Jenkins espoused the view that a reforming government should deal with the many restrictions that still constrained citizens' lives. In addition, in both groupings, there was an awareness of the electoral necessity of making a 'modernising' electoral appeal to the rising groups of professionals and white-collar workers.

The different reforms that were introduced from the late fifties onwards came about not through government legislation but through measures brought forward by individual Members of Parliament. By achieving a high position in the annual ballot for private members' bills, individual MPs could propose legislation on particular issues which, if parliamentary time did not run out, could become law. The actual voting figures on the different measures varied and MPs found in the reforming camp on one issue could be found among the opponents on another. Nevertheless, the strong presence of 'modernising' liberalism in both parties, overlapping with the views of the reforming pressure groups and currents in the Churches and the media, constituted a formidable force behind calls to change much of the legislation that had overarched cultural and sexual life in the country.

The legislation fell into two periods – the first associated with Conservative Home Secretary R. A. Butler and the second with Labour Home Secretary Roy Jenkins. The earlier, in addition to measures on the death penalty, suicide and gambling, changed the law on obscenity so that material would be judged as a whole and could be defended on the grounds that it contributed to the public good. The first period was also significant for the results of the deliberations of the Wolfenden Committee on Homosexual Offences and Prostitution. In the short term this resulted in legislation in 1959 on prostitution but, more importantly, the committee's view that it was not the role of the law to interfere in people's private lives or enforce morality would be crucial to the shifts that would follow in the second period of reform. This included the ending of theatre censorship, a second Obscenity Act and legislation concerning family planning, divorce and the death penalty. Above all, it involved two measures, the liberalisation of abortion and the decriminalisation of homosexual acts between adults in private.

This liberalisation of values and of law ensured that, whatever else it might be remembered for, the sixties would be irrevocably identified with 'the permissive society'. An elastic term that could stretch to encompass discipline in the classroom or hooliganism on the streets, 'permissiveness' was above all a term charged with the sexuality that the sixties seemed to symbolise. It was true, of course, that the legislation represented only a partial liberalisation – abortion, for instance, was not on demand but by the decision of two doctors; homosexuality was only decriminalised in certain circumstances and remained an offence with a partner under twenty-one or in the armed forces. But to both supporters and opponents, the law was seen as permitting what it had previously forbidden. It was true, as well, that sex outside marriage or abortion or divorce had been far from unknown before 'the swinging sixties' and, to raise a different argument, that sexual freedoms were to prove rather more double-edged for women than for men. But, with all these reservations, the term 'permissiveness' did capture important facets of what, to use another phrase taken up in the same period, was to become known as sexual politics.

For the reforming pressure groups, there had been little resistance. The long tradition within Conservatism of denouncing any inroads on traditional values of family and morality had weakened in the face of post-war developments, and few MPs felt as strongly as Sir Gerald Nabarro, with his vivid attack on the 'depravity in the Labour Party' shown by its support for liberalising legislation and his call for 'a Government of moralists'.[5] The Churches were no longer as central as they had once been and, as we have noted, no longer as sure what was right. The language of previous moral crusades, with their calls for social purity and the defence of chastity, had ceased to have the resonance that they once had. Indeed, in the latter part of the sixties, trends were emerging towards a belief that reforms had not gone far enough. For the newly emerging Women's Liberation Movement, women needed fuller access to abortion and contraception and an end to sexual stereotyping. Notions of homosexual reform were being overtaken by the idea of gay liberation, in which the taken-for-grantedness of heterosexuality and the family came under contention. In a more short-lived development, an underground press became increasingly visible, enthusiastically advocating sexual freedom and using nudity to shock 'straight' society. But there were also stirrings of a very different kind.

Initially these focused on television with the emergence of the Clean-Up TV Campaign. Launched by Mary Whitehouse in 1964, and renamed the National Viewers' and Listeners' Association (VALA) the following year, its attack on the BBC for encouraging 'disbelief, doubt and dirt' became increasingly generalised to other media and to permissiveness as such.[6] An anti-abortion campaign, the Society for the Protection of Unborn Children (SPUC) had also come into existence during the passing of the Abortion Act. While both these organisations were strongly opposed to key developments of the period, it is vital here to draw a distinction. Where VALA campaigns against sexual permissiveness and in defence of the family, for SPUC opposition to the Abortion Act is seen as defence of the unborn, as being 'pro-life'. As we will discuss, there are important overlaps between 'pro-family' and 'pro-life' campaigners, but there are also important differences.

Both VALA and SPUC objected to particular changes but, as with earlier crusades, they were also challenging the fundamental direction of society, seeing the issues which they raised as symptoms of a greater malaise. The reformers had treated the changes they championed as emblems of liberalism and modernity and saw the emergence of organised opposition as the mobilisation of religious bigotry. SPUC, although originating in part from discussions in the Anglican paper, the *Church Times*, drew much of its support from within the Catholic Church. VALA, in its early years, was dogged by claims of links with a controversial Christian grouping, Moral Re-armament (MRA), and received much of its support from among those sections of the middle class whose long decline we referred to earlier.[7] In a situation where Christianity was considerably weaker than a century earlier, both organisations could appear easy to dismiss. But the groups which gave such organisations their core following remained significant and in a society still rooted in Christian values, however attentuated, their concerns could reach more widely than those most committed in religious observance. More importantly, as we will see, 'pro-life' and 'pro-family' organisations were fully capable of arguing in a secular idiom and generalising their appeal beyond their Christian heartland. In different ways, both SPUC and VALA articulated a challenge to the sixties. But for those challenges to make headway, the circumstances that had proved so favourable to the reformers would have to alter drastically. Firstly, the liberal tide would have to be reversed, enthusiasm for the loosening of restrictions would have to give way to concern that permissiveness was having damaging effects upon the family and society. Secondly, where before the reformers had enjoyed the sympathy of government and opposition, politicians would have to be convinced that it was the demands of the moral crusades that needed addressing. By the end of the sixties, it has been suggested, this was coming about. The reformers were no longer in the ascendant and, in the general shift to the right that followed, it was the moral crusades which gained strength.[8] But this account needs revision. Not only have the legislative and social changes of the sixties proved extremely difficult to reverse but the rise of an ideologically combative Conservatism in the seventies did not mean that some corresponding form of sexual politics had come to the fore.

The liberalisation of the sixties had rested on what had seemed to be economic success. Yet what at the beginning of the decade had appeared minor worries about a weakening performance in comparison with foreign competitors had by the end become heated argument about rising inflation, worsening unemployment and an increase in industrial conflict. Both the Conservative government of the early sixties and its Labour successor were seen as unable to deal with the spiralling problems. Against this backdrop of increased polarisation and deepening anxiety, critics of post-war developments would achieve increasing support. But moral crusades were only one strand of protest and voices on other issues too were clamorous.

Already, opinions could be heard that the post-war consensus had been fundamentally misconceived. Such arguments were particularly associated with Wolverhampton Conservative MP Enoch Powell but it was not through his free market economics that he was to achieve national prominence. Instead it was through his series of speeches in 1968 on immigration that a challenge to consensus politics would first be successfully made. Powell himself was neither able to capture leadership of the Conservative Party nor willing to leave it and the massive popular support he received was to run away into the sands. But what he had done was show the power of a populist appeal against the party establishment. He spoke not only to anti-immigrant feeling but to bitterness with politicians and a sense of national decline and loss of direction. Credited in the 1970 General Election with winning key sections of Labour voters over to the Conservative camp, Powell widened out his argument during the campaign to encompass student rebellion, anti-apartheid demonstrators and the unfolding conflict in Northern Ireland as elements of an amorphous 'enemy within'. While Powellism itself was unsuccessful what it did do, in its combination of free market economics, nationalism and warnings of the danger of subversion, was map out much of what in the seventies and subsequently would become a full-blooded and far more successful attack on consensus politics.[9]

Before this could come to fruition, Britain's economy would considerably worsen and both parties fail in office once more.[10] First Edward Heath's Conservative government, committed to restoring the country's economic fortunes and curbing the power of unions, proved unable to do either and succumbed to a crippling miners' strike. Its Labour successor was to prove no more successful. In such circumstances, Conservative policies would undergo drastic change. After the Second World War, the party had felt it electorally vital to move in the direction of expanding the responsibilities of the state. With the apparent collapse of that strategy, Conservatives moved in a very different direction to embrace many of the arguments of what was increasingly being known as the New Right. The economic approach that Powell had championed was now considerably more appealing, its radicalism far less unsettling. Two key figures in Heath's ill-fated Cabinet became the most important converts. Initially Sir Keith Joseph was the more important of the two but it was Margaret Thatcher who, in 1975, would become the new party leader. The two would remain close allies in shifting the party to the right. At the core of this shift was economic policy, but it reached further than that. Concerns about crime, about race, about school discipline, about terrorism in both Northern Ireland and the mainland, all fed into what was to become known as Thatcherism. Disrupting any assumption that the Tory right is necessarily moralistic, Powellism had not taken up the concerns of the moral crusades. But would its successor?

Already during the fraught first half of the decade, moral crusades had become increasingly active. The creation in 1971 of the Nationwide Festival of Light brought many evangelical Christians into the fight against 'moral pollution', while secular arguments were raised by another body formed the same year, the Responsible Society. Other organisations, ranging from the Order of Christian Unity to the locally-based Community Standards Association, also entered the fray.[11] But while 'pro-family' campaigners were increasingly hopeful that that they represented the future, the developments which they opposed continued to unfold. Rather than seeing the sixties as having ended, from their vantage point permissiveness remained powerful as the issues that concerned them proliferated. They criticised sex education, the sexualisation in young people's magazines and the efforts of a number of pressure groups to lower the age of consent. Campaigners were bitterly critical of the Family Planning Association and the Brook Advisory Centres, particularly for providing birth control to young people, and it was this dispute which in 1976 brought together Conservative MP Jill Knight and a number of other parliamentarians to form a Lords and Commons Family and Child Protection Group.[12] There was opposition too to presenting homosexuality in a positive light and treating what moral campaigners saw as perversion as a valid choice of sexual preference. Anti-abortion campaigning also intensified, not only through SPUC, whose membership grew during the decade, but also through other organisations. In 1970, what would become an equally important group, LIFE, was set up while other organisations were established to mobilise 'pro-life' doctors and lawyers.[13]

The Heath government paid little attention to these campaigns, although, partly in response to over a million signatures collected by Whitehouse and other campaigners on a Petition for Public Decency, it did attempt to pass legislation to restrict indecent publications towards the end of its period in office.[14] In October 1974, however, following Labour's return to office, signs of a possible shift in Conservative strategy emerged in a much-publicised speech by Joseph.[15] Not only economic but other issues had to be raised, he argued, including those of family life and cultural values. They were the foundation of the nation but were being undermined by a new establishment which favoured permissiveness and collectivism. Socialists wanted to take responsibility from parents; by breaking down morals it would be easier to subvert society. Britain was facing increasing delinquency, truancy, teenage pregnancies and sexual offences. We should take inspiration, he declared, from 'that admirable woman, Mary Whitehouse'.

Joseph's argument developed into a dark warning of the threat to 'the balance of our population, our human stock' originating in the rising population of children born to young unmarried women in social classes 4 and 5 (the semi-skilled and unskilled working-class). The nation was faced by degeneration, Joseph suggested, and contraception was the lesser evil to these women bearing children. This section of the speech, with its eugenic implications, attracted a great deal of criticism and tended to obscure the significance of his overall argument. The themes he had raised earlier represented a vigorous re-emergence of traditionalist Conservatism and suggested the possibility that the moral crusades might find a valuable ally in the rising group within the Conservative Party. What would be crucial, however, was how strong these themes would be in the challenge to the consensus which Joseph and others were so powerfully formulating.

This increasingly successful attack on the Labour government concentrated on its economic failings and on the power of the unions but also accused it of weakness both towards crime and the Soviet Union. Denounced by the Opposition in Parliament, attacked in the newspaper columns of Paul Johnson, Ronald Butt and others, harried by the Centre for Policy Studies, the National Association for Freedom and other New Right pressure groups, the government came increasingly under pressure. Amidst the overall onslaught, issues of family and morality played their part. This took several forms. Addressing the 1977 Conservative Party conference, Margaret Thatcher declared that 'we are the party of the family' while, during a conference debate on the subject, the shadow social services secretary, Patrick Jenkin, told those present that 'The pressures on young wives to go out to work devalues motherhood itself.' The following year, addressing a National Children's Home Conference, he warned of the pressures that rising divorce, working mothers and other factors were putting on family life.[16] Conservatives were also active around the issue of pornography. In part, this was spearheaded by councillors on the Greater London Council and their concern over the increasing visibility of 'the sex industry' in the streets of Soho.[17] But it also

involved the more emotive issue of child pornography. In 1977, the
Labour government had decided, in response to an approach from
Mary Whitehouse, that there was no need for new legislation to
deal with such material. Margaret Thatcher, however, supported
Whitehouse and a Conservative MP, Cyril Townsend, took up the
matter through a private members' bill. The government, despite
believing that there was little such material in the country and that
it could be dealt with under existing legislation, was nonetheless
unwilling to oppose the Townsend bill and be portrayed as
unconcerned about the issue. Indeed, it gave government time to
the measure in order to get through all its stages and in July 1978
the bill became law.[18] The alliance between Whitehouse and the
Conservatives had forced Labour into giving way and could well
encourage those, both in the party and outside, who hoped that at
last the tide was turning. Indeed, addressing the VALA conference
earlier that year, the Shadow Home Secretary, William Whitelaw,
had declared that the bill and the GLC (Greater London Council)
drive to 'clean up' Soho were 'only the forerunners of a more
comprehensive reaction'.[19]

Yet while issues of family and morality played a part in the
attack on Labour, in the 1979 election campaign which finally
brought Margaret Thatcher to power neither pornography nor
pronouncements on divorce and working mothers were to figure.
Instead, amidst spiralling unemployment and industrial strife, it
was other issues that were to the fore. For Thatcherism, what the
situation demanded was a comprehensive alternative to the post-
war consensus in both its Labour and Conservative forms. At its
core was a commitment to the rolling back of the state's economic
responsibilities, the taming of the unions and the development of
an 'enterprise culture', a focus which shaded into the much more
difficult and long-term objective of reducing state responsibility for
welfare and encouraging its private provision. Thatcherism also
had ambitions of a more global character concerning Britain's role
as a major power. But where the family and sexual morality figured
within its concerns is far more contentious.

Our argument so far has been concerned to emphasise a number
of points. Firstly, that the development of a right opposed to the
post-war consensus did not have either in the late sixties or the
seventies a core concern with sexual politics. Secondly, that, while
the moral crusading organisations which emerged in this period

arose in and benefited from the same circumstances as the New Right, they had their own particular character. Thirdly, that the forces that gained control of the Conservative Party following Heath's failure, while not centrally concerned with issues of family and morality, were certainly aware of them. Not only were they part of the historic Conservative armoury, they were also a possible weapon against a Labour Party identified with permissiveness. As the seventies came to a close, it was by no means certain what the future held for the moral crusades or for the new government. In the chapters which follow we will examine how the relationship between them unfolded and what this tells us about the nature of Thatcherism and of moral protest.

2 The Battle Against Abortion

The Thatcher government was the target of protracted activity by a number of moral crusades. While Mary Whitehouse's National Viewers' and Listeners' Association has concentrated on issues of obscenity, the Responsible Society (subsequently renamed Family and Youth Concern) has been particularly concerned with sex education. Along with the Festival of Light, now CARE (Christian Action, Research and Education), these make up the main forces of the 'pro-family' movement. But of the different moral crusading organisations, the two that we will initially focus on will be the leading forces in the anti-abortion movement, SPUC and LIFE.[1] Of all the issues we discuss in this book, abortion has probably mobilised the largest numbers and certainly elicited the deepest feelings. Why has this been so? What do campaigners against abortion believe and what do they see as their strategy for achieving their goals? In looking at the fortunes of the abortion issue and of the anti-abortion organisations since 1979, we can begin to clarify these questions, and in subsequent chapters we will examine other aspects of the 'pro-life' movement. Firstly, however, we need to explore the way abortion became a political issue and the development of opposition to it in the years before the election of the Thatcher government.[2]

Before the 1967 Abortion Act, modern law on the subject dated from the Offences Against the Person Act, 1861, Section 58 of which made the procuring of a miscarriage a felony. This was subsequently modified by the Infant Life (Preservation) Act, 1929, which exempted those cases where abortion was necessary to save the life of the mother, and by a judicial ruling in 1938 which interpreted the 1929 Act as permitting abortion if the woman's health was at risk. The majority of abortions, however, remained illegal and it was only after a long period of lobbying by the Abortion Law Reform Association (which had been set up in the mid-thirties) that attempts to get a reform bill through Parliament began to be made. The earliest efforts, in the fifties, proved unsuccessful and, while publicity concerning the thalidomide tragedy in the early sixties generated sympathy for the idea of permitting abortion in such circumstances, the bills that followed continued to meet with failure. In 1966, however, the Liberal MP David Steel gained third place in the ballot for private members' bills and decided to introduce a measure on abortion. Allowed extra time by a sympathetic government, the bill finally became law in October 1967 and was put into effect the following year. It allowed a termination on two grounds – firstly, if there was a risk to the woman's life or of injury to her health or that of her existing children greater than the risks from abortion, and secondly, if there was substantial risk that a baby would be seriously handicapped. No specific time-limit was included since the 1929 Act already laid down that it was illegal to abort 'a child capable of being born alive' and this was held to apply to pregnancies over 28 weeks.

During the bill's passage through the Commons, opposition in Parliament and in the country had initially been weakly organised. The Society for the Protection of Unborn Children was not launched until January 1967 and, while it lobbied peers and MPs, wrote letters to the press and collected 530,000 signatures on a petition calling for a Royal Commission on abortion, it was unable to stop the bill becoming law. Consequently it set out upon a more protracted struggle to reverse the increased access to abortion but examination of the ways in which this could be done soon led to disputes within the organisation. For some, SPUC was too willing to compromise to achieve partial gains and there were also differences over whether to put energies into the establishment of provision for pregnant women who might otherwise have an abortion. In 1970, LIFE was set up as a separate organisation.[3]

Within Parliament, a number of MPs remained opposed to the 1967 Act and others were to reach the conclusion that it was being interpreted too loosely and needed amendment. Attempts were made as early as 1969 and 1970 to amend the Act but neither was successful, and the Committee set up by the Heath government in 1971 to investigate how the Act was working, although it proposed some restrictions, was largely favourable to the situation the new

law had brought about. In 1975, a restrictive bill was introduced by
James White, one of a number of Labour MPs critical of the 1967
Act. Having passed its second reading, it was referred to a Select
Committee which MPs who supported the 1967 Act decided to
boycott. The Committee, which received evidence from both SPUC
and LIFE, proposed in 1976 that the time-limit for abortions be
reduced from 28 to 20 weeks. But, unlike the White bill, the Select
Committee did not propose restricting the grounds for abortion.
Following its report, more attempts were made to amend the 1967
Act, notably a bill introduced by Conservative MP William Benyon
in 1977, but the unfavourable balance of forces in the Commons
made serious amendment of the Act elusive.

For both SPUC and LIFE, then, the approach of a General
Election offered real opportunities to change the balance in the
Commons. Both organisations had been canvassing prospective
candidates as early as late 1977 and the following year they
intensified their activities. In April of 1978, SPUC launched a
campaign with the slogan 'Value Your Vote' and announced the
intention to distribute at least a million leaflets by the time of the
General Election. In an advertisement at the beginning of this
campaign, it called for abortion to be made a 'primary' issue in the
election. It would be made clear to politicians, the advertisement
declared, that only those prepared to 'fight evil' would receive the
votes of opponents of abortion.[4] LIFE too was active, calling on its
members to find out the views of all candidates and campaign for
those who were 'pro-life'. Members were encouraged to concentrate on marginal seats and the organisation, wary of infringing the
law on electoral material, advised them how to produce leaflets that
would set out candidates' views without seeming to promote any
particular candidacy.[5] In the election year itself, SPUC published
MPs' voting records on the issue in its paper, *Human Concern*, and
sent them to 15,000 clergymen, and material was also sent out to
branches on how to campaign in the election.[6] LIFE too produced
material for voters and after the Conservative victory it declared
that the results in Dartford and in Gravesend owed much to its
efforts, while SPUC claimed to have influenced results in two other
constituencies.[7]

The granting of extra time by a Labour government had been
crucial for the passing of the 1967 Act and, while a non-party issue,
abortion had been supported more by Labour MPs than by

Conservatives. The influx of new Conservative MPs and the election of a Conservative government in 1979, then, seemed to increase the possibility of amending the 1967 Act. The first place in the private members' ballot that followed the election was won by a Scottish Conservative MP, John Corrie, who announced his intention of introducing a bill to restrict access to abortion. The bill, which reduced the time-limit for abortions to 20 weeks (except in the case of severe handicap), also altered the grounds for abortion to delete the reference to a risk to life or health from a continuing pregnancy being greater than the risk from an abortion. This phrasing, it was argued, had allowed too many abortions; instead the grounds should be changed to a 'grave risk' to life and 'substantial risk of serious injury'. In addition, the bill sought to make it easier for doctors or nurses to refuse to take part in abortion operations and render it impossible for such organisations as the British Pregnancy Advisory Service to both refer for abortions and provide them.[8]

The bill passed its Second Reading by 242 votes to 98. The size of the majority ensured that the Standing Committee set up to consider the bill in detail would have a clear majority of Corrie supporters. They were not, however, in agreement. In part, this concerned what attitude to take to the Health Minister, Dr. Gerard Vaughan, and the Department of Health and Social Security. For Corrie and William Benyon, gaining the Minister's support was important; for Jill Knight, Sir Bernard Braine and others the Department was a bulwark of abortionism. There was also disagreement over which clauses of the bill to prioritise. Corrie and Benyon were most concerned with the time-limit and the grounds for abortion; Braine and others with restricting the clinics and agencies. Connected with both of these areas of dispute was the issue of whether compromise on certain clauses was permissible, exemplified in Benyon's decision to change the wording concerning the grounds for abortion in the first clause of the bill, a decision which led to a split among the anti-abortion MPs on the Standing Committee. A similar disagreement took place over what restrictions would be placed on clinics and agencies.

The contents of the bill were also contentious among campaigners outside Parliament. While Corrie's measure was supported by anti-abortionists, LIFE and another organisation, Women for Life, had both expressed reservations about the detailed proposals.

LIFE had initially urged its supporters to press for amendments to tighten the bill, while Women for Life strongly opposed exemptions in the time-limit in cases of handicap.[9] On consideration, however, LIFE decided to support the bill as potentially 'the biggest step forward so far in the pro-life movement' and its chairman was quoted as saying that, if passed, it would cut the legal abortion rate by two-thirds.[10] But that reservations remained was evident in December 1979 when LIFE declared it supported the bill despite the measure falling 'far short' of LIFE's objectives.[11]

Despite their reservations, anti-abortionists did their utmost to support the bill. In late October a march organised by LIFE brought together some 3,000 people. Some 15,000 attended a subsequent lobby of MPs, organised by SPUC, and the Liberal MP Cyril Smith told a rally afterwards that 'This is our great chance.'[12] But neither lobbying nor letter-writing were to bring the 'pro-life' movement the victory it hoped for. The bill came to its crucial point, the Report Stage, on four Fridays in February and March 1980, during which it became increasingly clear that the whole bill would not pass. In particular, a 20-week time-limit was rejected by many MPs who could accept, however, some reduction from 28 weeks. Corrie himself was willing to accept 22 weeks, but Vaughan and much of the medical profession recommended 24, and an amendment along these lines was passed. With parliamentary time running out and large numbers of amendments still to be discussed, Corrie proposed dropping the questions of the conscience clause and the agencies facilitating or providing abortion. In addition, he offered to accept amendments extending the exceptions to a lower time-limit. But it was too late – on 14 March time ran out with amendments still to discuss and the Report Stage uncompleted. The bill was withdrawn a few days later.

The failure of the Corrie bill did not, however, demobilise the anti-abortion organisations. LIFE responded by urging those angered by the defeat to join its ranks, while SPUC publicised a call by MPs to 'join the fight *now*' for another private members' bill. 'We have learned a great deal' from the failure of the Corrie bill, SPUC stated, and this would help 'the next attempt to change the law'. A future bill, Phyllis Bowman declared, would probably be shorter but opponents of abortion would not 'give up until we get a decent law'.[13]

For a moment the initiative seemed to return to the anti-abortion movement with the decision by David Alton, the Liberal MP for Liverpool, Edge Hill, to introduce a ten-minute bill to lower the time-limit to 24 weeks. But, to his surprise, he was opposed by 'pro-life' groups who argued that since the 1929 Act already protected children 'capable of being born alive' its rigorous implementation would stop more abortions than a 24-week limit. (The reference in the Act to 28 weeks, it was held by campaigners, referred to definitive proof of life. Since children could be born earlier, they argued, they too came under the Act.) This view was put forward by, among others, Phyllis Bowman of SPUC and Dr Peggy Norris of the British section of the World Federation of Doctors who Respect Human Life. It did not, however, convince David Alton, who insisted that the only way forward was separate bills on the time-limit, the grounds for abortion and the clinics. He denounced what he termed as 'madness' on the part of anti-abortion groups but, opposed in Parliament by both defenders and opponents of the 1967 Abortion Act, the bill fell.[14]

Although they were not to know it, this was to be the last serious opportunity for several years for anti-abortionists to raise the issue in Parliament. A further opening seemed to offer itself shortly after when the Court of Appeal ruled that nurses who assisted in chemically induced abortions could be 'acting unlawfully'. This ruling, which arose from a case brought by the Royal College of Nursing, led to speculation that the British Medical Association would support a private members' bill to nullify the judgement and Phyllis Bowman announced plans to resist any attempt to introduce such a bill. On 10 December, however, the House of Lords overturned the Appeal Court decision and ruled that a nurse would not be breaking the law if a doctor in charge had given due instructions.[15]

Another opportunity also offered itself in late 1980. A Conservative MP, Timothy Sainsbury, came first in the ballot for private members' bills and announced he was considering a bill to restrict abortion.[16] The second place in the ballot was also won by another critic of the 1967 Act, the Scottish Nationalist Donald Stewart. By the following month, however, the possibility of a new bill came to nothing, with both MPs deciding on other subjects for their bills. A time-limit bill, Sainsbury had been persuaded, could stand in the way of SPUC's efforts to use the 1929 Act to restrict abortion.[17]

One development which took place in 1981 was interpreted by supporters of the 1967 Act as a victory for their opponents. In March new government regulations came into force, modifying the form doctors had to fill in after carrying out an abortion. While before, the form allowed for non-medical grounds, the new form did not, and critics saw the change as a Conservative attempt to make access to abortion more difficult. But the figures for abortions did not drop and SPUC, rather than supporting the form, criticised it as suffering from 'gross deficiencies'.[18] (Equally symptomatically, LIFE clashed with Dr Vaughan over his rejection of its argument that the 'morning-after' pill and the IUD (intra-uterine device) caused miscarriage after conception and were therefore abortificants, whose prescription would be an offence under the 1861 Act).[19]

The 'pro-life' movement was also disappointed the following year in terms of private members' bills. Surprisingly, John Corrie once again came top of the ballot and SPUC was hopeful that he might take up its bill. It had already been introduced in the Lords by Lord Robertson and sought to change the grounds for abortion to 'substantial' risk to the mother or her children. Corrie, however, shaken by the furious response of opponents of his earlier bill, decided not to take up the issue once more.[20]

As the end of the Thatcher government's first term approached, neither SPUC nor LIFE showed signs of waning determination. Equally importantly, however, there was no serious evidence of the major improvement in its fortunes that the election of a Conservative government had seemed to make possible. SPUC campaigned in the General Election, working in over 250 constituencies and claiming credit for the survival of all but one of those Labour MPs who opposed abortion amidst the general fall of the Labour vote. A number of MPs from different parties, it claimed, recognised that they owed their seats to SPUC's intervention. LIFE too was actively involved, distributing over 80,000 leaflets and playing a 'vigorous' role in 'several constituencies'.[21]

But no more than the first term did the second Thatcher government advance their cause. Instead, fissures opened up between the leading organisations not only over abortion but also, as we discuss in a later chapter, over the issue of embryo research. With regard to abortion, the problems arose over a parliamentary motion urging that the 1929 Infant Life (Preservation) Act be implemented. At the end of 1983 a Parliamentary Pro-life Group was set up and, in the motion shortly afterwards, 'pro-life' MPs called upon the government to circulate all maternity hospitals explaining that the Act made it illegal to abort any child capable of being born alive. Because the Act already gave protection, the motion's signatories held, a bill to lower the time-limit was unnecessary. SPUC too argued along similar lines. LIFE, however, argued that it had already tried to get the 1929 Act implemented and had been unsuccessful. It therefore wrote to the Health Minister, Kenneth Clarke, arguing that the Act should be amended to specify a 20-week limit.[22]

The following year, however, a working party report, produced by the Royal College of Gynaecologists, the British Medical Association and other medical organisations, proposed that the legal limit for abortion be reduced to 24 weeks. Kenneth Clarke announced that a meeting had been convened with the proprietors of those clinics approved to undertake late abortions. SPUC came out against the proposed change. 'We think', Phyllis Bowman declared, 'the minister could make the whole thing much worse... All this minister had to do was circulate hospitals and inform them that abortions carried out on babies older than 22 weeks are in breach of the Infant Life Preservation Act.' The government, rather than either resort to legislation or take up SPUC's suggestion, decided on a code of conduct by which clinics would be stopped from carrying out abortions after 24 weeks. For LIFE, however, the only solution continued to be the amendment of the 1929 Act.[23]

The only changes in abortion provision since 1967 (the 1981 alteration in the notification form and the 1985 lowering of the time-limit for clinics) had come about under the Thatcher government. Neither, however, gave much comfort to the 'pro-life' movement and, as the end of the government's second term and a fresh General Election began to come into sight, SPUC unveiled plans for a new campaign to mark its twentieth anniversary. It intended, it announced, to knock on 'virtually' every door in the country in order to find where voters stood. Parliament had to be made to understand, it declared, that those who opposed a 'pro-life' stance would suffer 'a huge drop in votes'.[24] LIFE, for its part, also issued leaflets for the impending general election urging voters to support candidates who opposed abortion.[25] 'Pro-life' supporters became increasingly active both in and out of Parliament. There was a false alarm when Conservative MP Peter Bruinvels, who had drawn third place in the private members' ballot, told the Catholic paper, the *Universe*, that he was considering a bill to amend the Infant Life Preservation Act to reduce the time limit for abortion from 28 to 24 weeks. In the event, he decided on a different issue.[26] The Bishop of Birmingham, however, did introduce a 24-weeks bill in the Lords. While private clinics had agreed with the government not to carry out abortions after 24 weeks, NHS (National Health Service) hospitals still carried out a few. (A total of 33 such abortions were performed in 1985.) More crucially, doctors, in order to avoid prosecution, would be likely, if the bill became law, to refrain from carrying out abortions after the twentieth week and this would stop a significant number of abortions. The bill therefore was strongly opposed by supporters of the 1967 Act. But despite receiving support from the government (which did, however, indicate it favoured some amendment of the measure) the Bishop was forced to accept that it would almost certainly not get through the Committee stage. It was therefore referred to a Select Committee and thus forfeited its chance to succeed in the parliamentary session.[27] While the bill had been supported by LIFE, this had not been true for SPUC (a difference which reflected the ongoing dispute about the 1929 Act and the 'pro-life' movement's tactics). The government, according to SPUC, was merely offering a 'sop to win the Christian vote' by supporting the Bishop's bill. Instead, John Smeaton declared, it should enforce the 1929 Act and stop the destruction of foetuses able to survive.[28]

All of this, however, was overshadowed by the publicity generated over the decision of an Oxford male student to go to court to attempt to stop his former lover from going through with an abortion. Arguing that the foetus had the right to mount a legal action through the father, he held that the 1929 Act forbade abortion of a foetus capable of being born alive. The High Court rejected both arguments and when the latter argument was taken to the Appeal Court and then to the Law Lords, it was rejected again. This sequence of unfavourable decisions was a blow to the anti-abortion cause. In response to this development, the parliamentary pro-life group declared its intention to introduce a bill to reduce the time-limit to 22 weeks while Peter Bruinvels announced plans for a bill to lower the time-limit and also allow the father to have the right to veto an abortion. For its part, SPUC decided to campaign for a parliamentary bill 'to enable an unborn child to be made a ward of court'.[29] In the weeks that followed, both SPUC and LIFE continued to press the government to enforce a lower time-limit.[30] In April 1987, Bruinvels's bill received its first reading in the Commons but was not supported by SPUC or LIFE. 'Pro-lifers' were more sympathetic, however, to another initiative in the shape of Conservative MP John Watts's decision to table a private members motion calling on the government to restrict abortion.[31]

LIFE meanwhile circulated a questionnaire to prospective parliamentary candidates on their views on abortion, embryo research and other issues. The protection of 'unborn children', Keith Davies told supporters, should 'become a major issue during this General Election' and people should attend hustings to raise the issues. SPUC too stepped up its General Election activity, encouraging its supporters to 'question candidates in detail about abortion and human embryo experimentation – not to ask their views, since politicians are experts in disguising them, but rather to ascertain their voting intentions'. As regards sitting MPs, SPUC added, 'we do not want to know their views' but would examine their voting records.[32] SPUC ran campaigns in over 300 constituencies, it later reported, and in many of these 'pro-life champions' from 'all the major parties won the day often against all the odds'.[33]

In early July, asked by Conservative MP David Amess to comment on the need to stop late abortions, the Prime Minister stated that the government had done all it could in circulating the College of Gynaecologists' report to all hospitals and making a 24-week limit a condition for the licensing of private clinics. But while government legislation was not possible, she added, private members legislation would be 'appropriate'.[34] Shortly after, Conservative MP Nicholas Winterton drew twentieth place in the private members' ballot and decided to introduce a bill forbidding financial links between abortion referral agencies and abortion clinics.[35] A more important development, however, lay in reports that Liberal MP David Alton, who held third place in the ballot, was considering introducing a bill to reduce the time-limit. Initially reported as a 20-week bill, it turned out to favour 18 weeks and was announced by Alton in late September. A third bill also appeared from Edward Leigh, sixteenth in the ballot. But, at third place, it was the Alton bill that was crucial.[36]

Many MPs were either wholly opposed to the bill or favoured a higher time-limit and exceptions for handicap. Faced with this problem, SPUC and much of the Parliamentary Pro-Life Group had long held that a weeks bill was not the way forward and that instead a tightening of the grounds for abortion was what was needed. SPUC activists had raised this with Alton when he announced his decision while speaking to their conference and, while publicly the movement appeared united behind Alton, internally significant sections had grave doubts about what an attempt to cut the time-limit might end up with. The Prime Minister, reportedly, favoured 24 weeks, although one account claimed that Alton supporters believed she would 'go as far as 22 weeks'. Alton, it was said, would compromise if necessary.[37] But whether he would and in what way remained uncertain. Published at the end of the year, the one-clause bill allowed exceptions where the mother's life was in danger or where the child was likely to be born with disabilities which would prevent it leading an 'independently sustainable' life. Other cases of handicap, Alton declared, were expressly excluded.[38]

An attempt by Winterton in the same month to get his bill through a second reading without debate was unsuccessful. LIFE meanwhile launched its 'Back the Alton Bill – Yes!' (BABY) campaign and urged supporters to write to MPs asking them to vote for the bill at its second reading in January and call on the Prime Minister for extra parliamentary time.[39] As the second reading approached, Alton described his chances of success as '50–50' and stated that he might allow exemptions at the committee stage in the case of handicap. (Indeed, although little noticed at the time, he made it clear that the bill was only part of a more long-term strategy: 'The only way to tackle the abortion issue is through numerous small measures, nibbling away at one area after another. If we fail on the question of disability this time, then that is the thing we tackle next. Then we must look at the private clinics and the grounds for abortion.')[40] As for the Prime Minister herself, one report claimed that she was likely to vote for the bill although, it added, she disagreed with an 18-week limit and would only support the bill on the understanding that Alton would accept a 22- or 24-week amendment later. However, according to another report, Alton had decided that while he would accept an amendment allowing late abortions for handicap he would not also accept a higher time-limit than 18 weeks for other cases.[41]

Shortly before the second reading, one question became clearer when the Prime Minister told the House: 'as the bill is drafted at present, I could not support it'. The bill nonetheless passed, by 296 to 251, a result greeted by its supporters. While CARE, which had been active in its support, called the vote 'a tremendous answer to prayer', LIFE declared that the bill had succeeded despite opposition from the BMA (British Medical Association), the media and 'Mrs Thatcher's disgraceful decision not to support it'. During the debate, Tony Newton, the health minister, had emphasised that the principal tests for handicap could not be carried out until the sixteenth or eighteenth week. Subsequently, Alton supporters were reported to be planning to put forward an amendment allowing abortion if tests had been started before the eighteenth week. (LIFE opposed any such proposal.)[42]

Fearing possible filibuster, 'pro-life' groups attempted to exert pressure on suspected opponents by approaching churches in their constituencies to fast and pray for their representatives. This, however, quickly led to criticism, with the Speaker of the House ruling that it 'amounted to an attempt to bring unacceptable pressure' on MPs. (The following month, it was also criticised by Home Office Minister Douglas Hogg.)[43] At the bill's committee stage, Alton supporters introduced amendments in an attempt to increase their support. An amendment by Sir Bernard Braine was passed, allowing abortion after 18 weeks where a consultant gynaecologist certified the severe nature of disability and Ann Widdecombe put through an amendment permitting late abortion if the woman had been the victim of rape or incest while under 18.[44] But despite appeals, the government declined to give extra time for the bill if it was unable to pass its report stage and a front page story in the *Universe* reported that SPUC feared a government 'plot' to support a 24-week amendment, in which the Minister of Health would speak for the amendment and government Whips encourage support for it.[45]

As the report stage approached, a crucial issue emerged as to the order in which amendments might be taken. For Alton, it should be in the order in which they had been tabled, with 18 weeks coming before 20, 22 and 24. For opponents, it should be in descending order, with 24 weeks coming much earlier. Whichever time first secured a majority, all others would fall. A news report that the Speaker had promised 'pro-life' MPs government time if the bill was blocked by its opponents came to nothing but he did decide the order of amendments in Alton's favour.[46] Nonetheless, on the day, opponents ensured that time ran out before the 18-week amendment could be reached and Alton, refused extra time, declared that 'the will of Parliament' had 'been thwarted by a minority of pro-abortionists aided and abetted by the Government'. He called on supporters to write to the Prime Minister and the Leader of the Commons urging the provision of government time for the bill and made clear his intention to take up the issue once more should this prove unsuccessful.[47]

All was not yet lost and Alton hoped that supporters would move closure motions on the discussion of two private members' bills the following Friday and thus give time for a vote on a 20-week amendment to his bill. Despite hundreds of campaigners singing hymns and praying outside his office, the Leader of the Commons rejected anti-abortionist MPs' appeals to give the issue government time.[48] When the next discussion of private members' bills took place, opponents ensured that only the first measure was discussed but Alton declared he would lay the bill before the House every day and pleaded for extra time. Over a hundred MPs had signed a motion in support of this and he was also reported considering reintroducing his bill by inserting a clause into the government's Health and Medicines Bill. This came to nothing and instead he attempted to amend the government's Criminal Justice Bill.[49] In the event, however, the Speaker ruled that the Alton bill could not become an amendment to another bill since it was still before the House in its original form. The Prime Minister, Alton claimed, had 'become an immovable object who has almost single-handedly prevented Parliament from considering the abortion issue further' and he urged supporters to increase pressure for government time for his bill. But the government did not shift and the bill fell.[50]

Later in the year, however, Phyllis Bowman told the SPUC national conference that at least 50 MPs had promised to enter the Private Members' Ballot in order to take up an anti-abortion bill.[51]

Taking a more absolutist position, LIFE's chairman suggested that, while the Alton bill should be reintroduced, it might be worthwhile considering a one-clause bill simply reading 'The Abortion Act 1967 is hereby repealed'. Although it would fail, he admitted, it would confront Parliament and the country with 'the whole truth' – that abortion was mass killing. (More radical still, another group, the Association of Lawyers for the Defence of the Unborn (ALDU), had argued that 'pro-lifers' should not support the Alton bill at all.)[52]

When the private members' ballot took place, anti-abortionists gained sixth and seventh place. The sixth, Labour MP Lawrence Cunliffe, considered taking up the issue but decided against. Ann Widdecombe, the Conservative in seventh place, decided on a bill similar to Alton's.[53] Although seventh position made success extremely unlikely, Widdecombe surprised opponents by also coming first in a ballot for private members' motions and deciding to use this to propose that her bill be debated 'until any hour', making it impossible to stop its second reading going to a vote. SPUC and LIFE announced that they would be asking supporters to lobby MPs to support this move while the government's business managers, it was reported, were increasingly annoyed at such uses of procedure.[54] In the event, however, opponents of the bill were able to block discussion of the motion by taking up parliamentary time discussing whether a writ should be moved for an impending by-election.[55]

The next month, Widdecombe was one of a large number of MPs who disrupted a speech by Dennis Skinner, the Labour MP who had played the leading role in blocking discussion of her motion. Speaking at SPUC's student conference the following week, she declared that those guilty of 'wrecking our Bills' would find their own causes wrecked. In March her bill finally failed, after only receiving four minutes' discussion following debate on the preceding bill.[56] However, with the government increasingly tired of the amount of parliamentary time being expended on the issue, signs of possible movement on the issue had emerged. The Prime Minister had agreed in reply to a parliamentary question that the law should be amended to stop terminations after 24 weeks and added that she regretted that this had not been the position of the Alton bill. This was followed by news of her reply to a letter from Ann Widdecombe. She would consider carefully, she wrote, whether the government would give time for a free vote on abortion reform, either through a special bill or as an amendment to embryo research legislation. While Widdecombe described this as a 'significant shift' from previous government views, the *Daily Telegraph* suggested that the government hoped for a 24-week amendment to the planned bill on embryo research, a change that would fall far short of 'pro-life' wishes.[57] Attempts to raise the abortion issue through different parliamentary avenues continued. Whether the issue would be dealt with by an amendment to the government's embryo bill or through some other channel remained unclear. SPUC did not support taking both issues in the same bill, concerned both that this would involve 'fighting on two fronts' and that the government would use its own bill to steer MPs towards embryo research and liberal access to abortion. In June the Society held a two-day mass lobby of MPs, calling on the government to support changes in parliamentary procedure to give more time for private members' bills and allow abortion measures to be voted on. The following month, however, plans were announced for the government embryo bill to also include provision for the reduction of the time-limit for abortion. While the government reportedly favoured 24 weeks, 'pro-lifers' favoured 18. Subsequently, Ann Widdecombe was quoted as expecting to achieve at least 20 or 22 weeks. If the vote was fair, she announced, then, 'pro-lifers' would cease to raise the issue for a time. It was such a possibility which led government managers to make the offer, although a closer examination of Widdecombe's view makes clear that anti-abortionists would turn to other aspects of the abortion issue in the meantime.[58] A flurry of reports towards the end of October suggested that the government intended to officially adopt a 24-week stance rather than leave it to a free vote, but this proved to be a false alarm. Nevertheless, it was indicated that ministerial support for 24 weeks would be made clear when it came to debate.[59]

As the vote fast approached, it became evident that there would be a considerable number of amendments to vote on. In addition to deciding between 24 weeks and less, there were other issues, in particular whether to have higher time-limits for serious handicap. 'Pro-life' MPs remained confident of victory, Ann Widdecombe declaring that 'We are sure of a huge Commons majority for 22 weeks and might even get 20 weeks.'[60] But, despite such predictions, it was not to be. MPs rejected 20 weeks by 358 to 189 and 22 weeks by 302 to 255. Not only did 24 weeks pass but so did the removal of any time-limit in cases of foetal abnormality or 'grave permanent injury to the physical or mental health of the pregnant woman'. In addition, MPs voted for the 1929 Act to no longer apply to abortion. It was, according to LIFE , 'kill, kill, kill – above all for the handicapped'. SPUC too described it as an 'appalling and barbaric decision' and while campaigners recognised that they would not be able to raise the issue again in that Parliament they did attempt to gain a fresh vote on the exemptions on the grounds that MPs had not understood what they were doing. As the bill's report stage approached, a number of 'pro-life' amendments were tabled. They proved unsuccessful; and in the aftermath the long-standing tensions between 'pro-lifers' once again came to the surface, with SPUC's political officer, Christopher Whitehouse, arguing that taking up time-limits rather than the grounds for abortion had been a disastrous decision, as had including abortion within a government bill. His criticism of a number of MPs, notably Alton, was in its turn described as 'lamentable' by LIFE's Keith Davis, as the public unity of previous months unravelled under the pressures of defeat.[61]

At the end of over twenty years of campaigning, restricting abortion still remained out of reach. But the movement would continue in its efforts. Intervention in the General Election to defeat those MPs who supported the liberalisation of abortion law will be particularly important, and both SPUC and LIFE also encourage their activists to join political parties to influence the selection of candidates. While we have focused on the movement's attempts to change the legal situation, much of its work involves, in LIFE's case, the running of pregnancy testing centres in which women unwillingly pregnant are encouraged not to have an abortion. The organisation also has a chain of houses in which such women can stay. Work in this area will continue, regardless of political reverses. So, too, will the work done by both organisations in putting over the 'pro-life' message in schools and, a more recent development, the setting up of organisations for women who have had abortions which they now regret. It is evident from talking to leading 'pro-lifers' that all these areas are seen as crucial for a long-haul strategy of changing the social climate concerning abortion. Its formidable level of activity ensures that, despite the raising of funds from within its ranks, the movement faces the perennial problem of financing. This is unlikely, however, to lead to any downturn in activity. SPUC is fortunate in the support it receives from within the Catholic Church and from other denominations, which not only provides it with facilities such as church newsletters through which to circulate its material but also, through what is called White Flower Day, an opportunity to collect money outside churches each year. LIFE too has substantial religious support and benefits from collections in some churches.[62] Even before its inevitable return to the private members' bill and the parliamentary lobby, the movement will have been active in numerous other ways. But why does it do so? It is only by examining the arguments that underpin these efforts that we can understand why it is so determined.

Anti-abortion arguments can perhaps best be initially understood from the leaflets with which the main groups attempt to win over public opinion. In one such leaflet, 'Abortion. Why You Can't Believe in it', LIFE argues, as it does elsewhere, that human life begins at conception and that from then until birth is an uninterrupted development. Abortion, it continues, discriminates against the unborn just as slavery or apartheid discriminates against black people. A civilised society, it suggests, would protect the weak and vulnerable, not 'kill him'. In one of its leaflets, SPUC likewise insists that 'Every Abortion Destroys A Human Life'. Instead of furthering women's rights, it argues, abortion presents 'the easy way out for the "male chauvinist" and for society'. Furthermore, it claims, the availability of abortion has led on to the euthanasia of handicapped children and is connected with a rise in the number of battered children and abandoned babies.[63]

Such arguments are developed at greater lengths in the pamphlets and books sold by 'pro-life' organisations and in the speeches at their public meetings. A particularly useful source here is the speeches given at SPUC's June 1983 Hyde Park rally, subsequently published in an edited form in the United States as *Who is for Life?*[64] One contributor, Alison Davis, a SPUC activist with spina bifida, argues against the provision of abortion on grounds of handicap and declares that everyone has the right to life. An evangelical cleric, John Stott, argues that the Bible sees the foetus as a human being and so do the findings of modern science. As a consequence, he continues, abortion must be recognised as 'feticide: the destruction of an unborn child. It is the shedding of innocent blood, and any society that can tolerate this, let alone legislate for it, has ceased to be civilized'. Other speakers addressed the rally along similar lines, the fullest argument coming from the prominent American evangelical, Francis Schaeffer. In his account, abortion is a 'symptom of a generally lowered view of human life', leading inevitably to infanticide and euthanasia: 'If human life can be taken before birth, there is no logical reason why human life cannot be taken after birth.' Through sonar studies, he continued, the baby can be seen in the womb; through test-tube fertilisation we can see it is not part of the mother but an independent being. Yet society carries out abortion and infanticide for convenience and is considering experimentation on human foetuses and euthanasia. Opposition to abortion was in the interests of even those who did not see it was wrong, for in a future in which the old would outnumber the young, the devaluation of life that had followed the acceptance of abortion would lead to the old being seen as a burden to be discarded. Western culture, he concluded, rested on the Judeo-Christian world-view that God created people with unique and intrinsic worth. But the relativism prevalent today lowered the esteem in which life was held. These values not only attacked life but were 'an attempted attack upon the existence of God'.

The arguments raised at the 1983 rally represented central beliefs of the 'pro-life' movement. There are a number of other arguments that I want to consider later, in particular anti-abortionists' concerns over population control and the assumptions current in the movement about sex, the family and the role of women. But the two arguments which constantly recur in the movement's views are the humanity of the foetus and the knock-on effect that legal abortion is believed to have on other areas of human life.

As exemplified in the very names of the leading organisations – LIFE and the Society for the Protection of *Unborn* Children (emphasis added) – the 'pro-life' movement sees the foetus not as part of a woman's body but as human life, an unborn baby. Although this can be argued in a religious framework this need not be so. Indeed in their publicity material 'pro-lifers' put great emphasis on medical science, arguing that it has established the soundness of their views. As we have seen, Schaeffer argues that ultrasound and test-tube fertilisation supports the view that the foetus is distinct from the mother. In late 1984, a controversial

American film using ultrasound, *The Silent Scream*, was premiered at SPUC's annual conference. It was then shown to MPs at the House of Commons before being released nationally. As its title indicates, much of the power of the film was in the emotive presentation of a foetus as opening 'her mouth in a scream' in a vain attempt 'to escape from the abortionists' instruments'.[65] Another vital element of the film was that it suggested that the most modern developments in science accorded with the anti-abortion view. For SPUC's general secretary, John Smeaton, speaking at a meeting reported in an evangelical paper, the argument was moving to the 'pro-life' side because of the findings of ultrasound, genetics and embryology. 'Pro-abortionists', he suggested, 'have been left floundering whilst science has shown that unborn children are complete members of the human race from the moment of fertilisation.'[66]

The 'pro-life' movement believes it is defending the weakest and most vulnerable and feels a sense of affinity for earlier movements against discrimination. Present in British literature and particularly in American material from which British 'pro-lifers' have often borrowed is an equation of 'pro-life' with anti-slavery, a vision of anti-abortionists as the twentieth-century equivalent of the abolitionists. John Powell is an American writer who has toured Britain as a SPUC speaker. In his *Abortion: the Silent Holocaust* he argues that, just as the American Supreme Court once ruled a slave was not a person, so in 1973 it denied the humanity of the unborn; just as the anti-slavery movement was right and eventually was victorious, so too with the 'pro-life' movement.[67] We find the same argument in the LIFE leaflet cited earlier. This identification of fighting against abortion with earlier movements is stated more sharply still in the equation of abortion of the 'unborn' with the destruction of the Jews. In the United States again, this argument is frequently used (as, for instance, in the title of John Powell's book). While in Britain the rhetoric of the movement has usually been less inflamed, the equation of the Holocaust victims and the 'unborn child' is to be found, for instance, in the leading activist Dr Margaret White's allusion at the 1983 SPUC rally to the work of the 'abortion chambers', just as in 1980 a Scottish organiser for the Society compared abortion to the scenes in the television film *Holocaust*.[68] Indeed, it may well be becoming a central theme in some sections of the movement – certainly three of the speakers at a recent LIFE rally drew on such imagery. According to one, a Labour councillor, abortionists were blood-brothers of the murderers of Treblinka; just as 'Work Makes You Free' had been the slogan of concentration camps, so 'Abortion Makes You Free', he claimed, should stand outside 'nursing homes'.[69]

The intensity of this language is crucially linked to recent developments with the rise of a direct action wing of the movement. LIFE and SPUC, as we have noted, are the dominant organisations of the 'pro-life' movement. LIFE is critical of SPUC's greater moderation, and in turn a smaller organisation has emerged more militant than both. The Human Life Council is affiliated to the American-based Human Life International, and takes a strong line in arguing for 'natural' contraception as against 'artificial' methods and, more importantly, advocates the tactics current in the American 'pro-life' movement, of demonstrating outside abortion clinics and attempting to stop women from entering.[70] For some time the Council remained the main proponent of such methods for the British 'pro-life' movement.[71] In the United States, however, such activity began to gain national publicity and a direct action organisation, Operation Rescue, achieved national prominence. In 1988, the Human Life Council announced that a Scottish activist, Jim Gallagher, had launched a new organisation, Rescue. The new organisation picketed outside hospitals and clinics, its literature arguing that Christians must disobey civil authority in order to 'end the holocaust' and that only by direct action would politicians be forced to enact legislation to stop abortion.[72] The *Mail on Sunday* reported that both SPUC and LIFE had disassociated themselves from Rescue's action, but a subsequent report in the *Catholic Herald* quoted a SPUC spokesman as saying 'We're not taking a stand against what these protesters are doing.' A later article in an evangelical magazine, however, quoted a SPUC spokesman arguing for a continuing focus on Parliament. Rescue, he suggested, was 'counter-productive' and, by diverting activists' energies, 'could endanger the long-term impact of the pro-life movement'. In interviews, Phyllis Bowman of SPUC emphasised that the organisation disagreed with Rescue, looking instead to 'the political fight', while LIFE's Keith Davies said that LIFE took no official stance but did make clear to its members that any pickets or vigils that they were involved in should remain within the law. But that there was at

least some sympathy for Rescue's methods among mainstream
anti-abortionists was evident from a LIFE rally in Manchester,
where Dr Peggy Norris spoke of her support for such activities
while Pauline Connor of the 'pro-life' Feminists Against Eugenics
urged those attending not to condemn direct action.[73] More
recently, the situation has escalated with the arrival in the country
of a number of American and Canadian activists and increasing
picketing and arrests. Nor has direct action been restricted to
picketing or blocking access to clinics. In one recent case activists
entered a clinic in order to damage equipment – 'sabotaging the
weapons', as one Rescuer described it.[74]

The 'pro-life' movement does not simply hold that abortion is
the destruction of human life and in all, or almost all, cases a
wrong act which should be against the law. It also argues that
liberal access to abortion has repercussions on society. 'Pro-life'
writers have put forward a generally negative picture of the
evolution of the West in recent years, often articulated as a
perception of medicine and science in general taking a dehumanis-
ing and alienating direction. Such views are to be found in the
campaign against under-sixteen contraception and, more particularly, in the opposition to embryo research, both of which we
discuss later. But its pertinence to the anti-abortion campaign is
also clear, as exemplified, for instance, in John Powell's book,
where he quotes from an article on morality and recent developments in biology. Advances in science, the article suggests, have led
to us seeing nature as something to be exploited and manipulated
and are eroding our idea of man.[75] This distrust of medicine or
science or both is equally evident when anti-abortionists take up
other bioethical issues. 'Pro-life' groups have been vehement over
what they have called 'the starvation to death' of handicapped
children in hospitals, and in 1981 SPUC's Chairman, the Rev. Alan
Rabjohns, reported on its demonstration outside the British
Medical Association conference to 'let the BMA know what it
thought of doctors'. Medical attitudes, he declared, had become
'more and more Hitlerian'.[76]

This fear of the medical establishment and of the implications of
scientific 'progress' is articulated particularly strongly in 'pro-life'
hostility to population control. For an organisation with strong
support among Conservative MPs, this antagonism is often
presented in surprisingly radical language, the most marked

expression of which occurred in 1979 when SPUC's paper, *Human Concern*, reprinted an article from what it called a 'first-class' publication by a left-wing organisation, the Canadian Movement of Labour. Unlike much of the left, SPUC noted in its introduction, the Movement of Labour opposed 'the new totalitarians' behind population control. In the article, the Canadian group argued that the function of population control was to divide the working class and distract its attention from the real cause of their problems. The root of these problems was not population but capitalism, the article went on, and it proceeded to explain the classical Marxist rebuttal of Malthus and to attack modern over-population theories as racist. Accusing international population control bodies of 'ruling class' connections and genocidal policies, the Movement of Labour concluded that only a 'fighting pro-gramme' could resolve workers' problems and that their interests and those of population controllers were 'miles apart'.[77]

SPUC is hardly to be seen as a Marxist organisation but the movement does not have a single language with which to address the issue of abortion nor does opposition to abortion have any necessary political association. The central points of the move-ment's argument – the humanity of the foetus and the 'knock-on' effect of legalising abortion – is advanced by the different sections of the diffuse 'pro-life' movement in a variety of ways. How we can untangle the different elements and reach a more rounded under-standing of the politics of the movement is something to which we will return. It is certainly true that Conservatives are prominent in the 'pro-life' cause and, as we discuss later, it is possible to argue that campaigns for a stricter sexual morality are closer to the political right than they suggest. We also discuss later to what degree either 'pro-family' or 'pro-life' organisations can be seen as *sexually* conservative in their views and assumptions. But to regard the 'pro-life' movement as politically right-wing or as part of an offensive orchestrated or even canalised by Thatcherism is to misunderstand its character. It is a diffuse and diverse movement as able to talk in left-wing (or feminist) intonations as it is to appeal to Conservatives or traditionalists. Its focus on abortion has brought it into conflict with a government with very different priorities, and its linking of abortion with other questions (population, embryo research, contraception, etc.) have given it a radical rhetoric which indicts civil servants, ministers, family planners and the medical profession. Despite evident resemblances, it is not the same as Thatcherism when it too invokes the people against the establishment. Nor does it yearn for the particular kind of remaking of society that would locate it as a movement of the radical right. Instead, it is a bringing together of people with different political predispositions to pressurise Parliament and government firstly, to reverse, the 1967 Act and, more broadly, to undo a whole series of legislative and administrative changes of recent years which, in its view, have cheapened life and devalued humanity. As such, it was not a part of a Thatcherite offensive but, on the contrary, was an attempt to force Thatcherism to move in a direction it was plainly unwilling to go.

3 Victoria Gillick and Under-Sixteen Contraception

Of the different morality campaigns that the Thatcher government had to face, one of the most important was the campaign against under-sixteen contraception. As we will see, the possibility of legal action against the government guidelines on the matter was being raised as early as 1974. But it was not until the election of the Thatcher government and its decision not to ban contraceptive provision to under-sixteens without parental consent that what had been a series of local campaigns, supplemented by a relatively low level of activity by national moral groups, took on the form of a national movement. It was this movement that brought to prominence Victoria Gillick, the most important moral crusader since the rise of Mary Whitehouse and the Clean-Up TV Campaign of nearly two decades before.

We have suggested earlier that it is misleading to see the tide of sexual reform as running out in the late sixties, and the roots of the Gillick campaign are strong evidence for this caution. The 1967 National Health Service (Family Planning) Act, introduced under the Labour government, had established that local health authorities could provide birth control advice or supplies but it was not until the Heath government's 1973 National Health Service (Reorganisation) Act that this became a mandatory part of health provision. During the Standing Committee discussion of the latter bill, Conservative MP Jill Knight had put forward an amendment to ensure that children under the age of sixteen would need parental consent to receive contraceptive advice or treatment. Social Services Minister Sir Keith Joseph, replying on behalf of the government, had proposed that the amendment not be accepted, arguing that doctors were already recommended to consult parents, and the bill duly became law.[1] In May 1974, however, the Department of Health and Social Security issued a memorandum of guidance on the provision of family planning. Drawing attention to the number of births and of abortions among girls under the age of sixteen, Section G of the memorandum stated that contraception should be available regardless of age. Any doctor, it advised, who provided contraceptive advice and treatment for a girl under sixteen would not be committing an offence 'provided he [sic] acts in good faith' to protect the girl against 'the potentially harmful effects of intercourse'. The memorandum went on to note that although it would be 'prudent' to consult parents this could only be done with the child's consent and that parents 'should not be contacted' without that permission.[2]

The memorandum was attacked by sections of the moral lobby from its inception and campaigners supported an Essex mother, Mrs. T. Wakeling, who leafleted MPs and took legal advice about the possibility of going to court on the issue. She was advised, however, that she was unlikely to succeed and the campaign all but disappeared from view.[3] But when subsequent plans to provide contraception to young people through local clinics began to attract press attention, opposition in the affected localities quickly received support from 'pro-family' groups. The Responsible Society was prominently involved, with Valerie Riches denouncing the DHSS (Department of Health and Social Security) memorandum as 'subversive' at a Doncaster parents' meeting in early 1978.[4] A local Community Standards Association was set up, which took legal advice on the feasibility of printing forms for parents to sign if they did not want their under-sixteen daughters receiving birth control or birth control advice from the Area Health Authority without their consent. If this was held to be legal, the Association hoped it would be the start of a national campaign.[5] The following year, Riches set out for the readers of the *Spectator* details of the memorandum and the resistance it was engendering.[6] An allied organisation, the Parents Advisory Group, also entered the fray with plans to approach all candidates, calling for support for legislation to restore parental rights over under-sixteen sex, while the Nationwide Festival of Light called for national action in its Bulletin in the latter part of 1978 and subsequently produced a document to enable parents to take action in their locality. (Local Responsible Society activists also raised the issue with prospective parliamentary candidates and Area Health Authorities.)[7] The

National Viewers' and Listeners' Association too moved into action on the question, with Mary Whitehouse accusing the Labour Prime Minister, James Callaghan, of evading the issue in his answers to a questionnaire VALA had circulated to party leaders. 'One is driven to conclude', she declared, that, if Labour was 'returned to power, such clinics before very long will become part of a way of life for our children.' Although, readers of VALA's newsletter were told after the election, this conclusion had been reached 'reluctantly', its implication for voters concerned with moral issues was all too clear.[8] After all, at the VALA convention the previous year, she had declared that there was 'no greater submerged scandal in our national life than the Department of Health memorandum which enables doctors and sex clinics to distribute the pill without parental consent'. What was needed, she announced, was 'a government which will not seduce our young-sters with the false security of the pill and abortion on demand'.[9] The issue had also been raised in mid-1978 with the Labour Home Secretary, Merlyn Rees, and the Opposition leader, Margaret Thatcher, when a delegation, which included Whitehouse, Valerie Riches of the Responsible Society and Ann Whitaker of the Community Standards Association, had called for the withdrawal of the 1974 memorandum as part of a series of proposals to end the 'moral manipulation' of young people.[10] Perhaps the most surpris-ing intervention, given that the issue was far more about teenage contraception than abortion, was by the Society for the Protection of Unborn Children. In Dudley a SPUC branch played a leading part in a campaign against plans for a local clinic, circulating a petition, organising a march and urging that letters be sent to the Prime Minister and the newly-installed Social Services Secretary, Patrick Jenkin, asking for the removal of the Area Health Authority Chairman.[11] But of the different local and national groups involved, it was the Ipswich-based Parents in Suffolk, led by Victoria Gillick, that was to be the forerunner of the drawn-out fight that lay ahead against the Department's guidelines. In what the *Sunday Express* in 1979 called a 'family planning 'war' ', Mrs. Gillick was already pioneering the campaigning tactics of petitioning and letter-writing that she was to use on a national stage in the early 1980s.[12]

Before the General Election, Patrick Jenkin, then Shadow Social Services Secretary, had promised that the guidelines would be reviewed should the Conservatives gain power. In June 1979, in a

speech to the British Medical Association Council, he announced
that he would be looking carefully at the matter and in January the
following year Victoria Gillick and her supporters delivered a five-
thousand signature petition to the Prime Minister.[13] The new
Minister of Health, Dr Gerard Vaughan, warned doctors later in
the month that to prescribe under-sixteen contraception condoned
an illegal act and should only occur under exceptional circumstances. 'We need to support and strengthen family life, not
diminish it', he declared, and the following month the Prime
Minister wrote to the Gillick group that both she and Jenkin
agreed that whenever possible the family should be 'the first source
of support and advice' and that the points the group had made in
its letter would receive 'particular attention' in reviewing the
guidelines. 'This is a tremendous boost for us', Gillick told the
press. 'I never doubted that Mrs Thatcher, as a mother herself,
would see how wrong the present system is.'[14]

In May, however, she responded sharply to reports that the
Prime Minister had agreed to new guidelines that would urge
doctors to involve parents but would allow them not to. In
Vaughan's statement, immediately after, he announced that the
original memorandum of guidance had been reviewed and it had
been concluded that 'greater emphasis' should be put on the 'vital
importance of parental responsibility'. He also emphasised, however, the importance of medical confidentiality. Professional bodies
would be consulted, he announced, before the guidelines were
amended. A new version was issued at the end of the year,
emphasising that a doctor should always 'seek to persuade the
child to involve the parent or guardian'. But, it went on, it had to
be accepted that consultation between doctors and patients was
confidential and that a breach of this principle in the case of
children might cause some not to seek professional advice and
therefore be exposed to the risks of pregnancy, sexually-transmitted
disease and other damaging consequences. There would then be
'exceptional cases', for instance where the parents were 'entirely
unresponsive, or grossly disturbed', where consultation with
parents was inappropriate. In such 'unusual' cases, it would be
legitimate for the doctor to prescribe contraception without
parental knowledge.[15]

That this should be the result of the government's review was a
bitter disappointment to campaigners, and their response was

exemplified in Valerie Riches's declaration that the government had effectively lowered the age of consent and surrendered 'to the tide of permissiveness'. 'We are not just surprised', she commented, 'that the present Government could act in this way – we feel betrayed.'[16] It was the BMA and key DHSS permanent staff that had decided the matter, the Responsible Society declared, citing a report in the medical publication, *Pulse*. Under their influence, the report had stated, government Ministers had turned 'full-circle' and decided to continue with under-sixteen contraception.[17]

Towards the end of the year, a furore had also broken out around the refusal of a Devon doctor, Dr Adrian Rogers, to provide contraception to under-sixteens in a local authority girls' home. Rogers, who came into conflict with the local social services department and was also reported to the General Medical Council (GMC), received considerable national publicity and, as we will see, was to become a stalwart of the campaign against under-sixteen contraception and of moral campaigning in general.[18] As for Gillick herself, she had moved from Suffolk to Cambridgeshire, to find that the Community Health Council in her new locality was about to consider the question.[19] This time, her campaign was to take on a national dimension. Initially, she attempted to extract a promise from her area health authority (AHA) that it would not give contraception to any of her daughters under the age of sixteen 'without my prior knowledge, and irrefutable evidence of my consent' and that it would contact her should any of them seek advice on contraception. Meeting with failure, she turned to the idea of court action.[20] Her intent was not only to stop the authority from giving such advice or treatment without her permission, but to obtain a judgement that the memorandum as such condoned breaching the law concerning the age of consent. For the AHA to ignore her wishes, she argued, was to deny her parental rights while, as for the memorandum itself, it advised doctors to encourage or connive at unlawful sexual activity.[21]

In court, however, her case was unsuccessful. Contraceptives, the court ruled in July 1983, did not directly assist in an act of unlawful sexual intercourse but rather were a palliative against its consequences. Government guidelines, then, that permitted the provision of contraception to someone under the age of consent did not break the law. Nor, the court held, was it the case that a child under the age of sixteen could not consent to receive medical treatment. If a child was mature enough, then her consent was valid and consequently a parent did not have the absolute right to be consulted before contraception could be provided.[22] But this judicial defeat was not to be the end of the matter. Gillick quickly decided upon an appeal while at the same time turning her attention to organising a national petition that would put direct pressure on MPs and the government. By this two-pronged strategy, it was hoped, the guidelines could at last be successfully challenged.

By early November, some 200 MPs had presented petitions to Parliament criticising the government's policy, and the press was talking of more than 500,000 signatures. (By the following month, it would be a million.) It was in this atmosphere that Vaughan's successor as Health Minister, Kenneth Clarke, announced that the guidelines were again to be reviewed. While Victoria Gillick was quoted at the time as saying that this was 'the first step on the way', Clarke had emphasised that the guidelines already did state that it would be 'most unusual' not to obtain parental consent.[23] A report a few days later showed Gillick as far more sceptical than she initially seemed. She had no confidence, she said, that Clarke favoured a change in the guidelines and had been told by a top government source that as late as two days before his Commons statement Clarke had had no intention of amending the document.[24]

Gillick was also meeting with opposition from the medical profession. The BMA had remained committed to the 1980 guidelines, holding that leaving such decisions to the discretion of doctors and maintaining the principle of doctor–patient confidentiality was crucial. This stand met with a furious response from Gillick and supporters of her campaign.[25] Even more heated was the response to a proposal that doctors who breached confidentiality and informed parents against their patient's wishes should be disciplined and even struck off. This proposal from the governing body of the medical profession, the General Medical Council, resulted in a row that included a declaration by Dr Adrian Rogers that he would defy the GMC ruling. The president of the Council then 'clarified' its ruling to allow for confidentiality to be breached if a doctor was sure that it was in the best interests of the patient or society.[26]

But if both Kenneth Clarke and the BMA were against changing the guidelines, sections of the Conservative Party felt otherwise.

Many Conservative MPs had spoken in support of the petition when presenting it to Parliament and the government, one report claimed in February 1984, was planning to override the DHSS and withdraw the guidelines following the Appeal Court hearing.[27]An account in the medical press, however, reported that this was inaccurate and that, on the contrary, the Prime Minister believed that ultimately the decision was up to the doctor.[28]

The Appeal Court's decision in late December 1984 in favour of Victoria Gillick changed the situation. In what Gillick called 'the finest Christmas present for millions of families', the court ruled that the DHSS guidelines were unlawful and that she should receive a specific guarantee that, except in an emergency or by leave of the court, none of her under-sixteen daughters would receive contraceptive treatment or advice without her consent. A girl under sixteen, they ruled, could not give valid consent to the provision of contraception, and parents had rights over their children that a doctor must not infringe.[29]

The departmental guidelines were immediately suspended. But, despite a parliamentary motion by pro-Gillick MPs seeking to pre-empt such a move, Clarke decided to appeal the case to the House of Lords. Such a decision could not but widen the gap between Clarke and sections of the party, with Jill Knight commenting that 'Some will see this decision as a very strange one from a government headed by a leader who is committed to the family.'[30] Outside Parliament, Dr Adrian Rogers echoed this sentiment: 'One really wonders why the Health Minister has made the decision to appeal to the Lords. It is meant to be a pro-family party to which I belong. It is very sad.'[31]

Tensions were also evident in medical reactions to the new situation. At the BMA annual meeting in July 1984, the chairman of its ethical committee had warned that doctors who refused either to prescribe contraception to under-sixteens or to direct them to someone who would would be liable to appear before the GMC.[32] But a significant minority of doctors opposed the BMA's stance, as was evidenced in petitions signed by some 2,000 doctors which were handed in to the GMC in late 1984, calling for a change in the policy of observing confidentiality for under-sixteen patients.[33] The Appeal Court's decision in favour of Victoria Gillick shifted the GMC's position, a new Council guideline in February 1985 retaining confidentiality but refusing contraceptive advice or treatment to an under-sixteen without parental consent except in emergency or by leave of court. This, however, was specifically described as an interim change pending the Lords' decision.[34] While the BMA, in order to remain within the law, also changed its own guidelines to accord with the Appeal Court decision, its secretary pronounced that what was meant by emergency remained unclear and that the Association would support any doctor who judged such a situation existed and was subsequently threatened by legal action.[35]

In the last of the legal decisions on the issue, the Law Lords in October 1985 came down in favour of the DHSS and reversed the Appeal Court decision by a majority of three to two. Provided she had sufficient understanding and intelligence, they ruled, a girl under sixteen could give her consent to medical treatment. As for parental rights, these were not absolute but, as had been accepted in Western Europe in modern times, gradually lessened as the child developed. This was an 'appalling defeat', Victoria Gillick declared, 'I never thought it could have been as bad as this.' Supporters in Parliament also spoke out, with Ann Winterton calling for government legislation on the issue and Peter Bruinvels accusing the Law Lords of 'effectively promoting under-age sex'.[36] In the House of Commons, the new Health Minister, Barney Hayhoe, announced that the guidelines had been reinstated but would be reviewed. A subsequent attempt by the Conservative MP Nicholas Winterton to have a form of notification introduced whereby doctors would have to obtain parental consent for contraception or give reasons why not was rebuffed by the Minister.[37] In early November, another Conservative MP, Harry Greenway, suggested to the House that the recent Lords decision was 'highly damaging to family relationships' and effectively abolished the age of consent. It would allow some doctors, he declared, 'to shell out the pill like jelly babies to very young girls'. Such views, Hayhoe replied, were exaggerated and a slur upon doctors.[38]

The legal battle, then, had finally gone against the Gillick campaign. But, while the Lords' decision marked the end of the battle in the courts, an appeal to the European Court being ruled out by Victoria Gillick, it certainly did not represent an end to the campaign itself. 'In a sense', she declared, 'the legal battle is done, but the social battle has only just begun.'[39] A decision by her own health authority to provide the written assurance she had long pursued was announced immediately after the Lords' decision and initially this was seen by her as a possible precedent for 'every parent in the land'.[40] This proved not to be the case, however, and instead she turned to a formal application to see the Health Minister to press for a systematic monitoring of the situation. Speaking after her subsequent interview with him, she declared that tightening up the guidelines would not be enough: 'I want a change in legislation and that can only happen if the government has sufficient evidence that things are going wrong.' If, she argued, doctors had to fill in detailed forms on the provision of under-sixteen birth control and figures were provided on the incidence of sexually transmitted diseases by age group, then Parliament and the public would be able to judge the appropriateness or otherwise of the DHSS guidelines.[41] This monitoring, it was hoped, would make it possible to secure a private members' bill on the issue and plans were reported to set up a network of local family centres as the basis for a national campaign. While local centres were not set up Gillick was, along with Riches, one of the speakers the following year at the launch of the National Campaign for the Family. The family must be made a central issue in the next election, Riches declared, and an action committee was formed to draw up a manifesto to be presented to main party leaders. A rally was also planned for the Albert Hall. The Gillick case, Family and Youth Concern reported, had been recognised by the conference as only part of a massive attack on the family over the last 25 years. But neither the manifesto nor the rally came about and, while the Campaign and its associated National Family Trust was to be frequently quoted in the press in the years that followed, it developed largely independently from the moral lobby.[42]

Efforts to influence Hayhoe also met without success, as was made clear when the government finally completed its review of the guidelines in the light of the Lords' decision. In exceptional circumstances, the new guidelines laid down, where a doctor believed that an under-sixteen girl who declined to involve her parents was sufficiently mature to understand the implication of using contraception, then its provision would be admissible. It was a decision that Gillick described as 'worse than ever'.[43]

Another possible avenue opened, however, with the decision of the General Medical Council, shortly before the Hayhoe statement, that doctors could inform parents if approached for contraception by an under-sixteen girl who, in their opinion, did not show the maturity necessary to use contraception. Despite opposition from the BMA, the GMC's stance represented a shift in policy that Gillick could utilise and she announced plans shortly afterwards to distribute forms warning doctors that they could be reported to the GMC if they prescribed contraception without parental consent.[44] Although the legal battle had been lost, the fight against under-sixteen contraception continued.

Plans were laid for a new national organisation, Inform, that would lobby government and hold a national rally the following year but the campaign was hit by crisis when newspaper reports appeared of Gillick's eldest daughter sunbathing topless while on holiday with her boyfriend in Greece. Victoria Gillick reacted furiously to the news and briefly considered abandoning the campaign rather than expose her children to such attentions from journalists. Valerie Riches, however, declared that this would only serve 'the enemies of the family' and that the campaign would go on regardless of Gillick's decision, and shortly afterwards Gillick announced that she would seek to protect her family while continuing with her efforts. Her next step, she announced, would be to launch Inform.[45]

This, it transpired, was solely a monitoring organisation with no plans to recruit members but statistics did, indeed, become central to Gillick's ongoing activity.[46] Thus, at the end of 1986, controversy emerged when a *Guardian* headline announced that 'Teenage births rose after Gillick victory' while the *Independent* claimed that 'Births and abortions fell after teenage Pill ruling'. According to the first report, official figures showed an increase in births to under-sixteens in 1985, indicating that the Appeal Court decision had led to a fall in contraceptive use but not in sexual activity. According to the *Independent*, however, both births and abortions among under-sixteens had fallen in the three quarters affected by the Appeal Court ruling.[47]

Why the discrepancy? As 'pro-life' campaigner Dr Peggy Norris pointed out to the *Guardian* in a subsequent letter, the key period for births after the December 1984 Appeal Court ruling was not 1985 as such but its last quarter and the first two quarters of 1986 since, after all, there is somewhat of a gap between conception and birth. But if the *Guardian* had been wrong, was Gillick right in arguing that 'These figures vindicate our campaign. We have ended up with fewer girls on the Pill, fewer girls having sexual relationships, fewer births and fewer abortions'? This was far less certain, with the Family Planning Association (FPA) arguing that the changes were very small and the Brook Advisory Centre suggesting that the fall in births might be linked to a rise in abortions in late 1985 and early 1986. What still remained unclear was the conception rates during the period, and these would not be released until the following summer.[48]

When these figures finally appeared, they showed a fall in conceptions to under-sixteens during 1985 and Gillick wrote to the Prime Minister and the Health Minister calling for the Appeal Court ruling to be implemented by Parliament. But the government did not agree, while for Gillick's critics the 1985 fall in conceptions was both extremely small and misleading – the number of young girls in the population was falling, they noted, and if the rate of conceptions was looked at rather than the total number, then there had been no reduction.[49] In mid-1989 an attempt was made to revive the issue when Ann Winterton proposed an amendment on under-sixteen contraception to the government's Children Bill, a move which Gillick supported but which did not succeed.[50]

As we have seen, Gillick received crucial support from Conservative MPs. But the campaign stretched wider than merely the political right. A devout Catholic herself, an important element of Gillick's support has come from within the Catholic Church and it was reported in 1984 that she had received letters of support from twenty-seven of the Church's bishops. Help also came from the Catholic Teachers' Federation and from among evangelical Protestants, notably the Salvation Army whose citadels were used as distribution points for the national petition campaign.[51] She also found support from a number of black organisations – the Afro-Asian-Caribbean Standing Committee, the Union of Muslim Organisations of the UK, the Confederation of Indian Organisations (UK) and the West Indian Standing Conference.[52] And, of course, there was the moral lobby, including Family and Youth Concern and the Order of Christian Unity, both of which issued pamphlets on the question.[53] SPUC too kept up its involvement, with Scottish activists issuing a leaflet condemning the Brook Advisory Centres' provision of contraception to the young.[54]

Such a wide span of support, however, was not without its tensions. Victoria Gillick's most noteworthy success, the gaining of support from black organisations, is particularly surprising in view of her own political history. She is an experienced campaigner and former anti-abortion activist.[55] But she also has had more controversial political connections. That she was once a member of a racist group in the early seventies, Powellight, is an involvement she initially denied but later stated had been due to her support for its stance on the Common Market. The anti-fascist magazine, *Searchlight*, which first uncovered her former connections, has shown, however, that her involvement in Powellight included writing a letter to her local paper in 1972 opposing government race relations policy and advocating repatriation. Indeed, her letter had specifically complained of the crowding of 'our once beautiful and fruitful cities' with immigrants while she and others who had 'lived in these isles for thousands of years' were told 'we must not have anymore of the children *we* want'.[56] Although she now disassociates herself from such views her relationship with black organisations is likely to have been strained by the revelations of her past activities, a development she has attempted to minimise by approaching the black press to clarify her present stance.[57]

A more surprising tension has emerged with the Catholic Church and Gillick has gone so far as to contrast its failure to fully support her with the support she has received from black organisations.[58] In early 1984, Cardinal Hume had written to her expressing his 'interest and sympathy' for her campaign. However, he went on, the issue had 'wider implications for the role of law, medical practice and social welfare in a pluralistic society' which needed to be taken into consideration in deciding the right policy.[59] Shortly afterwards the bishops approved a statement that opposed under-sixteen contraception and proposed amending the DHSS guidelines but did not declare support for the Gillick campaign and further suggested that there could be grounds for doctors not to consult parents about the provision of contraception to their children. It was a response that fell far short of what campaigners were seeking, and both Gillick and Riches wrote to the Catholic press criticising the statement.[60]

Not only the Catholic hierarchy but the government too was a bitter disappointment to the Gillick campaign. Certainly, many Conservative MPs had strenuously supported the campaign in Parliament. As for the former Minister responsible for the 1980 guidelines, Dr Gerard Vaughan, he had recanted, declaring that they had been misinterpreted by doctors who had given out contraception to under-sixteens too easily.[61] But none of this was to avail against the resistance of key ministers and much of the medical profession. Kenneth Clarke, in particular, was the object of Gillick's strictures (he was an old adversary from an earlier campaign against his closure of her local maternity hospital) and she was also deeply concerned about the pernicious influence of the 'Whitehall mandarins' who had drafted the guidelines.[62] Even the Prime Minister came under suspicion from the Gillick campaign. After all, she had personally approved the 1980 guidelines before they were issued. Indeed, Gillick declared in early 1984, the Prime Minister had written to her in 1980 that the decision to prescribe contraceptives must rest with the doctor.[63]

Nor did the replacement of Clarke by the Catholic Barney Hayhoe impress her. 'Mrs Thatcher's appointment of a Catholic as Minister of Health', she remarked, 'is one of the cleverest things she ever did. She bought off the Pro-Life vote.'[64] Distrust for the Conservative government's intentions on under-sixteen contraception had been expressed by, for instance, the Festival of Light, as early as 1980.[65] Gillick's criticism of the new Health Minister and the Prime Minister who appointed him carried on the long-running distrust that much of the moral lobby held for a government that seemed to offer so much yet delivered so little.

The Gillick campaign's unhappy experience with the Thatcher government has been a crucial element in the arguments it has developed against under-sixteen contraception. A central feature of these arguments is a defence of the family against what it sees as the intrusion of the state and the negation of the parental role. 'I have been told', Gillick argues, 'I no longer have the right to protect my children – that right has been taken from me by the state.'[66] This point, a frequent theme of her argument, is developed in her first book. The State, she argues, seeks to dictate to children how they should live and has reduced the status and role of mothers. The 'territory of parenthood has been encroached upon by "interested" outsiders' and only a 'supreme act of revolt against this growing tyranny' would push the Establishment back. The central issue, she goes on, is 'family integrity versus state interference' and only if resisted from without would the 'Nanny State' change its course.[67]

Along with this general theme of the family versus officialdom, Gillick argues that the state has become entangled with commercial

interests concerned to create a captive market for its products:
'When it became known that young people had a certain amount of
money to spend they actually invented the teenager in order to
provide a market in which they sold everything, including
sex...There was commercial pressure on Government departments from the huge combines who produce contraceptives.'[68]
Hostile to both government policy and the family planning
'industry', her campaign accuses them of responsibility for the
rates of sexually-transmitted disease and cervical cancer among
young women. Thus, the 'physical and mental ill-effects of early
sexual activity' play a prominent part in the argument in the Order
of Christian Unity's 1985 pamphlet on the question, while Gillick's
own reaction to her House of Lords defeat was to warn that
doctors would be unable to cope with 'the flood of disease' the
decision would unleash.[69] In its fight against under-sixteen contraception, the campaign focuses on the notion of permissiveness
and seeks to relate it to the theme of national decay. In a
particularly stirring assertion of this argument, a letter from 120
'concerned women', including Gillick and Riches, linked under-
sixteen contraception with teenage pregnancy, abortion, cervical
cancer, prostitution and violence.[70]

Like Mary Whitehouse, Gillick represents part of the challenge
to the sixties while maintaining a distance from and even a critique
of political Conservatism. For both of them, the Thatcher government was still too much influenced by the special interests – the
liberal civil servants, the commercial pressures, the doctors still
'trapped in the Swinging Sixties concept'.[71] In Gillick's argument,
this was closely connected with a baleful interpretation of what
really lay behind the Government's resistance to her demands. As
one account in 1983 noted, 'For her, the case seemed to have
unveiled a pervading feeling of something that cut across family
ties, a sort of "Big Brother" attempt by the government at social
planning. There was the idea, for instance, that pushing the Pill in
deprived areas would mean fewer births of undesirable people.'[72]
Another report, the following year, made her argument more
clearly, that 'government-backed family planning and abortion
services...[are] nothing less than an attempt at mass genocide of
the lower classes and the blacks' and that Joseph's 1974 comment
on the excessive birthrate of the lower orders was convincing proof
that 'The State is out to attack women's fertility rights.'[73] She

returned to this theme in a speech at Manchester University in 1985, only to have her attack on Joseph construed as anti-semitic conspiracy-mongering.[74] But, as her first book makes clear, what she is actually arguing is very similar to the argument made by sections of the anti-abortion movement. In 1979, a DHSS official had written to her suggesting that birth control could reduce the number of one-parent families and the amount of deprivation, delinquency and crime, a view she compares with that of Joseph in 1974. In 1981, she had written to the Secretary of State for Social Services stating her belief that the DHSS's policy was an attempt at social engineering aimed at 'certain religious, racial and social groups'. The existence of such a policy, she argues in her book, is demonstrated by the pressurised sterilisations, injected contraception and abortion perpetrated on 'unwitting women and girls'. It is also indicated, she suggests, by the confession of a GMC official to her that the provision of under-age contraception was particularly important because of the 'problems' in inner-city areas. It was this conviction of a deliberate population strategy that explained for Gillick why 'a Conservative Government . . . is prepared to fly in the face of the majority of its loyal supporters, and risk political suicide by so blatantly breaking one of its most basic manifesto pledges, of upholding "traditional values" and support for the family'. The reason, she claims, is 'because there is within its permanent officialdom, a core of very hard line social engineers, with a policy on population control that extends way beyond any party political considerations. Thus it is that every DHSS Minister, whatever colour his party bosses may sport, always ends up by promoting birth control facilities for the working classes and the poor'.[75]

Gillick's opposition to contraception for under-sixteens met with strong opposition not only from doctors but also from feminists. Another of the campaign's central themes, however, makes her sound peculiarly feminist herself. The provision of contraception to under-sixteens without parental consent, she argues, undermines the position of girls who 'are thrown on to the market to be exploited'. The original court ruling in her case, she declared, was a charter for boys. 'What the judge is saying is that as long as the girls don't get pregnant the boys can do what they like.'[76] She restated this view in an interview in 1985, arguing that Britain was moving towards a more aggressive male society in which younger girls were being prepared for men.[77]

But beneath this feminist-sounding point is a very different attitude to sexuality than that held by feminists. For, as she made clear in the Catholic press, she holds that contraception as such is 'wrong' even though for 'most people the argument was lost when procreation was separated from sexuality'. Eventually, she believes, 'the tide will turn against the anti-life mentality of contraception and abortion'. More recently, in her second book, she has raised the argument that birth control leads to infidelity and marital breakdown.[78] And, just as underpinning her campaign against under-sixteen contraception is a rejection of contraception per se, so too Gillick's opposition to under-sixteen sex is integrally connected with a positive view of the value of chastity. Chastity, she argues, 'is a woman's right. She came into the world whole, wholesome, exactly as she is. It is nonsense, this idea that she doesn't become a complete person until she's got a bloke in tow'.[79]

An examination of the Gillick campaign's arguments and a consideration of its diverse constituency makes clear its character as part of a politically independent moral lobby which rather than being part of Conservatism is profoundly dissatisfied with the fruits of Conservative government. But attempts have been made nonetheless to attribute a particular political character to the campaign. At its sharpest, this has entailed accusing Gillick, and, by implication, the campaign itself of extreme right-wing sympathies. In part, this involves the revelations noted earlier of her political past. But it also includes other components. In June 1985, the anti-fascist magazine that had broken the news of her Powellight involvement carried a report of her addressing a meeting of the British Housewives' League, an organisation it linked with a small far right group, the British League of Rights.[80] More recently, at a rally in Newcastle organised by local branches of SPUC and LIFE, she has spoken of the rise of Asian and Muslim numbers in Europe while white Europeans 'are busy stamping ourselves out' and in a later interview referred to the 'sadness' in seeing 'an indigenous population wiping itself out and being taken over by another. In our country it happens to be the Europeans taken over by an Asian force in sheer numbers'.[81] Finally, critics have claimed that she had written to the Overseas Development Administration in 1980 enquiring if the government had a strategy for curbing the birthrate of high-fertility ethnic groups.[82]

These charges however are not as compelling as they might first appear. Although certainly a supporter of repatriation in the early seventies, Gillick's campaign in the 1980s, as we have seen, deliberately encompassed black organisations and accused the government of pursuing a strategy aimed at reducing the birth-rate of poor and ethnic minorities. As for her address to the British Housewives' League, two points need to be made. Firstly, her reference during her speech to the support her campaign has received from Muslims and Jews hardly suggested a wish to attract far right sympathy. More importantly, the Housewives' League, unlike the National Front or other anti-immigration groupings, is an integral part of the moral lobby whose meetings have been addressed by other moral campaigners and whose magazine has published reports of VALA, Community Standards Association and Family and Youth Concern meetings.[83] Nor does the published extract from her letter to the government concerning population policy substantiate any claim for racism. Far from demanding that the government *should* pursue such a policy, the letter appears rather to represent part of her efforts to expose the government as already pursuing such a strategy, one that she opposes. Finally, in her Powellight letter and more recently, she is plainly concerned with racial numbers. But she no longer advocates repatriation and rather than identifying itself with specifically white concerns the Gillick campaign instead has endeavoured to build a multi-racial 'pro-family' movement. Similar efforts are taking place elsewhere in the moral lobby. The SPUC Conference was recently told by an Islamic speaker that 'For Muslims abortion is bloodshed' and ethnic organisations were among the signatories to a petition to the Prime Minister criticising embryo research. Given the importance of ethnic minorities in many localities, and the moral traditionalism particularly evident in sections of the Muslim community, an emphasis on achieving black support could well be an important development among moral campaigners in the future. If this is to be the case, then Victoria Gillick's campaign of the eighties will be a pioneer in moving away from an almost completely Caucasian movement.[84]

The Gillick campaign's argument that it is defending the family against the state, morality against promiscuity and young girls against exploitation is a powerful one which enabled it to tap a significant reservoir of support and gain extensive press coverage. Critics argue that, since sex is taking place under the age of consent, the responsible attitude is to protect young women from unwanted pregnancy. For the Gillick camp, however, their parental rights have been taken away, the state is usurping their role and the innocence of the young is being destroyed. In what Gillick has called the 'most important social issue to go before the courts this century',[85] a movement that held it was taking power away from doctors and from young men and restoring it to its 'rightful place' – the mother and father – came up against the opposition both of the medical establishment and those who favoured young women's sexual autonomy. As a force that championed the family and distrusted professionals, it looked hopefully to a force with the same predilection – the newly-elected Conservative government. That it did not obtain its demands gives us important clues about the nature of that government and its relationship with the moral lobby.

4 Embryo Research: From the Warnock Report to Government Legislation

The birth in 1978 of the world's first 'test-tube baby' opened up new possibilities for the infertile. Through the fertilising of human eggs outside the body and the transferring of some or all of the resultant embryos to the mother's womb, women who were unable to have children could now do so. But even with the advances in in vitro fertilisation (IVF) since 1978, its success rate remains low and the experience stressful. Much of the argument that has developed around IVF has been concerned with commercial surrogacy, the hiring of a woman to bear a child for someone else. For moral campaigners, however, there were fundamental problems with the very procedure itself, above all with the opportunities it gave to scientists to experiment on the human embryo. Concern about the issues stretched far beyond the moral lobby and in July 1982 the government set up a Committee of Enquiry 'to examine the social, ethical and legal implications of recent, and potential developments in the field of human assisted reproduction'.[1]

The committee, headed by the philosopher Mary Warnock, reported in June 1984. It was already clear, however, before the committee had even been established, that for 'pro-life' campaigners, in vitro fertilisation posed issues of the same gravity as the legal abortion which the movement had come into existence to avert. Thus, as early as 1979, SPUC's paper included a Canadian 'pro-life' article arguing that a process which involved the fertilisation of more than one egg and the discarding of those not used was completely unacceptable, while in 1982, before the Warnock Committee's inception, LIFE asked the Attorney General to rule on the legality of the discarding of 'spare' embryos during IVF.

This, it argued, was the destruction of human beings. LIFE also condemned suggestions of embryo research and whatever the Attorney General ruled, it declared, it would endeavour to get a private members' bill introduced in Parliament to stop all IVF except for the single fertilisation of an ovum and its immediate replacement in the womb of its donor.[2] Such a bill was not forthcoming and the approach to the Attorney General also proved fruitless. In Sir Michael Havers's view, the issue was as yet 'unregulated by the law' and could not be dealt with until the newly-established committee had reported. LIFE, however, had held that the matter could not be left to a committee of enquiry and that a test-case or legislation was needed.[3]

Both LIFE and SPUC submitted material to the Warnock committee. SPUC's submission, subsequently published before the Warnock report in pamphlet form, argued that IVF was immoral because it relied on discarding certain embryos and also submitted the unborn child to unknown risks. There should, the Society argued, be a moratorium until the public had properly considered the issue. As for embryo research, this should be banned unless carried out for the benefit of the embryo itself and a law should be passed to protect 'the test tube baby from zygote stage onwards'. LIFE's submission, also published before the report's appearance, argued that experimentation on 'spare' embryos was unacceptable. To accept the notion of the disposable embryo, it argued, would be as retrogressive as a belief in slavery.[4]

Other organisations also took up a stance on the issue. In May 1983, the Order of Christian Unity (OCU) organised a conference on the subject and the following year held a press conference to launch a book of the conference papers. In chilling tones that would recur during the campaign, one speaker, the former Royal gynaecologist Sir John Peel, spoke of the dangers of a breeding programme along the lines of Huxley's *Brave New World* while another, Professor Ian Donald, predicted that 'womb leasing' could be replaced by 'womb requisition'. This, he declared, 'could happen in an age which has seen concentration camps.'[5]

As the time for the Warnock report's appearance approached, CARE urged supporters to pray 'for a righteous, sensitive and understanding reaction in Parliament to the wonders and dangers of this new technology and for a strong resolve to curb its abuses by law'. The report, it hoped, would recommend that the production of spare embryos should be banned. Responding to reports that the Warnock recommendations would be sympathetic to embryo research, Nuala Scarisbrick of LIFE announced: 'We are very depressed to see all the predictions about Warnock seemed to be proved right.'[6]

The Warnock report did indeed reject 'pro-life' arguments. Some people, it noted, believed that the embryo was a human life and should not be used for research while others held that while the embryo was alive it was not yet a human person and that until such a status was attained, research was permissible. While it might appear, the report continued, that questions of life and personhood were 'straightforward...we hold that the answers to such questions in fact are complex amalgams of factual and moral judgements'. Instead, therefore, of directly answering such questions, the committee had decided to look at the ethical question of how to treat the human embryo. Having set out arguments against and for the use of human embryos, the committee turned to the legal situation and stated that, while the embryo as such had no legal status, laws concerning civil liability and the conditions under which abortion was legal did give it some protection. A measure of protection should, they argued, be extended to the human embryo but, in the view of a majority of committee members, this could be waived under certain circumstances to permit research and continued advances in medical knowledge and treatment. There was, it went on, no obvious point at which embryo development was more significant than at any other and different suggestions had been made about the point up to which research would be ethical. Some, for instance, had suggested the point at which the embryo could feel pain. The committee, however, thought that a somewhat earlier point, the formation of the primitive streak, was appropriate as this marked the beginning of individual development of the embryo. (This was the last point at which identical twins might develop.) Since this was around the fifteenth day after fertilisation, the committee proposed that 14 days should be the limit at which research might take place.[7]

The Warnock Report's arguments met with strong opposition from SPUC and LIFE. LIFE declared that no benefits from such research would justify 'experimentation on living human beings' and announced that it intended to promote a parliamentary bill requiring doctors to fertilise only those eggs that were to be reimplanted back into the mother. SPUC called for the lobbying of MPs to ban the use of the embryo 'as a guinea-pig' and the Order of Christian Unity and the Responsible Society also criticised the report.[8]

A campaign to ban all experimentation on human embryos was launched immediately after the report's publication. Prominent among its supporters was 'pro-life' campaigner Dr Margaret White, who declared that the acceptance of embryo research would open up a Pandora's box of horrors in which experiments would be carried out after the 14-day limit, babies would be developed in artificial wombs and attempts would be made to create hybrid species. 'Unless', she said, 'you put a firm ban on all experiments on human embryos you will go straight down the road to Brave New World.' Sir Bernard Braine, another early adherent, accused the Warnock committee of producing an expensive whitewash intended to mislead the public. At least a hundred MPs, he declared, were committed to oppose embryo experimentation and a further hundred would join them in supporting a bill to ban it. A bill had been prepared, he reported, to be offered to successful candidates in the private members' ballot. While he had not spoken to her, he said, he believed the Prime Minister would almost certainly support it.[9]

At its annual conference in mid-September, LIFE announced plans for a national petition calling upon the government to ban embryo experimentation, while later in the month the OCU escalated its involvement in the issue with a press conference calling for a two-year moratorium. Continued experimentation, Professor Donald declared, could lead to a Ministry for Babies with the powers to license potential parents and control which sex of child they would have.[10] The following month a letter signed by, among others, the OCU, LIFE and SPUC and other groups was delivered to Downing Street. It called for a moratorium on research until Parliament had decided on safeguards. The Prime Minister replied, declining to declare a moratorium.[11] By November LIFE's petition plans were in place and now included SPUC, ALDU, the World Federation of Doctors who Respect Human Life and CARE. A LIFE spokesman told the press that the petition would make Parliament hear 'loud and clear that the vast majority of people in this country are revulsed by the idea of using human beings as subjects for research and experimentation'. It would, it was hoped, be the biggest petition in the country's history.[12]

At the end of October the Report was discussed in the Lords, with a number of peers (including Lord Halsbury and Viscount Buckmaster) making clear their opposition.[13] More importantly, the following month the Report received its first airing in the Commons. It was not a favourable one. Government Ministers, the *Guardian* reported, had found themselves isolated as 'pro-life' Tory MPs demanded a ban on embryo research. While Harry Greenway insisted that the Social Services Secretary, Norman Fowler, recognise the sanctity of human life, Sir Bernard Braine described embryo experimentation as 'an affront to humanity'. The Warnock Report, he argued, was 'repellant' and without moral guidelines. Another Conservative, William Cash, warned of the possibility of animal–human hybrids, claiming that 'The nightmare creation of a super-race and with it the super-prole seems nearer at hand.' Fowler, however, was unwilling to meet the demand of his back-benchers while the Health Minister, Kenneth Clarke, also rejected their arguments.[14]

Unsatisfied by the government's response, MPs opposed to the Warnock Report turned to support a private members' bill presented to Parliament by Enoch Powell, who had come fifth in the ballot the previous week. Powell's plans to introduce an Unborn Children (Protection) Bill immediately attracted support from SPUC, LIFE and the All-Party Parliamentary Pro-Life Group.[15] By the end of the month, with the bill's second reading fast approaching, the *Guardian* was reporting that a 'formidable lobbying operation' had unleashed a 'deluge of petitions' upon Parliament. Letters and petitions had been pouring in, it reported, the latter at a rate of some 150 a week. This, it was suggested, could well begin to exert the kind of pressure on some MPs that anti-abortion protests had done earlier and would make the situation difficult for government ministers as they decided whether to recommend support for a 14-day limit in an eventual free vote on the issue.[16]

In the run-up to the second reading, the campaigners kept up their pressure. In late January the OCU and the World Federation of Doctors who Respect Human Life held a joint press conference to denounce embryo research while SPUC called for as many letters as possible to be sent to MPs urging them to vote for the Powell Bill on 15 February. 'It is essential', the society declared, 'that we have a huge vote to outlaw human vivisection.' The other groups involved in the petition, LIFE and CARE, likewise urged supporters to write to their MPs.[17] There were, however,doubts among some of the campaigners. Published at the beginning of February, the bill laid down that doctors would have to apply in every individual case to the Secretary of State for permission to carry out IVF and that it would only be legal to possess an IVF embryo in order to enable a specific woman to give birth. Responding to this, Nuala Scarisbrick described it as 'woolly' and failing to deal with the creation of spare embryos. She would not be calling on LIFE members, she said, to press MPs to support the bill. LIFE did, however, subsequently decide to support the measure. SPUC, while supporting the bill, was also unhappy. Its spokesperson, Phyllis Bowman, however, was confident that problems with the bill could be resolved at committee stage.[18]

The petition, as we have seen, had been expected to attract over a million signatures. When it was finally presented, however, it far surpassed these predictions – over two million had signed it. Professor Jack Scarisbrick, LIFE's chairman, describing it as the largest petition since the days of the Chartists, was concerned to insist that it was not aimed at IVF. 'What we are protesting at', he stated, 'is the manipulation and exploitation of life which run-away IVF technology threatens'.[19]

The result of the parliamentary debate itself was a significant victory for the Powell bill, which passed its second reading by 238 to 66, a majority of 172. It was, Ann Winterton declared, 'an attempt...to step where the Government have been too slow or lacked the moral courage to tread'. 170 Conservatives voted for the bill, including 35 government ministers and whips. Norman Fowler and Kenneth Clarke voted against but only one other minister joined them. While Norman St John-Stevas, supporting the bill, called for a clear indication that the government would provide time for the bill, this was not forthcoming, although Clarke did promise a government bill dealing with the Warnock report proposals within the life of the Parliament. The Powell Bill itself, he argued, was 'extreme and fundamentalist'. Those groups who had lobbied for the bill were unmoved by Clarke's argument. SPUC described the vote as an 'immense victory' and an indication to the government that it had to pass legislation without delay while LIFE pronounced it a 'victory for democracy and justice...For the first time in history, the forces of darkness are on the retreat'. Fearing attempts to derail the bill, however, LIFE also announced that it would 'mount pressure on the Government to ensure this kind of underhand business does not take place'. CARE, meanwhile, was not only concerned that the bill should pass all its stages but also expressed the hope that it could be strengthened at a later stage.[20]

When the bill returned to Parliament in early May, only one amendment was discussed and voted on. Supporters were furious, SPUC accusing opponents of 'shabby and dishonest tactics' and demanding that the government 'stop the butchery' of the bill, while CARE urged supporters to write to the Prime Minister asking for adequate parliamentary time. LIFE, which had given the bill only a 'one in ten chance' of proceeding, had circulated MPs in advance calling on them to press the government for extra time.[21]

Although the bill had been outmanoeuvred, parliamentary supporters struck back. Andrew Bowden, a Conservative MP, used his first place in the private members' motion list to move for another discussion of the bill for 7 June. If he was successful, discussion of the bill could continue throughout the weekend if necessary. It was a move which pleased 'pro-life' groups but SPUC warned that the government might abandon its neutral stance on the bill and called upon supporters to ask their MP to cancel all arrangements to be at the debate for all Friday and Saturday if necessary.[22] When 7 June came, however, it was to see the Powell Bill's defeat. Labour MP Dennis Skinner moved the writ for a by-election, which took precedence over Bowden's motion. The government, it was reported, had regarded Bowden as misusing parliamentary procedure and had given tacit support to Skinner.[23]

Not only was the bill thus talked out but signs had emerged of divisions among its extra-parliamentary supporters. Before Bowden's motion, LIFE's chairman had described the bill as already 'dead' while SPUC believed it still had a chance. Beneath this difference of interpretation lay a greater difference about what legislation was needed. LIFE, as we have seen, argued that the Powell Bill allowed the production of spare embryos and that any adequate law would stop such production. SPUC favoured pressing the government to take up Powell's proposals, believing that any stronger measure was politically unwinnable. As with abortion, so with embryo research, LIFE's stance was significantly different from SPUC's more pragmatic view.[24]

Following the bill's defeat, the government had to deal with backbenchers' anger over a Cabinet decision that it could not introduce a bill on the Warnock Report in the next session of Parliament. Mrs. Thatcher announced during Prime Minister's Question Time that the Government would bring in a bill 'as soon as practicable'. She had noted the strength of feeling around the Powell bill, she stated, and shared some of the feelings. Outside Parliament, opponents of the Warnock Report regathered their forces. SPUC announced a proposed mass meeting in Westminster to be addressed by Powell and others. At the rally, Powell told those present that he would continue to fight to ban embryo research while Sir Bernard Braine declared that many MPs had entered the private members' ballot in order to put forward such a bill and he announced a new campaign to press the government to introduce its own bill banning embryo research or give time to a private members' bill.[25]

But while 'pro-lifers' were by no means defeated by the fate of their bill in Parliament, the differences between them as to how to proceed were worsening. William Cash and other MPs tabled an early-day motion in mid-July calling on the government to set up a select committee to look into embryo research and genetic engineering. But while this was supported by LIFE, it met with hostility from SPUC and the Parliamentary Pro-Life Group. For LIFE, the virtue of Cash's motion was that it would keep the issue alive in the public mind, allow an examination of developments that had occurred since the Warnock committee had collected its evidence and was more likely to reflect parliamentary feeling than an independent committee. But according to SPUC, Cash's proposal was 'idiotic'. A bulletin was sent out to its branches and supporters warning that such a move was potentially disastrous for the impetus of the campaign. Instead of letting the government 'off the hook' by allowing it to set up another Select Committee, Phyllis Bowman argued for pursuing the campaigners' aims through private members' bills.[26]

Towards the end of August, the *Guardian* reported that the government was on the verge of putting forward proposals in the next parliamentary session along the lines of the Warnock Report. The government, the report stated, had intended to postpone such a move rather than risk wrecking its parliamentary timetable. But concerned by the possibility of a version of the Powell bill being successful, it was now 'on the brink of reversing' the earlier Cabinet decision to defer Warnock legislation. There was, however, a problem, the report noted, in the likelihood that Kenneth Clarke, a supporter of Warnock, would be moved from his post as health minister in the imminent government reshuffle.[27]

When Clarke was indeed moved, his replacement by Barney Hayhoe, a Powell bill supporter, suggested that embryo research might not be favoured. The new junior minister of health, John Major, was also a Powell bill supporter, and only Norman Fowler remained in place as a defender of the Warnock Report. Peter Bruinvels, who announced that thirty-five MPs were willing to take on a bill against embryo research, was enthusiastic about the new appointment, declaring that 'Barney Hayhoe is a pro-Life man. It's very good news for the pro-Life lobby, he has strong moral and religious views.' SPUC, however, gave a more chary welcome. 'Although we know that he would most certainly not follow the Clarke line', the Society said in a statement, ' it could well be that his appointment will be used to mollify the Christian vote, yet with the Government following the same line as before...It has to be made clear to Mrs Thatcher that such tactics simply would not work...'[28]

Although Hayhoe had made it clear that he would not introduce a bill in the present session or give government time to a private members' bill a fresh attempt was made in late 1985, when Kenneth Hargreaves, who had gained ninth place in the private members' ballot, announced he would adopt the Unborn Children (Protection) Bill. Once again, SPUC urged supporters to write to MPs to support the bill. A second reading in early 1986, however, was blocked by opponents.[29] There was still a possibility that the bill could proceed when brought back to the House on 2 May and Hargreaves made it clear that he would continue in his efforts. Thus at the end of February he tabled a motion, signed by 51 MPs, calling on the government to find time for the bill.[30]

In March SPUC announced plans for a mass lobby of MPs on 21 May, a date subsequently changed to 9 July. In the meantime, it kept up its pressure on the government, Bowman telling a meeting at Chiswick that Hayhoe was only a 'kind of window-dressing' for a government that had failed to support the Powell bill and, she believed, was likely to put forward a bill along Warnock lines. (Bruinvels too had changed his mind from his earlier view, declaring in the early part of the year that 'Hayhoe is a tight-rope walker. He has convinced both sides he is on their side and we are very disappointed with him'.)[31]

At the rally following the SPUC lobby in July Bowman repeated her attack on the government and her description of Hayhoe as 'window-dressing'. From the platform, Tory MPs attacked the government. 'Today we are here', proclaimed Nicholas Winterton, 'to leave not the tiniest doubt in the minds of the Minister of Health and the Prime Minister that the human embryo may be small, but our anger at Government delay is *not*'. James Pawsey, criticising the idea of a Select Committee, argued that it would be good news for the government, but not for the 'pro-life' cause.[32] Hargreaves's efforts to get parliamentary time for his bill had met with failure but, following its demise, he announced that it would be introduced as a ten-minute bill, tabled for 21 October. It passed its first reading by 229 to 129, although, with the parliamentary session nearly over, its sponsor acknowledged that it was unlikely to become law. Opponents had obstructed earlier bills, he stated, but 'we are determined today, even at this late stage in the parliamentary year, to have a vote to show the British public that the majority in the House is concerned to see something done to protect the human embryo'. In the last twenty years, he argued, legislation had been passed that degraded society and a parliamentary minority had obstructed any attempt to reverse them. 'We have an opportunity', he concluded, 'to give a moral lead to the world.' At a subsequent House of Commons meeting, he appealed to 'pro-lifers' nationally to 'put more pressure than ever before on the Government, and demand that it recognises the strength of feeling in the House.'[33]

The Queen's Speech included no reference to embryo research. Shortly afterwards, however, the Health Minister, Tony Newton, told the Commons that the government intended to publish a consultation document before the end of the year asking for further views on the issues. Following this, the government's intention was to bring forward legislation in the next Parliament with alternative draft clauses on embryo research so that MPs could freely vote on the subject. Hargreaves responded by warning the government that it would not be allowed to postpone the matter to after the General Election, while SPUC's reaction was to emphasise that the proposed alternative clauses should be part of the consultation document so that it could be ensured that they were acceptable.

According to Christopher Whitehouse, SPUC's campaign co-ordinator, the Conservative Party leader and its whips should realise that they were 'way out of step with their own grass roots supporters'. A survey of Conservative prospective parliamentary candidates, the Society reported, had shown that a substantial majority opposed both the abortion law and embryo experimentation. LIFE, too, was opposed, repeating its preference for a select committee. The proposed consultation document would 'only scratch the surface', it claimed.[34]

The consultation document was published the following month. Inviting comment on an array of questions connected with Warnock report recommendations, the document emphasised that embryo research would be decided by a free vote. The government recognised, it stated, that there was 'great disquiet' about the present situation. 'Pro-life' groups were strongly critical. Professor Scarisbrick, for LIFE, accused the document of failing to discuss 'Warnock's awful muddle on 14 days' and scarcely touching on genetic manipulation. The latter, he said, needed to be investigated by a select committee. SPUC likewise attacked the document, seeing it as 'a deliberate delaying tactic' intended to 'bamboozle the public'. The government, Phyllis Bowman stated, was 'obviously determined to do everything possible to prevent legislation reaching the statute book before a general election'.[35]

Another MP, Alastair Burt, had adopted the bill as a private members' motion, and at a meeting with MPs, Thatcher described herself as 'deeply concerned' at the implications of human genetic engineering, a view she reiterated in a subsequent interview during the General Election campaign.[36] But in a leaflet issued before the General Election, SPUC denounced the government for remaining officially neutral on the Powell bill while allowing Ministers to do all they could to support the Warnock proposals. Many people, it noted, had voted Conservative because they thought the party would protect the weakest members of society and 'strengthen the value of the family'. Instead it had appointed the 'totally biased' Warnock committee. The government, it went on, had failed to carry out its election promise and failed its supporters. '*Wake up Tories and start listening before the next General Election!*', the leaflet concluded, '*You will lose many thousands of votes.*'[37]

Following the General Election, government proposals for legislation on embryo research were again absent from the

Queen's Speech, an omission which was strongly criticised in an
Early Day motion by Hargreaves, Burt and a large number of other
MPs.[38] Immediately after, however, it was reported that the Health
Secretary, John Moore, would publish a White Paper in the
autumn, to be followed by a bill which would be in line with
Warnock recommendations but allow a free vote on a 14-day
limit.[39] The following month Nicholas Winterton, who had come
twentieth in the private members ballot, announced his intention to
introduce a bill either to restrict abortions or stop embryo research,
while in the House a question from Jill Knight on government
plans for legislation elicited the reply from the Prime Minister that
it was hoped that a bill would be introduced the following year.[40]
In August, however, the Cabinet decided to postpone its plans for a
new bill. Official sources, it was reported, had admitted that a free
vote would have gone against the government.[41]

The White Paper, however, was still to be published and as its
publication date approached, SPUC warned the government that it
should be 'under no illusions' about the depth of feeling in the
Commons and the country and the widespread outrage that would
result if the document took a pro-Warnock line.[42] When it
appeared, it met with hostility from the 'pro-life' lobby. While it
promised a free vote on embryo research, it also envisaged that
surplus embryos could be stored and discarded and, LIFE declared,
had failed to 'prove that human embryos are not human beings and
to justify the 14-day rule'. In SPUC's view, it was 'scandalous',
while for LIFE it was 'a mere re-run of Warnock, a put up job'.
(Continued opposition to the Warnock report was equally evident
in the reintroduction of the Powell bill by 'pro-life' MP Kenneth
Hind. His position of seventeenth in the places for private members
bills, however, ensured that this would attract little attention.)[43]

The following year Tony Newton confirmed to the House that a
bill, with alternative clauses on embryo research, would be
introduced during the Parliament. In the debate that followed,
familiar fears were voiced – William Cash warned of 'genetic
supermarkets' and eugenics experiments reminiscent of Nazism,
while another MP, Sir Trevor Skeet, reminded the House of
Hitler's plans for a master race.[44]

In July SPUC was informed by 'sources close to the Whip's
office' that the bill would be dropped from the Queen's Speech.
Ann Winterton immediately raised the question of embryo legisla-

tion with the Prime Minister, to be told that it was not possible to 'anticipate everything that will be in the Queen's Speech' and that 'a very great deal of debate' would be necessary before deciding on legislation. When, soon after, *The Independent* reported that legislation on embryo research had been dropped from the Queen's Speech, Christopher Whitehouse, SPUC's parliamentary adviser, declared that, if true, 'it would be an outrageous betrayal of trust by the Government'. Despite its manifesto promise to bring forward legislation as soon as possible, he claimed, the government was stalling for time because it feared a majority vote against embryo experiments.[45] CARE too expressed concern while the following month, at the annual meeting of Doctors Who Respect Human Life, its secretary, Dr Peggy Norris, attacked the government for its failure to act.[46] But, to the outrage of Sir Bernard Braine, LIFE and others, once again no reference to the subject appeared in the Queen's Speech.[47]

In the House of Lords the following month the Duke of Norfolk announced plans to introduce a private members' bill based on the Powell bill while in the Commons John Watts, the Conservative MP for Slough, called for a ban on embryo research in a private members' motion. The Minister of State for Health promised MPs that legislation on embryo research would be brought forward during the current Parliament.[48] This was soon followed, as we have seen, by reports of plans for a government bill which would also be concerned with the time limit on abortion. In March the Duke of Norfolk's bill passed its second reading in the Lords while 'pro-lifers' were far from happy with the government's plans. By combining the issues in one bill, Keith Davies of LIFE feared, the government could be trying to secure embryo research by offering its opponents change in the abortion law.[49]

In April the Norfolk bill was withdrawn in the Lords, government whips having indicated they might introduce a motion blocking discussion in order to clear the way for government legislation on the issue in the Commons. The bill would be reintroduced, Norfolk warned, if the government failed to introduce legislation in the next parliamentary session.[50] 'Pro-lifers' remained concerned over government plans and in September Keith Davies of LIFE warned that the government might not live up to its promise while SPUC's John Smeaton spoke of the need to be 'extremely watchful' and the danger of 'a massive betrayal if proper restrictions' were not introduced. In November details of an embryology bill with alternative clauses were announced but opponents of embryo research remained distrustful. Where some pointed out that its introduction first in the Lords could lead to the deletion of the clause banning research before it reached the Commons, criticism focused more on the phrasing of the bill, 'pro-lifers' arguing that it contained loopholes which would still allow experimentation for a brief period after fertilisation.[51] When the bill received its committee reading in the Lords, it was this point that was strongly emphasised and the government agreed to reconsider the matter. (The wording was subsequently changed.) In a free vote, however, the Lords decided by 234 to 80 to support embryo research. While 'bitterly disappointed', SPUC announced, it was not surprised and it looked to greater support in the Commons to defeat embryo research.[52] In the weeks that followed, SPUC and LIFE intensified their efforts, LIFE, for instance, producing a postcard to be sent to MPs while SPUC brought supporters to Parliament to lobby MPs.[53] At the bill's committee stage, Kenneth Clarke, the Health Secretary, told the House that the government took no position on the subject but that he personally supported research. While Sir Bernard Braine argued that the issue was one of human life, MPs voted in favour of research by 364 to 193, a decision which SPUC criticised as 'misinformed and tragic'.[54]

Despite the repeated failure of the Powell bill, 'pro-life' groups had successfully pressed the government to allow a free vote on embryo research. But, at the culmination of their long campaign, embryo research had been supported by Parliament and their efforts had met with defeat. Why did they so much want to defeat the Warnock Report's key recommendation? Why is embryo research so abhorrent to them? We have referred earlier to SPUC's submission to the committee, subsequently published as part of the Society's pamphlet on the subject. LIFE, CARE and the Order of Christian Unity also published pamphlets on the issue. Their arguments can be seen to fall into two main areas: the humanity of the unborn and the effects on society that would follow the acceptance of embryo research. Not accidentally, these two central concerns are exactly the same as those which lie at the core of the 'pro-life' critique of abortion. (Importantly, however, a third element sometimes appears in the discussion – the argument that IVF as such is a threat to the family. Thus, LIFE's pamphlet contrasts the procedure with 'authentic parenthood' within 'married union' while SPUC's 1983 leaflet characterised members of the Warnock committee as holding values 'alien to the family and to traditional moral values'. But this does not play as central a role as the other elements. Discussing the issue, CARE explicitly argues that, while the protection of marriage and the family is an important element of public policy, the defence of human life is the central question.[55] In this chapter, we will concentrate on the main 'pro-life' arguments concerning embryo research. We will, however, return to the relationship between the movement and the family in our later discussion of moral crusades.) On the first of its two main arguments, SPUC argued that human beings are such from the moment of conception and that by substituting an arbitrary definition of personhood for biological fact those who favoured embryo research were doing to the human embryo what Hitler had done to the Jews or slaveowners to the slaves – denying their humanity. The only defensible philosophy towards human life, the society held, was that which argued that human beings had an equal right to life and liberty.[56]

In the publications that appeared after the Warnock Report, this view was reiterated and contrasted to that of the Committee. Thus Raymond Johnston, in CARE's critique of the report, argued that its views were only to be expected considering the committee's composition, 'the prevailing civil service secularist stance', the ethical ambiguity of the medical profession and the moral confusion of society. Despite its stated rejection of utilitarianism as morally unsatisfactory, Johnston argued, the report had fallen into such a stance when it held that research on embryos was justified on grounds of the gains to humanity. To claim that a human embryo deserved a measure of respect beyond that of other animals, he continued, was to evade recognising that the embryo was a human individual and hence could not be experimented upon. LIFE, likewise, argued that the report was a 'betrayal of human life' which proposed the creation of 'second-class and disposable' laboratory human beings. This, it believed, was as discriminatory and unjust as the 1967 Abortion Act.[57]

If the embryo's human status and rights were the moral lobby's first concern, it was also disturbed by the deleterious effects it believed embryo research would have on society. Here, as with

abortion, moral campaigners evoked fears of scientific irresponsibility and medical abuse. Both the cover and the introduction of
the OCU's pamphlet alluded to Huxley's dystopia, *Brave New
World*, while one of the authors speculated that a totalitarian state
might 'choose to breed people like racehorses to produce varieties
like H. G. Wells's Eloi and Morlocks', creating a society in which
an elite ruled over slaves. It was this writer, Rex Brinkworth of the
National Centre for Down's Syndrome, who put the argument
most vividly, linking embryo research, abortion and 'the elimina-
tion of handicapped children' to a 'modern and increasingly self-
centred idea of life' which threatened civilisation in both West and
East. Such views, he argued, had allowed the Nazis to kill the
handicapped and there were 'dangerous currents' in society that
could 'make us...a totalitarian state' as Orwell had predicted 'in
his book *1984*, a year now only seven months ahead of us'.[58]

SPUC's pamphlet too was influenced by literary precedent. One
of its contributors, an American ethicist, Paul Ramsey, pointed to
three British authors – George Orwell, Aldous Huxley and C. S.
Lewis – as important for understanding what was at stake. The
latter two, he wrote, 'had the prescience to discern that the final
assault upon humanity was not to be from the abuse of political
power but of our knowledge of pharmacology and genetics'. How
far, he asked, were 'we from Huxley's East London Hatchery with
its "decanting rooms"?' If Huxley was one symbol of the moral
lobby's concerns, then Hitler was another. There was, he argued
later in his submission, 'already the odour of totalitarianism' in
proposals for embryo research and...Hitler would have gladly
abandoned his 'natural' methods of eugenics for the possibilities
science were now offering.[59]

We noted earlier the OCU's fears of hybrid experiments and
selective breeding. LIFE, in a front-page article in its paper, had
likewise been fearful of the implications of recent developments,
evoking 'the frightening new world of controlled human breeding
and genetic engineering'. Drawing on his experience as a Jewish
refugee, Erwin Chargaff, a member of the Parliamentary Pro-Life
Group's Medical and Scientific Advisory Committee, evokes even
more terrible images. 'I have seen all this before', he declared.
'What I see coming is a gigantic slaughterhouse, a molecular
Auschwitz, in which valuable enzymes, hormones and so on will
be extracted instead of gold teeth.'[60]

Images of Auschwitz and Brave New World underpin the 'pro-life' movement's opposition to embryo research just as they do its stance on abortion. But the very same images are also to be found in publications of very different provenance. Among the strongest critics of recent developments in reproductive technology have been sections of the feminist movement. Is there any common ground between the two arguments?

At first sight, they are very different. In the introduction to *Test-tube Women*, a collection published in 1984, the editors argue that reproductive technology represents the manipulation of women's biology by male experts. The American 'pro-life' movement, they suggest, (which they characterise as part of the New Right), was opposed to embryo research and IVF on grounds of human life and the threat to the family. But this was mistaken, for IVF was being promoted in ways that propped up the family. In 'clashes between conservative groups and biomedical research', they ask, how could either group be supported, 'knowing that what they both share is to dismiss the *women* involved in these technologies...?'[61] In another collection, published the following year, reproductive technology was described by one of the editors of the earlier volume, Renate Duelli Klein, as 'violence against women' and compared with pornography and Nazi breeding programmes. Brave New World, she suggested, was neither brave nor new but just 'more of the same for women', this time more dangerously so. Referring to fellow-contributor Robyn Rowland's image of 'the final solution to the woman question', Klein suggested that 'When the "glass womb" is perfected, women as a group might be obsolete as childbearers.'[62] Rowland, in her contribution, suggested that it might be necessary to 'call for an end to research which would have helped infertile women to conceive, in consideration of the danger to women as a social group of loss of control over "natural" childbearing'. Feminists might also, she suggested, have to 'consider align-ments' with 'right-wing women'.[63]

Where the earlier argument had claimed that 'right to lifers' were right-wing while feminists were concerned with defending women, Rowland now argued that feminists and 'right-wing' women might well be allies. Such a suggestion was necessarily deeply controver-sial and it was another feminist, Marge Berer, who later drew attention when Rowland spoke at a press conference organised by anti-abortion MPs in support of Powell's Unborn Children

Protection Bill. Rowland had made it clear that she supported
abortion rights but, Berer argued, her support for the Powell bill
undermined any such position.[64]

The Order of Christian Unity had organised the press conference
at which Rowland had spoken and its Spring 1985 newsletter
published her speech, in which she criticised the title of Powell's
bill while arguing that it could 'stimulate informed public debate' in
the fight against eugenics and the use of women as 'living
laboratories'.[65] Both her speech on such a platform and Berer's
critique pointed to an important divide among feminists. Where
Klein, Rowland and others saw embryo research as a genocidal
threat to women, Berer spoke of 'Science fiction scenarios' which
encouraged 'fear of... technology' rather than a critical evaluation
of which aspects of science could represent a widening of women's
choices and which a foreclosing. Arguing that existing feminist
accounts often exaggerated how 'advanced' reproductive technology had become, Berer disputed the likelihood of a 'glass womb'
future and the plausibility of a vision of the mass murder of women
as science's aim.[66]

Subsequent work has reiterated this argument. In a review in
another feminist journal later in the year, Rose Shapiro argued that
real concerns were being overwhelmed by 'borrowed images and
second-hand fears'. Instead of considering how reproductive
technology could benefit women the authors of *Man-Made
Women* seemed transfixed by the apocalyptic vision of 'techno-
docs' as 'mad patriarchs'. As a result, she suggested, they considered alliance with the right and telling infertile women that IVF
was against their interests.[67] Later material has also advanced such
arguments, most importantly in collections of essays edited by
Michelle Stanworth and by Lynda Birke, Susan Himmelweit and
Gail Vines.[68] As with pornography, the overlap in argument
between the moral lobby and sections of the feminist movement
was only a partial one. *Human Concern* has recently devoted two
pages to a discussion of feminist critiques of reproductive technology and, as it points out, such arguments have important
differences from those of 'pro-lifers'. Despite the hopes expressed
by Phyllis Bowman in a subsequent interview, co-operation
between the two strands is hard to envisage.[69] But, the very fact
that areas of agreement was possible was significant, not only in
generating dissent from other feminists. As with the division

between the Conservative government and many Conservative MPs, it shows how we cannot expect conflict over moral issues to coincide with the divisions in other areas of political dispute.

5 'Sex and Violence': The Whitehouse Campaign

Obscenity, it has been held since a legal judgement in 1868, is the tendency to deprave and corrupt and in the years that followed this ruling a number of literary and scientific works fell foul of the law.[1] It is hardly surprising, then, that with the shifts in values we discussed in the first chapter, pressure from the Society of Authors and others should have brought about reform in the law at the end of the fifties. The 1959 Obscene Publications Act permitted those accused of obscenity to argue that the material in question had been taken out of context or had redeeming qualities of literary, scientific or other value. Materials held to be obscene are not merely regulated by the 1959 Act (and the minor changes introduced in a similarly named act in 1964). While legislation passed in the late seventies extended the Act to film shows, cinema was primarily the province of the British Board of Film Censors, established early in the century, which viewed films and decided whether or not to grant them a certificate indicating that they could be exhibited. If this was decided, however, this did not automatically mean that they could be shown since local authorities were entitled to refuse their showing within their area. As for broadcasting, it was not covered by the Obscene Publications Act but instead was regulated, in the case of independent companies, by the Television Act 1954 which set down that broadcasters should avoid offending against 'good taste and decency'. The BBC, in 1964, agreed to accept the same obligations.

There are other areas of the question, not least the important but lesser offence of indecency, which does not go so far as to deprave but instead shocks and disgusts. But while we might expend some considerable time in exploring the different aspects of obscenity law, the key areas have already come into sight. Firstly, that the

1959 Act permits material to be defended that critics would wish to be convicted. Not only novels but pornography too can be championed on the grounds that it contributes to society or that it is impossible to demonstrate that those who have come into contact with it have been corrupted. Secondly, films could well be certificated which campaigners would never wish to see the light of day. And thirdly, that television is policed not by obscenity law but more informally, giving leeway to broadcasters to deny that they had offended against their obligations. Books and magazines, films, television programmes – in all these areas moral crusaders found from the sixties onwards a profound cause of concern. Spearheaded by Mary Whitehouse's thirty-thousand strong National Viewers' and Listeners' Association but involving most of the moral lobby, the opposition to 'sex and violence' on television, in magazines and, to a lesser degree, in other media, has been a constant source of press reports and parliamentary activity.[2] Far more than the 'pro-life' movement, campaigners against obscenity have been successful in achieving legislative changes and in inserting some of their demands into Conservative party manifestos. But, while their campaign gained more from Thatcherism than did supporters of abortion restriction (or of the Powell bill or Victoria Gillick), it still has not achieved the full-blooded reversal of recent social and political changes that it seeks. In Chapter 1, we discussed the rise of VALA and similar groups prior to the election of the Thatcher government. In this chapter, we will outline the moral lobby's campaign against obscenity from 1979, before going on to examine the nature of its arguments and its relationship to the emergence of campaigning against pornography from outside the moral lobby.

In an earlier chapter, we have discussed the activity of the anti-abortion movement in the run-up to the 1979 General Election campaign. VALA too was active during this period and in mid-1978 members were urged to approach their MP with the organisation's questionnaire and then inform their local paper of the response. Moral issues 'could decide the result of the next General Election', VALA claimed, and its Organising Secretary, John Beyer, urged members to form constituency Action Groups which could exert pressure on MPs.[3] The following year the organisation set out its plans to send MPs' responses to their local paper as soon as the election was called. In this way, it stated, it hoped 'to bring

these moral issues to the very forefront of the election'. When, at
last, the election campaign began, Mary Whitehouse made clear
where her sympathies lay. Questionnaires had been sent to each of
the party leaders, she announced, and while David Steel had failed
to reply for the Liberals, James Callaghan's response, although
'very interesting' had been unsatisfactory. Mrs. Thatcher, however,
had promised to fight pornography and expressed the view that sex
education should be based on Christian principles. If Labour was
re-elected, Whitehouse declared, 'we shall see a steady deterioration
of moral standards'.[4] As we have already noted, Whitehouse's
remarks focused above all on Callaghan's failure to condemn the
provision of under-sixteen contraception without parental consent.
But while this had played the leading role in VALA's General
Election intervention it had only been one of the items in the
organisation's questionnaire. In the period after the election under-
sixteen contraception all but disappeared from its agenda. Instead
it was the core issues of VALA – the representation of sexuality
and violence in the media – that returned to the fore.

The first major campaign of moral crusaders against obscenity
after the election of the Thatcher government came with the
publication later that year of the Williams committee report on
obscenity. The committee, headed by the philosopher Bernard
Williams, had been appointed in 1977 by the Callaghan government to examine the state of obscenity legislation and film censorship and make proposals. The report which eventually appeared
proposed that a new law should be introduced which would define
obscene material as that which gave offence to reasonable people
on account of its sexual or violent content. Such material would be
restricted in its availability so that only those over the age of
eighteen who positively wanted access to it could do so and it
would only be available by post or in special premises or sections of
premises. While most obscene material would thus be restricted in
availability, the premises having to have blank windows and
display a warning notice concerning its contents, the committee
recommended that live sex-shows should be prohibited, as should
photographs or films that involved the sexual exploitation of
someone under the age of sixteen or the infliction of actual
physical harm. As regards cinema, it proposed the transfer of the
powers of pre-censorship from local authorities and the British
Board of Film Censors to a new statutory board which could refuse

a certificate to films judged 'unfit for public exhibition' and would operate a system of classification which would include an 18R category for showing under restricted circumstances in designated cinemas. In the committee's view, film was a more powerful medium than the written word or the still photograph and, as such, should be subject to greater restriction.[5]

As was to be expected, the moral lobby's response to the report was sharply critical. The committee had concluded that there was no satisfactory evidence that pornography caused harm other than offence, a view that was particularly objectionable to its critics. Pornography, Whitehouse replied, did 'incalculable harm to all involved'. Increasing availability of such material, she argued, was followed by a rise in sex crimes and the committee's proposed legalisation of hard-core pornography could not be accepted. The report was, in her words, 'a pornographer's charter' and VALA would be seeking an interview with the Home Secretary in order to make clear that its acceptance would destroy people's faith in the government. She could not see, she went on, that the Prime Minister would accept the report, 'not only because she is Prime Minister but because she is a woman, and especially because she is a mother'.[6]

Press reports following the completion of the Williams report had suggested that the government was unlikely to support it.[7] At the beginning of the following year, a House of Lords debate on the issue made it clear that agreement on new legislation would not easily be forthcoming. Following a succession of speakers, many opposed to the report, Lord Belstead, Under Secretary at the Home Office, suggested that the committee's recommendation not to restrict the written word need not be accepted and that the difficulty of proving that pornography caused harm did not mean that it was not damaging culturally and morally. The recommendation that the licensing powers of local authorities and the British Board of Film Censors should be replaced by a new film examining board was also open to question. Much thought, he told the House, needed to be given to whether the committee's proposed balance between prohibition and restriction was generally acceptable.[8]

The following month, Whitehouse led a delegation to William Whitelaw, the Home Secretary, to discuss the report. The delegation asked Whitelaw to publish all the submissions to the committee and to reject the report as biased. It was told that the government hoped to deal with the issue when the report was debated in Parliament.[9] While the Home Secretary in late April called for comments on the report to be sent to the Home Office by the end of July, VALA decided to launch a 'STOPORN NOW CAMPAIGN' and concentrate its efforts on what Whitehouse termed 'arguably the most important petition that has ever been launched'. The report, she declared, was a threat 'to our children, our culture and indeed our health and safety'. The petition, which was also circulated by the Festival of Light, called upon the government to tighten up obscenity legislation, prohibit the publication of pornography and bring broadcasting under the legislation. In early July, VALA brought Dr John Court, an Australian researcher criticised in the Williams Report, to Britain to defend his view that there was a link between pornography and sex crime. The visit received considerable press and broadcasting attention and included a meeting with the Home Secretary.[10] In addition to the petition, VALA also issued a memorandum to the Home Office in which it urged the report's rejection. The government, it argued, should immediately bring in legislation to control video pornography while, to curb obscenity, it should bring in a measure to specifically define the sexual acts which it would not be legal to depict or describe.[11] The Responsible Society, too, attacked the report and urged its rejection. The committee, it argued, had failed to see the connection between pornography and the general breakdown of stable sexual relationships.[12]

The petition campaign continued for some months and later in the year Whitehouse announced to supporters that the Home Office had made it clear that the government would take no action on the report during the new session of Parliament. This had the advantage, she went on, of giving more time to collect signatures but, she feared, the report's recommendations would 'come to be accepted in practice' and fundamentally shift the boundaries between 'decency and responsibility'.[13] At the beginning of the following year, Patrick Mayhew, the Minister of State at the Home Office, told the Commons that the majority of responses to the report had been hostile and there was no early likelihood of general government legislation on the subject, but it was not until late June that MPs at last had the chance to discuss the report. Opening the debate, Mayhew reiterated that there was no 'early prospect' of general government legislation on the subject but held out the hope of some changes. Discussing the report he expressed sympathy with some of its suggestions but rejected both the call for a new film examining board and the proposal to end restrictions on the written word. Many people, he noted, believed strongly that a degraded view of human relationships damaged society and, he added, sex crimes, in part, might be due to pornography.[14] Soon after the Home Secretary announced that no legislation on the subject would be introduced in the 1981–82 parliamentary session. As a result, VALA members were encouraged to continue collecting signatures with a view to presenting them 'at a strategic moment' in 1982 in order to force the government to introduce legislation tightening up the law. (In the event, the half-million signatures collected were finally presented in December 1981 in protest against government plans to license sex shops.)[15]

During the same period, Parliament and moral campaigners were also concerned with private members' legislation on the public display of indecent material. In July 1979 details were published of a bill by Conservative MP Brian Mawhinney, who had come seventh in the private members' ballot. The bill proposed that magistrates would have the power to decide whether a particular magazine-cover, book-cover, cinema-hoarding or window display was indecent and, if so, the offender could be fined up to £2,000 and could be sent to prison for up to three months.[16] Given its position in the queue for parliamentary time, the bill was unlikely to proceed and, the following year, it failed for lack of time, the Home Secretary having refused the request by the delegation led by Mary Whitehouse to give government time to the bill.[17]

In January 1981, however, Timothy Sainsbury, Conservative MP for Hove, who had come first in the new private members' ballot, announced his intention to introduce an Indecent Displays bill. The bill sought to restrict the display of indecent material to paying premises or to shops with warning notices and at its successful second reading at the end of January, Patrick Mayhew, on behalf of the government, expressed support for the bill's broad objectives. Whitehouse, however, who had been present in the public gallery, described the government as 'running scared' of dealing with the issue. 'People', she said, 'wanted action but the Government has given no assurance at all when it will do anything. When the Tory Government came in we thought they would have the

courage to do something.'[18] In a letter of protest to the Prime
Minister, Whitehouse criticised the government's Commons announcement that it saw 'no early prospect' of comprehensive
obscenity legislation and in a subsequent statement described it
as incredible that a Conservative government was presiding over
what was effectively the legalisation of pornography. If all the
government was going to do was control the display of indecency,
she said, then 'shops with blank windows' would be 'selling all
kinds of pornography'.[19]

In an article in the *Universe* the following month, journalist and
moral campaigner Joanna Bogle reported that campaigners were
far from satisfied with Sainsbury's bill. One MP, James Dunn,
urged a tightening up of the bill during its committee stage so that
television would be included, while Mary Whitehouse argued that
the bill 'merely' dealt with indecent display and would be 'useless'
unless the government introduced effective pornography legislation.[20] In April, in a meeting with the Home Secretary, she again
criticised the bill, but the following month saw the completion of its
report stage and third reading. During the debate, Sir Bernard
Braine criticised the bill as effectively allowing pornographers free
range as long as they put up a warning notice, but the bill passed
and, after passing through the Lords and receiving the Royal
Assent, came into force at the end of October. Whitehouse,
interviewed immediately before, made it clear that she continued
to oppose the warning notice clause and was concerned that the bill
lacked a definition of indecency. What was needed, she suggested,
was to specify exactly what was indecent.[21]

While campaigners were concerned about obscenity in general,
much of their activity in the early 1980s has been concentrated on
sex shops and in this too they achieved some important success. As
such shops spread out of London into the provinces numerous
local campaigns sprang up, often involving national moral groupings. In Walsall, for instance, VALA was active in trying to stop
such a shop opening in the area while the Bristol Family Life
Association picketed premises in its area.[22] While such campaigns
often received the support of local MPs, the issue became most
politicised in London itself. Having campaigned on the issue for
some time, in late 1980 the Conservative group on the GLC
published its Campaign Guide for the May 1981 elections. 'The
Conservative GLC', it stated, 'is taking a strong line on the

question of pornography.' Since the Williams Report, it claimed, indecent display had worsened in Soho and Piccadilly Circus and what was needed was new legislation through which 'sex establishments' could be placed under strict controls with their numbers limited and their windows blacked out.[23]

In April 1981 the GLC and other bodies approached the government with the proposal that controls be included in the next GLC General Powers Bill and received a sympathetic response. Such a measure, however, would only affect the capital and campaigners elsewhere continued to press for a more general solution. In June, facing questions on the situation, the Under Secretary of State for the Environment, Giles Shaw, acknowledged concern over the issue and indicated that the government intended to see how the GLC provisions worked before deciding what could be done nationally.[24]

The government's caution was unacceptable to campaigners and later in the year Whitehouse attacked the spread of sex shops across the country. Without new and strong obscenity laws, she said, 'Britain is rapidly becoming another Denmark by default – and this under a Conservative Government.'[25] An attempt by Whitehouse to gain a sponsor for a private members' bill on the subject proved abortive but, in December, under pressure both nationally and locally, the government agreed to legislate for the licensing of sex shops. Early the following year Timothy Raison, Minister of State at the Home Office, told Parliament that a new clause in the Local Government (Miscellaneous Provisions) Bill would allow local authorities to control sex shops but this could not, he added amidst objections, be purely on moral grounds. Both Labour and Conservative MPs criticised the proposal for falling short of what they believed was needed, Sir Bernard Braine being particularly forceful in arguing that the bill permitted sex shops rather than banning them.[26]

In response to criticism, however, the clause was subsequently toughened to allow local authorities to rule that the appropriate number of sex shops in any locality was nil. In March, the new clause was accepted in the Lords, a Festival of Light amendment from Lord Nugent allowing a formal ban being withdrawn.[27] Whitehouse's initial response had been to condemn the government's proposal to license sex shops as 'ill-conceived Civil Service obscurantism'. She had never thought she would see the day, she subsequently wrote, in which 'a *Tory* government would "license" pornography'. But in the light of the toughening of the clause, for which it partly claimed credit, VALA was eventually to welcome the new measure while criticising it for not going far enough. Licensing, John Beyer stated, would 'give sex shops an aura of respectability' but the new law could be effective if people demanded that their councillors refuse licences to sex shops. It was also necessary, he added, to press for stronger legislation on the material sold in such shops: 'If all these things were illegal, the shops would cease to exist.'[28]

Local campaigning has continued against sex shops subsequent to the new legislation.[29] More importantly, however, the energies of campaigners began to move in new directions. If limits were being put on what people might encounter in the public sphere (another private members' bill, passed in 1982, put restrictions on sex cinemas)[30] then this did nothing about the very concerns with broadcasting and the home which had brought about VALA's creation. Television remained outside the Obscene Publications Act, new developments were occurring in cable and satellite television and, crucially for its next campaign, there was the rise of video. As early as August 1980, VALA had described video pornography as 'the biggest single media threat to the quality of life in Britain' and, in a memorandum to the Home Office, it had called for obscenity laws to cover the showing of videos in the home.[31] It was not, however, until 1982 that the subject of obscene videos was taken up in a major way and by then the exact nature of the object in question had changed. Instead of pornography, it was violent videos which were the target of concern (although, as her later book shows, Whitehouse equates the two, tracing the origin of the later campaign to her 1980 attack on video porn.)[32] A number of newspapers rather than Whitehouse herself had led the attack on 'video nasties'[33] but she had quickly moved into action when plans were revealed for a voluntary classification scheme involving the British Board of Film Censors and the British Videogram Association. Film censors, she declared, had already passed unacceptable material, and what was needed was new obscenity legislation.[34] In June, a number of videos were sent to the Director of Public Prosecutions (DPP) to consider whether prosecutions should be brought. After some deliberation, it was decided that charges could be brought under the Obscene Publications Act and in hearings in

September distributors of several videos were found guilty. The DPP had decided to bring charges under Section Three of the Act where forfeiture was the penalty, rather than Section Two, where imprisonment was a possibility. Following the first hearings, Mary Whitehouse, who had called for prosecutions under Section Two, attacked the proceedings as a farce and called for the Director's resignation. Relations, worsened if anything, later in the month when the DPP told magistrates that police had been mistaken in plans to proceed under Section Two. This was a public scandal, Whitehouse announced, in which the DPP had taken the distributors' side against the police.[35] Speaking at the launch of her new book, which coincided with the later case, she urged the Prime Minister to act quickly against 'video nasties'.[36]

A ten-minute bill to ban the rental of adult videos to young people was unsuccessful.[37] The Prime Minister, however, in a letter to Whitehouse immediately afterwards, declared her concern that pornography was undermining standards of decency and family life and noted that while the Home Secretary was still looking into the effectiveness of voluntary controls on videos she did not rule out legislation. This, however, in Whitehouse's view was inadequate. What was needed, she argued, was a parliamentary screening of 'video nasties' to convince MPs of the need to legislate.[38] Some 150 MPs had replied to a letter from her, supporting the need for legislation and, with an election pending, she urged the Conservatives to include the strengthening of the obscenity law in their manifesto. Pornography, she predicted, would be a major issue.[39]

The Conservative manifesto for the 1983 Election did indeed include a pledge to introduce legislation to deal with 'violent and obscene video cassettes'.(As Marsh *et al.* point out, the Conservative Campaign Guide issued shortly before had claimed credit for opposing pornography but made no reference to 'video nasties', showing how rapidly they had become an issue.)[40] Shortly after the Conservative victory, the Prime Minister told the Commons that the party manifesto had recognised 'the great concern' over the matter and that voluntary regulation was not enough. Instead, legislation would have to be brought in. In a separate statement, the Home Secretary, Leon Brittan, told the House that he was urgently considering the form of statutory control. But rather than the government introducing a bill, it was reported that Graham Bright, the Conservative MP for Luton South, would introduce such a bill and had already met Whitehouse in the House. (Indeed, unnoticed by the national press, the two had met earlier. While VALA had urged supporters to press parliamentary candidates to support a new obscenity law, Whitehouse herself had toured marginal constituencies in a van bearing the slogan 'CHILDREN AT RISK! VOTE FOR THE CANDIDATE WHO WILL FIGHT FOR DECENCY'. Among the candidates with whom she discussed her hope for a private members' bill on 'video nasties' was Graham Bright).[41] In a subsequent interview Brittan made it clear that Bright's bill was based on the government's policy on the issue but, when the details were revealed in mid-July, they did not meet Whitehouse's wishes. Bright, who had come top in the private members' ballot, proposed that all videos should be classified and anyone selling or renting one in breach of its classification conditions could be fined up to £10,000 or imprisoned for up to two years. This, in Whitehouse's view, did not go far enough and did not specifically list 'those elements of violence and obscenity which should be deemed to be illegal'.[42] Later in the month, she led a delegation to the Home Secretary to express 'serious misgivings' about the bill. She also called on him to stop pornographic videos – 'That was an absolutely new idea to him and he promised us he would take it very seriously indeed.' Brittan also promised that he would ask Bright to introduce the bill earlier than had been anticipated.[43] A little over two months later, Whitehouse organised a twice-daily showing of 'video nasties' at a fringe meeting at the Conservative conference.[44]

Shortly before the bill's second reading, a showing of extracts from 'nasties' took place at the Commons and, in a separate development, the Lord Chief Justice, Lord Lane, spoke out against pornography and 'video nasties'. Asked by a Conservative backbencher during question time to endorse his views, the Prime Minister did so and added that she hoped that the Bright bill would be passed as quickly as possible. Whitehouse, however, continued to have doubts and was reported to favour the introduction of an amendment to restrict what type of videos could be seen in the home.[45]

Briefly, it looked as if her wish to extend the bill's reach would be successful. As it stood, the bill allowed people over 18 to buy pornographic videos. Whitehouse's argument was that these could be seen in the home by under-18s and instead should be banned, a view which Bright rejected on the ground that a ban would merely lead to a 'flood' of black market material. During the second reading, however, the Home Office Under Secretary of State, David Mellor, stated that both he and the Home Secretary understood the concern expressed by Whitehouse and others and that they saw the argument for extending restriction. If, he went on, after the matter had been considered in committee, the House decided there should be a ban on pornographic videos the government would not stand in its way.[46] Whitehouse soon after called upon her supporters to approach their MPs urging a ban on pornographic videos and the creation of a new broad-based classifying body rather than the proposal in the Bright bill that the British Board of Film Censors be responsible. This body, she claimed, had already proved too lax in classifying films.[47]

During its committee stage the argument about pornographic videos continued, with Mellor for the government and Sir Bernard Braine (who had put down an amendment on the issue) arguing that they should be banned and Bright continuing to argue that this would merely force them underground. Outside Parliament Leon Brittan also argued the government's new and tougher position, which, most importantly, was supported by the Prime Minister.[48] By this time, however, a new element had entered the situation. While other sections of the moral lobby had also been involved in the argument, only VALA had played a prominent role. Now, a new group emerged in the shape of the Parliamentary Group Video Enquiry. This official sounding body had had its origin in a meeting during the summer of 1983 called by Viscount Ingleby and chaired by Lord Nugent, in which representatives of the main churches had been invited to attend and were presented with a paper by Raymond Johnston, the leading figure in CARE. This paper urged the setting up of a working party to produce within six months a report on the danger video posed to children and what should be done about it. Amidst some misgivings, this was agreed and a report appeared on 22 November (immediately before the first meeting of the Standing Committee on the Bright bill), which claimed that over 40 per cent of children aged between 6 and 15 had seen a 'video nasty'. While the report was quickly to run into trouble with academics and church representatives disassociating themselves from it, its effect at the time was to strengthen the campaign.[49]

The amendment against pornographic videos, however, did not succeed, the committee on the bill voting by 11 to 5 to remove it, a defeat which led Whitehouse to once again urge the need for 'a really effective Obscene Publications Act'.[50] The bill received an unopposed third reading in March 1984 with amendments being added to increase the proposed maximum fine to £20,000 and limiting the sale of pornographic videos to sex shops.[51] The bill then went to the House of Lords and, albeit after a contentious Report Stage, passed into law.

During this period, the government had also introduced legislation to bring cable TV under the Obscene Publications Act, a decision which Whitehouse supported.[52] Following the passing of the Bright bill, however, for a period obscenity declined in prominence as an issue. But VALA and other groups remained active and in October of the following year the Video Enquiry issued a new report while Whitehouse again organised a videoshowing at a fringe meeting at the Conservative conference, this time on obscenity. Time, she said, was running out for the party to fulfil its 1983 election pledge to take action.[53] Then in November a speech by Norman Tebbit attacking the permissive society led Whitehouse to urge Conservative MPs who had been successful in the private members' ballot to take up a bill strengthening the 1959 Obscene Publications Act. 'I would have thought', she said, 'that after Mr Tebbit's speech one of the Tory members would be prepared to act.' Meeting the Home Secretary, Douglas Hurd, she received no promise of government support but individual members proved more sympathetic. Sir Nicholas Bonsor, Conservative MP for Upminster, had achieved sixth place in the ballot and decided to take up a measure to tighten up the definition of obscenity by specifying exactly what activity it would be obscene to depict.[54] More importantly, Winston Churchill, Conservative MP for Davyhulme, had second place and he decided to take up a measure to extend the 1959 Act to cover TV and radio and deal with obscene magazines. Bonsor dropped his bill in Churchill's favour and the government itself began to show more concern with the issue. Speaking to the Conservative trade unionists' conference at the end of November, the Prime Minister announced that the government was considering very carefully whether anything further could be done about scenes of explicit violence on television. (This, it turned out, was in response to a question from a VALA activist.) In a Commons debate on juvenile crime days after, David Mellor suggested that research had established that TV violence did have an effect on children and this, he said, was what commonsense would suggest. People, he stated, should make clear to the television companies their concern over TV violence.[55] This was quickly followed by a warning from the Home Secretary (who had just received a report on TV violence from VALA) that broadcasters should put their 'house in order'. Hurd promised 'to look carefully at what Winston Churchill is proposing' since, he said, legislation might well be necessary. Later in the month, he held a meeting with the heads of the BBC and IBA (Independent Broadcasting Authority) and warned that the government would step in unless they dealt with the problems. VALA and similar groups, he subsequently announced, deserved a hearing and the government had not as yet decided its stance on the Churchill bill. While the government remained unsure, the bill was supported by Whitehouse, who warned that the government would suffer electorally if it opposed it and Churchill too urged the government not to do so.[56]

In a letter to Whitehouse shortly after his meeting with TV heads, Hurd agreed that broadcasters needed to be strict concerning violence and obscenity. She, for her part, called upon supporters to press MPs to back the Churchill bill.[57] The bill received its second reading in late January. It included a so-called 'laundry list' which specified acts which it would be obscene to show on television or in magazines. The bill passed by 161 to 31. David Mellor, for the government, however, warned that, given the existence of broadcasting guidelines already stricter than the 1959 Obscene Publications Act, careful thought was necessary about Churchill's proposal to bring broadcasting under the Act.[58] For Churchill, however, the exclusion of broadcasting from obscenity legislation had been proved wrong by the recent showing of two films – *Jubilee* and *Sebastiane* – on Channel 4. *Jubilee*, he declared, had been obscenely violent. (While it received less attention in the Commons debate, objections to *Sebastiane* partly involved its homo-erotic nature and one Labour MP, Jo Richardson, had argued that the bill would be used against the 'visual depiction of a homosexual relationship'. VALA had sent reports on the two films to a large number of MPs and then shown extracts from them at a House of Commons screening three days before the Second Reading.)[59]

The following month, the Prime Minister told the Commons that the government was monitoring the situation before deciding what to do.[60] The bill itself had come under heavy criticism, particularly for its potential effect on artistic and documentary coverage, and in late February, Churchill amended it by discarding the list of activities held to be obscene. In its place he introduced a clause under which a jury would decide if a broadcast was obscene with 'regard in particular to the probability of it being viewed or heard by children and young persons'.[61] As the Report Stage approached, Whitehouse called on her supporters once more to write to MPs urging them to vote for the bill.[62] Instead, however, a five-hour filibuster killed the bill. Whitehouse, undeterred, announced that the Prime Minister had told her in a letter that legislation was possible if there was sufficient agreement. If it really wanted, Whitehouse declared, the government could produce a bill. In an interview shortly after, Hurd urged the broadcasting authorities to do more to deal with sex and violence on television.[63]

Within months Whitehouse returned to the offensive, presenting a report to the Home Secretary that called for a new Obscene Publications Act which would cover TV, an annual parliamentary debate on complaints about broadcasting and the issuing of an instruction to chief constables to record those sex crimes associated with obscene material. In reply later in the year, Hurd agreed to ask chief constables to monitor such incidents. More importantly, commenting on the recent defeat of the Churchill bill, he stated that the government would be considering further whether broadcasting should be brought within the Obscene Publications Act.[64] This was quickly followed by the news that the Prime Minister now favoured reforming the Act and that a commitment along these lines would probably appear in the party's General Election manifesto.[65]

It was reported, following the private members' ballot, that the Home Office was hopeful that one of the successful MPs would take up an obscenity bill. The following month, it was announced that Gerald Howarth, Conservative MP for Cannock and Burntwood, would take up the issue of broadcasting's exemption from the 1959 Act. Once more, Whitehouse used the tactic of a video showing, this time showing MPs extracts from late-night Channel 4 films and the BBC series, *The Singing Detective*. And again, supporters were encouraged to write to their MPs asking them to support the bill.[66] In April the bill, which also attempted to extend the definition of obscenity to that which was 'grossly offensive' to a 'reasonable person', received its second reading. (As Howarth made clear in his speech, his proposals were not only aimed at broadcasting but also at magazines.) Supported by the government, it passed by 160 to 23, Whitehouse describing its progress as 'a great step forward' and urging a strong campaign to ensure it became law.[67] But, with the General Election approaching, attempts to complete the committee stage of the bill foundered on the large number of amendments tabled by critical MPs. The Conservative manifesto, however, contained, as expected, a promise to bring forward proposals to deal with 'the display of sex and violence on television', a pledge described by Whitehouse as 'something that will strike a chord in many hearts'. A new Broadcasting Bill would be introduced, the manifesto stated, and in order to protect standards broadcasting would be brought under the Obscene Publications Act and new arrangements established to effectively reflect public concern.[68]

Following the election, it was reported that Hurd was confident that agreement over a new body would be reached between the Home Office and broadcasters and legislation would not be necessary. Citizens could, he stated in a BBC interview, turn to the body if they felt 'violence or sex have been portrayed in a particularly offensive or dangerous way on television'. However, it was evident that a non-statutory body might be decried as too weak at Conservative conference the following month and within days Hurd had announced that an independent watchdog would be set up quickly and would subsequently be given statutory powers. At the Conservative conference, all thoughts of a voluntary body forgotten, the announcement of a statutory Broadcasting Standards Council (BSC) met with the representatives' support.[69]

What powers the BSC would have, however, remained unclear. Towards the end of the year it was reported that it would have the power to order companies to screen 'apologies' but, in a more muted account early the following year, the government was credited with intending to give broadcasters a six-month trial period of co-operation with the Council before deciding whether to legislate to make 'the screening of sex or violence warnings mandatory'. In a further sign of possible tension on the issue, a report also appeared that the Prime Minister had come into conflict with the Home Office over who should be in charge of the Council. 'Mrs Thatcher', it was reported, wanted someone who would 'stand up to powerful TV executives'.[70]

The Home Office, however, denied this report, claiming that the delay in announcing an appointment was due to the problem of finding a suitable candidate and soon after it was reported that Sir William Rees-Mogg, former editor of *The Times* and vice-chairman of the BBC Board of Governors, was the likely candidate, a possibility that was warmly greeted by Mary Whitehouse.[71] Later in the month, the Home Office minister in charge of broadcasting, Timothy Renton, was the guest speaker at the VALA Conference. The Council, he reiterated, would have powers to broadcast its views on programmes, television would be brought under the Obscene Publications Act and the Council of Europe would establish joint rules to stop indecent material on satellite television. Furthermore, he added, the government was reconsidering whether the BSC would be entitled to preview programmes.[72]

The following month, however, any idea that the Government intended the Broadcasting Standards Council to be able to preview programmes was denied by a government spokesman. The Home Office, it was reported, was moving away from potential conflict with the IBA and BBC and was now most concerned about the risk of violence and pornography from cable and satellite broadcasters. Subsequently announcing Rees-Mogg's appointment in the Commons, Douglas Hurd indicated that previewing might be feasible but only of certain fictional material acquired from abroad.[73] At a Press Association lunch the following month, however, the Prime Minister warned that if TV companies failed to show self-discipline then the government 'would simply have to protect our young people from some of the violence and pornography we have seen'.[74] Nor was the situation uncomplicated on the European front. Problems emerged later in the year, following an agreement between broadcasting ministers to stop the transmission of indecent material. This would be difficult to implement concerning satellite broadcasts, however, and it was unclear if one suggestion, to penalise advertisers, would be effective. Another possible response, the blocking of satellite signals, also appeared impractical.[75]

In 1989, the Broadcasting Standards Council issued a draft code of practice urging that programme-makers should be careful in the depiction of violence, particularly towards women, while sexual scenes should avoid exploitation. It did not meet with Whitehouse's approval, who compared it to 'a civil service document' in trying 'not to come down firmly on one side or the other', and Rees-Mogg came in for some criticism when he attended VALA's silver jubilee convention as its guest speaker. He rejected the Association's view that there should be a list of behaviour prohibited from showing on television, proposing instead an advisory code, and suggested that 'adult' films should be allowed on satellite television as they were in video shops. This view was not well received and was in direct contrast to Whitehouse's earlier speech in which she insisted that there should be no distinction between what could be shown on broadcast and satellite channels.[76] The possibility of a two-tier system, with certain material allowed on subscription channels which were not permitted on BBC or ITV, continued to be the subject of the BSC's deliberations.[77]

In September, Hurd announced that foreign programmes would be monitored and services could be suspended through the Council of Europe. Subsequently, however, the director of the BSC suggested that, given the state of European negotiations, satellite soft porn could not be stopped.[78] As for the domestic situation, there appeared to be some uncertainty whether the forthcoming BSC code of practice was mandatory or not but its subsequent appearance did at least resolve one question, with the decision not to permit different standards for subscription channels. The new Broadcasting Bill, announced in September, included provisions to prosecute anyone in Britain supplying a station beaming offensive programmes and to penalise advertisers and in the debate on the Queen's Speech the new Home Secretary, David Waddington, emphasised that obscenity law would be extended to broadcasters.[79]

As our account suggests, obscenity has rivalled abortion as the most important issue for moral campaigners in recent years. But what does the moral lobby mean by obscenity and why does it believe campaigning against it is so important? VALA and other organisations have produced a considerable amount of literature on this subject, and it is a major theme of the books and other writings produced by Mary Whitehouse and other leading campaigners. Through examining some of these we can get a clear picture of the moral lobby's objections.

Following the Williams Report's publication, for instance, VALA produced a joint response with the Community Standards Association. In this response, VALA and the CSA championed the work of Dr John Court in arguing that pornography did affect behaviour, suggested that increased violent crime was connected with violent material on television and in the cinema and argued that, if it was available, it could fall into the hands of children.[80] Other sections of the moral lobby have also been forceful in their opposition to obscenity. Thus in *Pornography and Hate*, a Responsible Society publication of the seventies still sold by Family and Youth Concern in the eighties, David Holbrook describes pornography as sexual fascism, a malicious attack on human values. It reduces women to things, to sex objects and where democracy rested on mutuality and equality, pornography rested on exploitation and selfishness. Just as racist materials should be suppressed so too should pornography.[81]

If we turn to Whitehouse's own writings, we find in the index of one of her books four entries for pornography – one of which concerns her argument that it is connected with 'communist strategy', to which we will return later, while the others examine it in relation to 'human relationships', 'sex crime' and 'social decay'. What does she argue? Once again strong links are suggested between increased availability of pornography and rising rates of rape and other sexual offences. The head of the San Francisco police sex crime detail, she reports, has pointed out that 'attacks on women cluster abundantly in the areas around the dirty cinemas'. In Japan, however, low incidence of rape is connected with strict enforcement of legislation against pornography. As for its effect on human relationships, Whitehouse draws on the Moors murders, correspondence from pornography consumers and their spouses and the views of psychologists to argue that pornography can lead to marital discord, exploitation and violence. While pornographers promise us emancipation, she writes, 'we are driven either into ourselves or into brutal fantasies which are often in essence destructive. Far from being a fulfilment of true sexual drive, pornography is an emasculation.' Finally, on the link between pornography and social decay, Whitehouse argues that our culture has become degraded and both personal and public morality have collapsed. Sexual anarchy will be followed by political anarchy and that in turn by 'either dictatorship or destruction' unless we defend standards and 'the family, the foundation-stone of civilised life' against 'the perversion and inhumanity of pornography which is already characterising Western society'.[82]

Whitehouse's argument is frequently pivoted not on the depraved adult consumer of pornography but on the innocent child who suffers as a result of its existence. This was particularly noticeable at the time of the child pornography and 'video nasty' campaigns but is a constant theme throughout her argument. Along with sex education, pop music and trends in teenage magazines, the availability of pornography is indicted for putting at risk children's healthy development. Her deepest fear, she argues, is that the debasement of our culture will lead to the destruction of childhood. Pornography cost the lives of 'the dead babies in the moors' and while it is true that this type of child murder is rare, 'it is equally true that their minds are constantly being raped by the kind of material which meets their eyes on every side'. In allowing adults 'rights' to buy pornography, she writes, we are turning our backs on our responsibility to protect children's right to childhood and to develop at their own rate rather than under the pressures of 'sexual manipulators'.[83] For Whitehouse, a central theme of the fight against obscenity is the fight to protect childhood innocence.

Whitehouse's concern with childhood also connects with her concern over obscenity in another way – that we are each a 'child of God'. Pornography, she argues, undermines respect for women and for the family, and a society that tolerates it will lose a sense of guilt, a sense of sin and as a consequence a capacity for redemption. The Cross itself would become without meaning in such a society, she fears, and sexploitation will have destroyed the ability to resist evil that comes from Christian culture.[84] Whitehouse's fight, then, is for 'faith and...family'[85] rather than a merely negative fight against objectionable representations. It is a fight of cosmic proportions, of good against evil, but it is also a fight between earthly forces. 'Who's getting at our kids?', she asks in one chapter title and her reply is that we are witnessing 'a calculated assault upon a whole generation' and that the increasing evidence of Marxist infiltration in industry can open our eyes to their use of sexual anarchy too.[86] A VALA pamphlet on pornography likewise makes clear its views on both the centrality of religion and the

threat of subversion in its discussion of obscenity. 'Who wants it?',
the pamphlet asks, and it replies by claiming that Communists
deliberately seek to break down people's moral values by 'focusing
their attention on sexy books'. In Denmark, the pamphlet reports,
the spread of porn is now being followed by live sex shows. 'And
when it's impossible to think of more methods of defiling man', it
goes on, 'these forces will throw off their mask. Their ultimate
effect is to defile the holy things of God.'[87] Although some sections
of the moral lobby, notably Family and Youth Concern, argue in a
purely secular way, for VALA and others the struggle against
pornography is a Christian battle against degradation, against the
causes of sexual crime, and ultimately against the forces of
subversion and Satan. But Whitehouse and allied groupings are
not the only forces arrayed against obscenity. In recent years much
activity against pornography has been carried out not by the moral
lobby but by feminists. This development has generated a debate
within the feminist movement, leading to the recent emergence of a
group, Feminists Against Censorship, concerned that anti-pornography campaigns could lead to a strengthening of a state hostile to
feminism and an open discussion of sexuality. In this discussion,
however, we will focus on one particular question – whether there
is any common ground between the moral lobby and feminist anti-
pornography campaigners.

Emerging in the Women's Liberation Movement of the seventies,
such organisations as Women Against Violence Against Women
(WAVAW) have argued that pornography 'encourages a climate in
which sexual violence against women is seen as acceptable'.[88]
Feminists have marched to 'Reclaim the Night', demonstrated
against such films as *Dressed to Kill*, picketed W. H. Smith and
other shops selling 'soft' porn magazines and supported demands
by feminist Labour MP Clare Short for an end to Page 3 of the
Sun. Moralists, they argue, oppose pornography for very different
reasons. Laura Lederer, in an influential early collection of
American essays, argues that conservatives say pornography is
immoral because it exposes the human body, while feminists see it
as the ideology of an anti-woman culture. More recently, Sam
Chugg of the feminist Campaign Against Pornography has argued
that 'Mrs Whitehouse is a straw opposition to pornography',
manipulating women's anger 'to get support for an actually
reactionary project. It is not because selling pornography is to do

with women's rights or sexual violence – it is to do with imposing their morality on others'.[89] Other feminist anti-pornography campaigners have seen some common ground between the two movements even though they are at loggerheads. Thus, writing in the late seventies, Ruth Wallsgrove agrees with Whitehouse that porn is degrading but argues that their reasons for opposing it are 'precisely the opposite', Whitehouse wanting 'to maintain the sexual status quo...the nuclear family and the sanctity of marriage'.[90]

To suggest that moralists do not concern themselves with women's position is to misrepresent their argument (Whitehouse, for instance, explicitly attacks 'the misuse and gross exploitation of women')[91] and it is, as Wallsgrove suggests, more useful to separate out the argument that pornography degrades women, common to both camps, from the very different forms of society and gender relations they wish to establish. As we discuss later, Whitehouse, Raymond Johnston and others explicitly oppose feminism. What is more surprising, however, is the attitude of moral campaigners towards feminist opposition to pornography. The Festival of Light, in particular, has seen feminists as political allies. In 1979, commenting on 'Reclaim the Night' marches, its Bulletin suggested that feminists, whose 'views probably conflict with many aspects of Bible teaching' understood that pornography 'turns some men into potential threats to any woman', recognised 'the connection between freely available pornography and a rising rape problem' and realised 'that pornography...puts all women at risk'. Similarly, discussing a feminist article in *Cosmopolitan* magazine on violence in films, the bulletin commented that it emphasised 'the point we have been making for 10 years' that film was a major source of incitement to rape. Finally, and most interestingly, Raymond Johnston himself, in response to a Channel 4 feminist programme on the subject, praised its argument that pornography turned women into sex objects and reduced them to their bodies. Would they, he asked, be willing to co-operate with those who believed in a 'complementarity of gender' and 'lifelong covenant fidelity' in a coalition to end pornography?[92]

CARE, which has recently launched a new campaign against pornography, continues to argue that pornography degrades women, valuing them only for their body rather than for personality or intelligence. Its journal has praised a radical feminist pamphlet on the pornography industry (despite, it noted, 'minor misgivings' over its revolutionary language).[93] It is perhaps not so surprising, then, that a separate initiative, the Off the Shelf campaign against 'soft' porn magazines, brings together Clare Short and Jo Richardson from the Labour left with Jill Knight of the Conservative right or that Short was a platform speaker for a CARE fringe meeting on pornography at the 1989 Labour conference. More recently, CARE's approach to six MPs (ranging from Conservative Michael Alison to Clare Short), asking them to sponsor an Early Day motion criticising pornography and calling for research into its effects resulted in over 200 MPs signing.[94] Just as pornography divides feminists and, as we will see, Conservatives, so, conversely, it has produced surprising alliances.

6 The Politics of Sex Education

Sex education has gradually developed in Britain since the First World War. By the early seventies the Departments of Health and Education shared responsibility for the subject but sub-contracted much of the work to two advisory bodies, the Health Education Council (HEC) and the Schools Council. While these bodies were the source of reports and recommendations, at a local level the Local Education Authority had an overseeing role, while the actual delivery of sex education in the classroom was the task of teachers but also involved outside bodies such as the Family Planning Association. In this somewhat complex situation, neither central nor local government set down how sex education should be taught. Instead they provided the funding and made decisions which facilitated or discouraged particular approaches. By its very nature, the subject was inevitably to generate controversy and in 1976 even became the topic of debate in the House of Lords, during which speakers attacked rebellious teachers who encouraged 'young girls to have 5 condoms in their handbag when they go out at night', family planners who favoured contraception without restricting it to marriage and extremists who sought to 'write off a country' by persuading 'children to become homosexual'. Moral campaigners were involved in opposition to sex education from early on but, from the eighties, this has taken on a more central role in its activities. The Responsible Society, with its combination of one or two thousand individual members and a much larger corporate membership (voluntary organisations, churches etc.) has been at the forefront but other forces too were involved, as we will see.[1] Later in the chapter we will discuss the argument in recent years over 'positive images' of homosexuality. But this is closely linked with the moral lobby's general objections to sex education and it is to this that we will turn first.

With the election of a new government new measures on education were all but inevitable and in 1980 an Education Bill was introduced. Following a meeting with the local Responsible Society group, George Gardiner, the Conservative MP for Reigate, tabled an amendment proposing that school heads should inform parents of any provision for sex education and invite them to inspect teaching materials. Furthermore, it added, they should be entitled to withdraw their children from such classes. The amendment, Gardiner suggested, was 'fully in line with the objectives of the Education Bill and I hope Ministers will support it'.[2] The amendment failed because of lack of time but the issue was taken up again in the Lords by Viscount Ingleby, who also raised the question of efforts to promote the view that homosexuality was 'natural and normal'. In reply, Lady Young, Minister of State for Education and Science, expressed her sympathy for the aims of the clause. While expressing doubt over withdrawing children from sex education, she emphasised that parents would receive information about sex education under the bill's provision for parent governors. She would read the debate, she added, and see if there was a possibility of advancing parental rights in the area.[3]

When the Bill reached the report stage, Ingleby, who had withdrawn the clause at the end of the committee stage, reintroduced it. Lady Young remained unpersuaded of the need for special arrangements for the exemption of children from sex education. School governors, she reiterated, should play a significant role in deciding how the subject was taught and should take parents' views into account. In order to make sure that parents were properly informed of the content of sex education, however, she intended to consider carefully how provisions for local education authorities to publish information could be used concerning sex education. She had discussed the matter with local authorities since the committee stage, she reported, and had received an encouraging response. Declaring that Young had made a 'most valuable contribution towards meeting the great anxieties' which had been expressed, Ingleby withdrew the clause once more.[4]

Having promised to reconsider the matter, Young held meetings with Gardiner and agreed that in future schools would be directed to publicise their sex education provision and indicate whether parents could inspect teaching materials. When the bill received its Third Reading in the Lords, Young announced the new arrangements. (In the Commons, however, Tory MP James Pawsey, who had co-sponsored Gardiner's amendment, again called for legislation to allow children to be withdrawn from sex education. The Minister of Education, while agreeing that parents' wishes should be taken into account, replied that there was no need for legislation.)[5]

Having made a partial gain on the question, moral campaigners did not retire from the field. The following month the Conservative MP John Stokes launched a ferocious attack on what he called 'the sex education industry' for encouraging promiscuity and 'undermining the institution of the family which is the basis of our civilisation'. The FPA and the Brook Advisory Centres, he alleged, issued 'vulgar and distasteful' propaganda which incited to early sex and denied the need for self-control. 'It is tantamount', he declared, 'to the encouragement of the widest promiscuity with the result that fornication and adultery are the normal condition of affairs.' Government grants to the FPA and the Brook Centres should be withdrawn, he urged, and sex education only provided if parents agreed.[6] In August Jill Knight, as chairman of the Lords and Commons Family and Child Protection Group, also strongly criticised the DHSS for funding the FPA and other agencies concerned with sex education and contraception. In reply, the Minister of Health, Gerard Vaughan, defended an increase in government provision for family planning. He also noted, however, that some sex education literature had been withdrawn and that the Family Planning Association had agreed to a request to cease stocking a particular book.[7]

Outside Parliament, the Responsible Society took the initiative by producing a much-publicised leaflet aimed at young people arguing the case for pre-marital chastity. Entitled 'Saying No Isn't Always Easy' and with a cover-illustration of a Valentino-like figure seemingly attempting to seduce a young woman, the leaflet warned of the dangers of sexual disease, cervical cancer and contraceptive failure before concluding that sex was 'only really fulfilling when it's part of the total commitment of marriage'. Some 20,000 were scheduled to be distributed to schools and youth clubs, it was reported, and the leaflet was described to the press as an

alternative to the sex education material of the FPA, the Brook
Centres and the Health Education Council. 'Frankly, I think its
time this Government got its ideas sorted out', one of the leaflet's
authors declared. 'They have virtually admitted that the heavy
promotion of abortion and contraception has not worked, and yet
they keep offering more of the same medicine.'[8] Immediately before
the release of the leaflet, Responsible Society member and
journalist Joanna Nash interviewed Gerard Vaughan and drew a
picture of a man and a government that had lost their way on the
issue. His office, she wrote, had the atmosphere of a place where
others 'presented him with the bits of information they felt were
relevant'. It was evident, she suggested, that he supported the
family, was worried about its instability and recognised that recent
government policies on family planning had not worked. Yet, she
complained, he supported an increased grant to the FPA and failed
to deal with the Health Education Council's unacceptable activities. There were signs in the interview that Vaughan was willing to
respond to moralist approaches, notably in his comment that the
FPA's grant was by no means guaranteed for the following year
and that he would 'take note of any complaints' and watch the
situation carefully. But overall, Nash suggested, 'he seemed obliged
to maintain exactly the same policies as were pursued at the
Department of Health under the previous Government'.[9]

In November the Secretary of State for Education, Rhodes
Boyson, turned down another approach from Pawsey for legislation allowing parents to opt out.[10] Soon, however, increased signs
of government movement began to be detectable. This first came to
light with a speech by Sir George Young, the junior Health
Minister, at a conference on the consequences of teenage sexual
activity in April 1981. In the last twenty years, he declared,
'Traditional family values have been undermined. This Government wants to reassert them.' The Health Education Council, he
announced, would be launching an autumn campaign, aimed at
discouraging the increase in teenage pregnancies. The campaign
would be concerned with persuading teenagers to seek contraceptive advice but, he declared, it was also important to discourage
premature sex. 'I consider it necessary', he said, 'that any material
for this age group makes it clear that the option of chastity is not a
vestigial concept of the 19th century but something which has
relevance today.' That the government planned to spend money on

encouraging the use of teenage contraception led to the Responsible Society attacking Young's speech in a subsequent issue of its bulletin. Furthermore, during his speech, he defended the provision in exceptional circumstances of under-age contraception without parental consent. But, despite the Society's strictures, Young's speech, taken as a whole, showed all the signs of a balancing-act between what he called the government's support for traditional family values and the need to stem unwanted teenage pregnancies.[11] This came out even more clearly when the campaign was eventually launched, several months later than originally intended and including an advertisement bearing the words 'NO. Still the most effective form of birth control.' Ministers had blocked earlier Health Education Council proposals, it was reported, owing to concern at possible attack by Conservative backbenchers and the Responsible Society.[12]

But by then the heat had increased considerably on the issue. At the beginning of June 1981, James Pawsey used a late-night debate in the Commons to attack Brook Advisory Centre sex education teaching material. A teaching pack produced by the Centre, he claimed, was pornographic: 'This literature shows full frontals and goes into considerable detail about sexual intercourse. There is very little left to the imagination and even less left to prayer.'[13] This was quickly followed by a letter in the *Daily Telegraph* from Valerie Riches of the Responsible Society drawing a connection between sex education material and Parliament's third reading of a bill on indecent display. Children, she argued, were exposed to sex education material which would be deemed indecent if publicly displayed. Since, she concluded, the Department of Education was unwilling to protect children from this kind of assault, Parliament should allow parents to exempt their children from sex education.[14]

Very soon afterwards, details of a letter from Lady Young to Riches were announced. In it, Young expressed her concern about the Brook Centre's sex education material and noted that she had said so at a recent meeting with Brook representatives. 'You may be glad', she went on, 'to know that they welcomed the suggestion that there should be much closer liaison and mutual planning.' Within days, a further announcement reported that certain of the Brook's sex education material was to be withdrawn as a condition of increased DHSS funding. While James Pawsey described the decision as 'a victory for common sense', a Brook spokesman was quoted as welcoming close liaison but regretting 'the other conditions'.[15] Still unsatisfied, however, the Responsible Society later in the year issued a pamphlet, aimed at teachers and parents, denouncing the government's policy on sex education. Once again Sir George Young was criticised for encouraging the use of teenage contraception and the Department of Education too came under attack. 'It is sheer folly', Riches declared, for the Department 'to encourage schools to introduce sex education at a time when so much of the material available is amoral, pretentious and subversive of the family.'[16]

The following year the argument re-emerged. In February representatives of the Responsible Society met Health Education Council officials to discuss the presence of certain material on its lists of resources for schools and the absence of 'pro-family' and 'pro-life' literature. In the Commons John Stokes returned to the offensive with an attack on the 'sexual propaganda' of the FPA and the Brook Centres and a call for the right of parents to exclude their children from sex education. The junior Education Minister, Rhodes Boyson, was sympathetic. Certain sex education teaching materials had been removed the previous year, he declared, and 'we are asking for more to be taken away now'. Schools should provide information on how sex education was taught and parents should be consulted. The following month a Conservative MP, John Blackburn, called on Boyson to introduce legislation to allow parents to vet school sex education material. Boyson replied by emphasising the importance of consultation with parents and agreed with another Conservative MP that parents should be allowed to withdraw their children from sex education. Certain books, he announced, had, as a result of Department of Education pressure, been removed from school libraries and were now only available to teachers.[17]

The *Daily Telegraph* had accompanied its report of the Commons exchange with details of some of the materials listed by the Health Education Council for schools and, while the Council agreed to include some 'pro-family' literature, its lists, in the Responsible Society's view, continued to include 'perverted and amoral publications'.[18] Later in the year, Boyson announced to the Commons that he and Geoffrey Finsberg, the Under-Secretary for Health and Social Security, had seen the Health Education Council and asked it to review 'the purpose, balance and content' of its list.

It had responded, he stated, by promising to take account of criticisms. Subsequently, Finsberg told the Commons that the Council had agreed to review its recommended list. Ministers, he announced, had asked for it to be reconsidered following the outcry earlier in 1982. Some of the material listed, he said, was 'quite unsuitable' and schools needed to co-operate with parents and be sensitive to their feelings.[19]

As the new year dawned, the *Telegraph* was able to announce that the HEC would suspend circulation of its list and review recommended materials as a result of Boyson and Finsberg's approaches. Boyson, who had been in contact with Valerie Riches, had produced a 16-page document containing extracts from contentious material, and had suggested to the Council that it should consider whether such books should be recommended and 'whether its list can be considered balanced'.[20] But the tension between the Council and its critics in government and the moral crusades was not to end that easily. The Department of Education continued in its efforts to have some material no longer listed while, in 1986, the Conservative Family Campaign attacked the HEC's continued reluctance.[21] By then, however, the focus of criticism was shifting.

A Government White Paper, *Better Schools*, published in early 1985, had stated that sex education should be taught in 'a moral framework' but it was not until the Third Reading of the 1986 Education Bill in the Lords that the critics of sex education achieved the beginnings of a breakthrough. During the committee stage, Lord Buckmaster had put forward an amendment to ensure sex education complied with parents' values and was taught 'in the context of enduring family life'. In addition, parents would have the right to withdraw their children from sex education lessons. This stance, he told the House, was supported by Family and Youth Concern, the National Council for Christian Standards in Society, the Parliamentary Family and Child Protection Group and others. While the government was unwilling to support Buckmaster's amendment, it did decide, subsequently, to bring forward its own amendment in an attempt to satisfy critics. Baroness Hooper, on behalf of the government, informed the Lords that in response to fears expressed in the House the government had decided to introduce a new clause into the bill. This amendment stated that local education authorities, school governing bodies and headteachers should 'take such steps as are reasonably practicable' to ensure that sex education would be 'given in such a manner as to encourage... pupils to have due regard to moral considerations and the value of family life'. It was the government's view, Hooper told the House, that teaching about the physical side of sexuality could not be treated in isolation but had to be placed in a moral context. Young people, she continued, needed to be taught the necessity for self-restraint, loving caring relationships and stable family life.[22]

As news reports quickly made clear, moral campaigners welcomed the government's move. The *Daily Telegraph* reported Mary Whitehouse's support for the new clause while Valerie Riches of Family and Youth Concern told the *Daily Express* that 'We have been working at this for years and at last we have had success.'[23] CARE, however, although it too welcomed the decision and described it as 'exactly the sort of lead' that it and other groups had wanted for years, made it clear that the clause alone was not enough. What was needed was determined action on the government's part.[24] A newly-formed organisation, the National Council for Christian Standards in Society was also 'disappointed' over developments. The earlier amendment by Lord Buckmaster had referred to 'stable marriage', while the government had not used the word 'stable' in its clause. As for the government's phrase 'reasonably practicable' this, it feared, could easily be used by schools to evade implementing the new amendment.[25]

It had been suggested at the time of the announcement that the government had been influenced by speeches by Norman Tebbit against the 'permissive society' and this was quickly denied by the Minister of State for Education, Chris Patten. Characteristically, however, Tebbit commented that the clause's support by all parties in the Lords made him 'very glad the Labour Party, at least in the House of Lords is now following the lead I gave'.[26]

The following week, the amended bill received its second reading in the Commons. Moving the reading, Kenneth Baker, the newly-appointed Secretary for Education, made clear the government's belief that, while much of sex education was satisfactory, this was not always the case. The Department of Education, he stated, was preparing a circular on the subject which would make it clear that parents could examine teaching materials. Pupils should be helped to recognise the risks, both physical and emotional, of promiscuity and while, he went on, it was difficult to legislate on such matters it was vital that both Houses should 'give a clear signal reinforcing the institution of marriage as the foundation of a healthy family life and the very bedrock of our civilisation'. It was crucial, he declared, to build up children's respect for a 'happy family life'.[27]

At the end of June, a Schools Inspectorate document appeared, calling for sex education to be taught in a moral framework but urging sensitivity towards those children whose backgrounds did not correspond to the 'ideal' of family life. It was particularly important to consult parents, the report noted, because they had no legal right to withdraw their children from sex education lessons. Such topics as homosexuality, abortion, birth control and sexually transmitted diseases should be taught in an objective and honest way, it proposed, but teachers should bear in mind that, while there had been a shift away from condemnation of homosexuality, many individuals and groups in society continued to object on moral grounds.[28]

In August the promised Department of Education draft circular appeared. Sent to local education authorities, teaching unions and churches for comment, the circular emphasised once again the importance of covering controversial topics in a sensitive way and the right of parents to be informed and shown teaching materials. While parents had no legal right to withdraw their children, it noted, their anxieties should be considered sympathetically by schools. Sex education, it reiterated, should be taught so as to encourage due regard for morality and family life and the risks of promiscuity should be pointed out.[29] Within days, however, the government's proposals began to come under attack. In the Commons an amendment by Labour and Conservative MPs called for parents to be given the right to remove their children from sex education. This peculiar alliance appears to have originated (and was eventually to succumb) amidst some considerable confusion. Labour members reportedly sought to allow parental exemption in order to avoid legal clashes between schools and outraged parents. The government clause, Labour frontbench spokesman Mark Fisher stated during the committee discussion of the Bill, would be 'an open invitation to someone like Mrs Victoria Gillick'.[30] On the Conservative side, Peter Bruinvels rapidly emerged as the leading force behind the amendment and the Education Minister wrote to dissident backbenchers, opposing parental right to exclude children from classes and defending the government's clause as a satisfactory safeguard for their concerns.[31] While it was not yet clear how strongly Bruinvels and his colleagues would argue against the government, there were already signs of support for his challenge in the announcement by Chris Kelly of Family and Youth Concern that her organisation would campaign for parents' rights to opt out. 'Some teachers have strange life-styles', she commented, 'and this could be reflected in their teaching'.[32]

In September the confusion caused by sections of both major parties uniting against the government cleared. The Conservative rebels, now 70 strong, had their own amendment while Labour's, signed accidentally by some of the Conservatives, was now being described as a holding action until Labour had finished consulting teachers, local education authorities and others over what stance to take. The consultation produced the decision to withdraw the amendment and to oppose Bruinvels (who by mid-September was claiming nearly 100 supporters.) The *Guardian* suggested that Labour's initial support for the parental right to withdraw their children had originated in the concerns of ethnic minorities and an article in the *New Statesman* likewise suggested that Labour's stance derived from the fear that ethnic groups would withdraw their electoral support. According to Labour's shadow spokesman, Giles Radice, however, Labour's initial decision to support parental exemption had solely been in order to pressurise the government to abandon its clause.[33]

Events now began to move more rapidly. The recently-launched Conservative Family Campaign (CFC), echoing Family and Youth Concern's earlier comment, decried 'teachers living in irregular relationships' using sex education 'as a means of proselytizing to children for their own lifestyles'. Parents had been concerned for years, it stated, about the nature of certain sex education provided by 'pressure groups with a vested interest in breaking down the structure of the family by promoting promiscuity'. In addition to the amendment to allow parental exemption others had been introduced urging an emphasis on 'stable family life' and removing the 'as reasonably practicable' phrase and the Campaign called for support for both. (As it noted, Viscount Buckmaster, one of its sponsors, had favoured these changes and Ivor Stanbrook, who took this up in the Commons, was, like Bruinvels, also a Campaign sponsor.)[34] The ministerial reshuffle a few days later replaced

Patten with Angela Rumbold as Minister of State for Education, emboldening the rebels who believed that she and the junior minister, Robert Dunn, supported their position and would attempt to persuade Baker to change his stance. Bruinvels wrote to Baker demanding that the family unit be 'safeguarded...morality instilled in every child [and]...sexual deviance within the teaching profession weeded out' and Baker was reported to have told colleagues that the subject needed to be re-examined. Ahead lay the crucial debate on the issue when the Commons returned from recess on 21 October.[35] First, however, lay the party conference where the Conservative Family Campaign was confident that the strength of representatives' feelings would force Baker to produce his own parental exclusion amendment. As part of its campaign, the CFC distributed large numbers of copies of its pamphlet, 'Sex Education and Your Child'. 'Our intention', the Campaign declared, was 'to save a generation from the immoral propaganda for promiscuity, homosexuality, contraception, anti-marriage views, fornication, and encouragement of children to experiment with sex, which has passed in too many schools during the past two decades as health education.'[36] Outside the party, the onslaught was joined by CARE which announced in mid-September a campaign to pressurise the government to accept both amendments. The Education Bill, its chairman stated, would be the last opportunity in the present Parliament to seriously affect the sex education of 'the nation's children' and CARE intended to do its utmost to strengthen parental rights and 'the moral backbone of sex education generally'.[37]

At the Conference, on the fringe of which a Conservative Family Campaign meeting took place, Baker's speech to the representatives made it clear that a compromise was on offer. Instead of allowing parents to opt out of sex education for their children, Baker proposed to transfer control of the subject from teachers and local authorities to strengthened school governing bodies, answerable to an annual parents' meeting. It was these bodies which would decide what, if any, sex education should be available and whether particular parents would be allowed to withdraw their children from such classes.[38] Subsequently Graham Webster-Gardiner was to claim that 'in two months' the CFC had succeeded in changing Conservative policy on sex education and persuaded Baker to announce the new initiative. At the time, however, campaigners

Sex and Politics

were far from satisfied.[39] Chris Kelly, for Family and Youth
Concern, although describing it as 'a most encouraging change in
the Government's thinking', added that the society would like the
end of school sex education altogether, while Bruinvels not only
continued with his amendment but introduced a new one proposing
a proscribed list of 'corrupting' sex education books and the instant
dismissal of teachers who continued to use them. Parents, Bruinvels
proposed, should be able to submit 'suspect' books to a Department of Education unit which would revise the list monthly and
send it out to governing bodies.[40] While, he wrote to the press
shortly before the Commons vote, he welcomed Baker's change of
position, he remained unconvinced that enough parents would be
able to withdraw their children or that teachers would be stopped
from promoting 'their own sexual prejudices and proclivities'.[41] But
if Baker had not stopped the opt-out amendment from being put,
he had succeeded in paring down the numbers willing to follow
Bruinvels in rebellion. Instead of the 70 of early September, let
alone the nearly 100 of mid-September, only 43 Conservative MPs
(along with 2 Liberals and Enoch Powell) voted for the Bruinvels
amendment. (Nor were the other moralist amendments successful.)
The bill, Rumbold assured the Commons, would ensure that
unsuitable materials would not be used in schools.[42] Bruinvels,
however, was not persuaded and he appealed to parents to send
offensive sex education books to himself or to Baker in the hope
that governing bodies could be advised of such material. A Private
Members' Bill or Ten Minute Rule Bill might have to be
introduced, he suggested, to ensure that parents had responsibility
for the sex education of their children.[43]

CARE too was disappointed by the result while conceding that
the government had made some move towards its view. Soon after
it made it clear how much it still dissented from the government's
stance. In response to the DES draft circular on sex education,
CARE argued that the document made no reference to marriage,
ignored the breakdown in family life which accompanied the
growth of sex education and by not defining what it meant by
'moral framework' would allow children to be presented with ideas
which were 'deeply offensive' to their parents.[44] Family and Youth
Concern too at its AGM in November 1986 also made it clear that
it did not accept the status quo, with Riches telling those in
attendance that the government had mutilated Buckmaster's

amendment after she had approached him to raise the issue and Christopher Whitehouse warning that local education authorities would define a gay relationship as a family in order to stay within the law on teaching sex education in a family context. The organisation would fight on, he told the audience.[45]

But the context of this fight was already changing. As we have already seen, a recurring theme of critics of sex education was that it not only encouraged a precocious and promiscuous heterosexuality but also might encourage homosexuality. In the May 1986 local elections the explosive issues of homosexuality and sex education finally came together with the furore over proposals by some local Labour parties that children should be taught about homosexuality in a positive manner. In Haringey, where the black left-wing council leader Bernie Grant had become a controversial national figure, Labour manifesto proposals outraged both the local press and local Conservatives. In a scathing report, the local paper, the *Journal*, gave front-page coverage to a statement by Tottenham Conservative chairman Peter Murphy that 'no person who believes in God can vote Labour now. It is an attack on ordinary family life as a prelude to revolution.' A local Conservative leaflet reproduced a *Daily Express* article on the 'Storm over "Barmy" Bernie's new gay teach-ins' and, in a confrontational situation, Conservative gains in one hitherto Labour locality combined with Labour's increased majority on the council to make conflict on the issue all the more embittered.[46]

Following the election, the new council Lesbian and Gay Unit wrote to school heads calling for proposals for 'promoting positive images of lesbians and gays'. While local Conservatives described the policy as 'a bigger threat to normal family life than even the bombers and the guns of Adolf Hitler', more widespread opposition began to emerge.[47] In July a 'mums' petition' collected 1,500 signatures, and the following month, amidst some dispute among activists about tactics, a newly-created Parents Rights Group (PRG) launched a vociferous campaign against council policy. Protests at a similar policy were also taking place in Ealing and as the issue began to take on national importance, Kenneth Baker, the Education Secretary, stepped in, demanding the council provide him with full details of its proposals. This followed a Lords statement by Lord Swinton, the education spokesman, that the government would deplore any policy to promote homosexuality,

while, in Haringey itself, Councillor Murphy offered the view that
the policy was 'part of a Marxist plot to destabilise society as we
know it'.[48]

As the arguments escalated, the Conservative Family Campaign
announced plans for its fringe meeting at the Conservative
Conference on 'the teaching of homosexuality in schools'. According to the Campaign, the Department of Education circular on sex
education had encouraged councils to pursue such policies.[49] In
mid-September, Kenneth Baker attacked the availability in libraries of *Jenny Lives with Eric and Martin*, a book portraying a young
girl's sharing of a household with her gay father and his lover.
Locally, opponents of the council's policy were highly active.
Tottenham Conservatives had collected over three thousand
signatures for its own petition (the figure would ultimately reach
five thousand) and in a local leaflet accused the council of
attempting to make the 'normal abnormal and abnormal normal'.[50] The Parents Rights Group threatened to withdraw children
from school if the policy was implemented and suggested that it
might set up private classes with the aid of teachers who were
willing to resign rather than carry out the council's policy. It also
announced that members had gone out to borrow the book named
by Baker from public libraries and would burn copies publicly. A
referendum for ratepayers was also under consideration by the
group while a breakaway organisation, the Tottenham Parents'
Group, which viewed the PRG as too militant, also pressurised the
council to drop its plans.[51] The following month the Parents Rights
Group turned towards the organising of pickets at selected schools
calling for one-day strikes. Two of these actions were only partly
successful but one, at Belmont primary school, forced it to close for
the day with the group setting up an alternative school in a nearby
church hall.[52]

With the Parents Rights Group and the Tottenham group active
at a local level, at a national level Rachel Tingle, the religious
affairs correspondent of the Freedom Association paper, the *Free
Nation*, entered the fray with a booklet, *Gay Lessons*, which
accused local authorities and teachers' organisations of promoting
'homosexuality on the rates'. It was an intervention which received
considerable attention in the press.[53] Paul Johnson also entered the
dispute with an article in the *Daily Telegraph*, 'Assault on the
young', which called upon the government to stop homosexual

propaganda in the classroom.[54] Both the launch of Tingle's pamphlet and Johnson's article immediately preceded the Conservative party conference, at which the Conservative Family Campaign held its fringe meeting.[55] Shortly afterwards, CARE too announced it was launching a 'campaign to oppose the propagation of homosexual and lesbian practices among children in Britain'.[56]

If nationally new forces were coming to the aid of the Haringey council's critics, locally problems among the Parents Rights activists were re-emerging. The group continued to be active, sending schoolpupils to a public library, for instance, to establish if children could borrow a gay novel, *The Milkman's On His Way*.[57] But tensions worsened and dispute over a leaflet issued in its name led to a clash in which two of the group leaders, Terry Wise and Patricia Headd, argued that their critics had taken the PRG from its parents-only origins and given a platform to 'people who just want to gay bash and read out Tory speeches'. In the event, however, Headd remained with the group and Wise was expelled.[58]

The Lords and Commons Family and Child Protection Group, chaired by Jill Knight, had become involved and in December the issue came before the House of Lords. A private members' bill, introduced by Lord Halsbury, proposed that local authorities should be banned from 'promoting homosexuality as an acceptable family relationship' or financing the teaching in schools of its acceptability. Supported by Baroness Cox, Viscount Ingleby and others, the bill received an unopposed Second Reading but did not receive government support. Lord Skelmersdale, the Environment Under-Secretary, speaking on behalf of the government, emphasised that it was opposed to promoting 'homosexuality as a normal way of life' but argued both that there were problems with the bill's wording and that it was unnecessary since the new Education Act would protect pupils and needed to be given a chance to prove its effectiveness.[59]

In Haringey itself the battle continued and a surprising connection emerged between the Parents Rights Group and the Union of Democratic Miners (UDM). Having organised the schools pickets and petitioned to no avail, the group had turned towards the idea of court action and Headd announced at a meeting of the group that its legal case would be taken up by David Negus, a solicitor who had acted for working miners during the miners' strike. The meeting was also addressed by John Liptrott, general secretary of the UDM, who declared that the parents' fight was comparable to that against Arthur Scargill: 'It's a battle over who controls the country. There's a saying: corrupt the morals and you defeat the people'.[60] Shortly afterwards, *The Times* published an article supporting the Parents Rights Group and drawing parallels between it and working miners' opposition to the strike. The comparison was no accident. Its author, David Hart, had earlier been in close contact with the Prime Minister and the Chairman of the Coal Board while engaged in organising a working miners' movement during the coal strike and, as will be seen, he was to appear again during the 'positive images' controversy.[61] Equally remarkably, a new force entered the situation in the form of the New Patriotic Movement. Formed in late January 1987, the movement demonstrated outside Haringey Civic Centre with banners reading 'Do You Want Your Child To Become A Homosexual?' and 'Gay equals AIDS equals Death'. The movement, which claimed to speak for 'ordinary people who follow the normal standard of sexual behaviour' also went to Manchester to demonstrate in support of Chief Constable James Anderton, following his much-publicised speech on AIDS.[62] The movement had definite political sympathies, concerned not only with a 'return to God-centred moral and ethical values' but also with 'atheistic communism as the greatest threat to world peace'.[63] Journalistic investigation soon uncovered the stance that underlay its arguments. Michael Balcomb, the movement's spokesman, Hamish Robertson, its press officer and Timothy Read, another prominent member, were all, it transpired, leading activists in CAUSA UK or CARP (Collegiate Association for Research into Principle), front organisations of the Rev. Sun Myung Moon's Unification Church, the 'Moonies'.[64] While Moonie involvement, condemned by the Parents Rights Group's Patricia Headd, attracted some publicity, a further split in the PRG passed off almost unnoticed, in which eight committee members resigned, accusing two leading figures in the group, Betty Sheridan and Patricia Headd, of running the group in an authoritarian manner. The main objector, Patrick Harte, subsequently launched a new organisation, the Haringey Parents Association.[65]

In February the Halsbury bill, slightly amended, passed its Third Reading (in the face once more of government criticism) while in the Commons Angela Rumbold told MPs that Kenneth Baker had ordered an urgent investigation into allegations that Ealing and Haringey councils were encouraging homosexuality.[66] Shortly afterwards, CARE announced its plans to encourage Christians to intervene in the May local elections to oppose pro-gay policies. This campaign, it explained, would include not only asking candidates where they stood on such issues but encouraging supporters to stand for election and to join political parties in order to influence policy.[67] In Haringey, the issue of 'positive images' of homosexuality remained a bitter issue, with the Council's decision in April to distribute a leaflet to households on equal opportunities for gays and lesbians coming under attack. The leaflet described an American book, *Young, Gay and Proud*, as suitable for 13-year-olds and Murphy denounced the book as encouraging homosexuality. During the month the Tottenham Conservatives gathered 15,000 signatures for a petition calling on the Labour Party to drop its 'positive images' policy.[68]

In May the Halsbury bill, which had proceeded to the Commons and passed its Second Reading, reached its committee stage. Its sponsor, Jill Knight, argued that there was a shocking amount of evidence that 'the teaching of sex in our schools' was such that children were 'frequently' being encouraged into homosexuality and lesbianism. The aim of all this 'filth', she claimed, was the abolition of the family and the perversion of children 'from normal family life to a lifestyle which is desperately dangerous for society'. Speaking for the government, Rhodes Boyson made clear his support for the bill's principles. 'All of us', he declared, had 'noticed in recent years an attack on the institution of the family'. However, he added, the government continued to have reservations about aspects of the bill. It could be described as premature, he suggested, in light of the 1986 Education Act's changes to sex education and a forthcoming code of practice for local government publicity. It was evident that his tone was less critical than the government spokesman had been in the Lords and in his conclusion he declared that while the bill had shortcomings the government would not oppose it and that he himself supported it. Strong criticism, however, both of the bill and of the way it was being dealt with, was voiced by Labour's home affairs spokesman who called for a division on the bill. The clause passed by 20–0, but in the absence of the requisite quota of 40 MPs, the committee was stood over to the next sitting, which, given the imminence of a general election, effectively sealed its fate.[69] The following week Jill Knight, accusing Labour of blocking the bill, called on the Prime Minister to introduce legislation in the next Parliament to 'protect both children and the concept of the family'. The Prime Minister replied that it had been 'a great pity' that the bill had not passed and that she hoped it would be brought back to the House and become law.[70]

During the General Election, the issue played a part in an anti-Labour press advertising campaign by a new and initially mysterious group, the Committee for a Free Britain. The advertisements featured individuals explaining why they feared a Labour victory, one of whom was Betty Sheridan of the Parents Rights Group: 'I live in Haringey./ I'm married with two children./ *And I'm scared.*/ If you vote LABOUR they'll/go on teaching my kids about/ GAYS & LESBIANS instead of/ giving them proper lessons.' After the election, the Committee was formally launched. Led by David Hart, the author of *The Times* article referred to earlier, supporters included Baroness Cox and Betty Sheridan. The PRG had been partly funded by the Committee, it was subsequently revealed, and at the end of the year, when the issue of the 'promotion' of homosexuality would once again receive national attention, Hart declared that the Committee would fund action by local people against councils on the issue.[71]

In September the Department of Education and Science issued a circular on sex education which, the Order of Christian Unity noted approvingly, stated that pupils should be helped to appreciate stable married and family life. Equally importantly, it pronounced that there was 'no place' for 'teaching which advocates homosexual behaviour, which presents it as the "norm", or which encourages homosexual experimentation by pupils.'[72] Haringey and Ealing, however, both declared their policies were compatible with the circular and would continue while Pat Headd of the PRG declared that 'The battle still isn't over'.[73] That this was indeed the case became very clear when, in early December, David Wilshire, Conservative MP for Spelthorne, introduced an amendment to the government's Local Government Bill during discussion in Standing Committee. This amendment (subsequently to be known as Clause 28), once again, sought to prevent councils from the 'promotion' of homosexuality or promoting the teaching of its 'acceptability' as 'a pretended family relationship', and was supported by the Local Government Minister, Michael Howard, on behalf of the government. Jill Knight's earlier bill would probably have passed had it not been for the General Election, Howard told the Committee, and 'The Government has always supported that Bill's objectives.' In view of the concern expressed in Parliament and by 'the general public', he announced, 'the Government wish to support the progress of the proposal.' However, he added, in light of the reservations expressed on the government's behalf during the discussion of Knight's bill, he proposed some changes including the addition of a section ensuring that local authorities would not be affected in their work against AIDS. These changes were acceptable to Wilshire.[74]

During the subsequent Commons debate on Clause 28 critics made repeated reference to the government's change of line on the issue, suggesting it could be attributed to populist motives. The clause passed and, having proceeded to the Lords, efforts were made, early the following year, to amend it. But 'Government whips marshalled their troops' and the challenge was defeated, although the government did decide to alter its wording to refer to 'intentional' promotion of homosexuality.[75] The bill returned to the Commons in March and, despite efforts to amend it once more, passed. No amount of abuse from opponents, Jill Knight declared, was 'going to stop me protecting children and protecting the family unit'.[76] In a subsequent bulletin to its supporters, the National Council for Christian Standards in Society claimed that 'We were behind' Clause 28. Its President, the Earl of Halsbury, had originated it while Jill Knight, it pointed out, was one of its patrons.[77] But the clause's success was more than the work of one pressure group. The Conservative Family Campaign, which Knight also supported, claimed credit too for the clause and other groups had also been active. Most importantly, Clause 28 had support at the highest level. According to government sources, the *Guardian* reported shortly after the clause's acceptance in the Commons, Thatcher had pressed to retain it against other ministers' hesitancies.[78]

In Haringey, both the Parents Rights Group and the Parents Association had supported the new clause, as did local Conservatives, and in late April an emergency council meeting met to consider a Conservative demand that the authority 'recognise the

wisdom of the Local Government Bill' and close down its Lesbian
and Gay Unit, cease attempting to introduce 'positive images' in
the classroom and drop all reference to homosexuality from
Council policy. The move, however, was defeated, while a section
of the local Conservatives, at loggerheads with Peter Murphy,
supported an amendment that Clause 28 was not intended to
encourage prejudice and discrimination.[79] The Council itself,
meanwhile, had produced an extensive working party report on
lesbian and gay issues in education envisaging raising issues of
sexuality in history, literature and other classes. The document had
been carefully phrased in light of the new law, Patrick Harte stated,
but 'the essential message . . . hasn't really changed' and the Parents
Association might take court action. The Parents Rights Group too
remained opposed and took legal advice about the possibility of
using Clause 28 while also announcing that members would
withdraw their children from local schools if the report was
implemented.[80]

The situation soon became more complicated. Since the 1986
Education Act, decisions on sex education and the curriculum were
no longer the responsibility of local authorities but of school
governors and at the end of May it was reported that, according
to a Department of the Environment circular, Section 28 (as it now
was) did 'not affect the activities of school governors nor of
teachers'. 'This has got to be a mistake', Jill Knight declared.
'The major point of it was to protect children in schools from
having homosexuality thrust upon them.' The Department of the
Environment, in response to the press reports, pointed out that
local education authorities still had an advisory role in schools and
Knight subsequently announced at a meeting of the National
Council for Christian Standards in Society that press reports had
been misleading and that the Section could still be deployed.
Despite expectations, however, it has not played the role that its
advocates (and opponents) had anticipated.[81]

In discussing the battles over sex education in the eighties, it is
necessary, without losing sight of the connections, to separate the
fight against sex education in general from the specific battle over
the 'promotion' of homosexuality. What exactly are moral
campaigners arguing when they criticise sex education? A number
of different organisations, ranging from the Conservative Family
Campaign to the Order of Christian Unity, have produced material

on sex education.[82] The leading organisation in the field, however, has been the Responsible Society, which was already espousing the key arguments in material produced before the arrival of the last Thatcher government. In *Education or Manipulation?*, published in 1975, the Society argued that a combination of 'financial interest' and 'ideologies hostile to the family' was subverting young people and putting the family and society at risk. While the pamphlet attacked a variety of targets including girls' magazines, pornography and the provision of under-age contraception, a key target of its strictures was described as 'new explicit forms of sex education' and in its conclusions the Society called for research to establish what role sex education played in 'the ever-increasing tide' of unplanned pregnancy and venereal disease.[83]

The Society quickly followed with a pamphlet specifically on sex education by K. H. Kavanagh, a senior probation officer and chairman of the Parents Advisory Group. Kavanagh argued that sex education was undermining codes of right and wrong and counterposing what was called reason (but was in fact amoralism) to religion and absolute values. The pamphlet warned of the dangers of gay activists 'using sex education to propagate the idea that homosexual feelings and activities are as natural as heterosexual' and attacked the Family Planning Association for 'presenting homosexuality in a positive light' and distributing contraception to young people. In Kavanagh's view, sex education, rather than contributing to young people's development, instead encouraged intercourse and a rise in unwanted pregnancy, sexual disease and child prostitution. If it was to be taught in schools, then it must be taught in the 'context of family life' with the involvement of parents and their right to withdraw their children if they so wished.[84]

Following the 1979 election, the Society continued to dispute the direction which sex education was taking. During the debate on the 1980 Education Act, for instance, in an article in the *Daily Telegraph* on 'The Sex Industry Versus the Parents', Riches argued that those who had 'a vested interest in the sale of contraceptives and sex education' were naturally opposed to parental involvement in sex education and their right to remove their children. They had a 'rooted contempt for parents' and manipulated sex education with 'little or no accountability to the public'. The Family Planning Association, she held, was using unacceptable material and when this had been drawn to the attention of the DHSS, an official had replied that the FPA's activities were 'generally compatible with Government policy'. This, she declared, was outrageous – if it was compatible with government policy for 'boys and girls to be encouraged to engage in sexual activity of any variety at any age' then parents must resist the loss of their children 'to the ideology of those who envisage a system in which self-appointed sex experts gain the control they seek to influence and change the *mores* of society'.[85]

A pamphlet published in 1986 developed this argument further. In the pamphlet, *Sex and Social Engineering*, she reiterated that, if sex education was provided in schools, it should be given with parental co-operation, 'with the aim of preparing young people for marriage and parenthood'. But there were powerful organisations engaged in amoral sex education, part of a world-wide 'assault on the family'. In Britain, she argued, the Family Planning Association stood at the centre of a network linked by personnel, ideology, vested interest and funding – 'a power structure with enormous influence'. Its tentacles reached into publishers, medicine, marriage guidance and elsewhere; it exerted influence over the media and over civil servants and systematic research, Riches claimed, had revealed that the network had international connections – it was part of 'a carefully planned international attack upon the nature of the family and the value of human life'. Sex education, Riches argued, was linked with the forces which promoted population control, who also advocated compulsory sex education, support for homosexuality, abortion on demand, under-age contraception and liberalised divorce, all of which had been implemented in Britain. It was the FPA, she argued, which had achieved the provision of under-sixteen contraception, thus undermining parental rights while in sex education it sowed 'confusion in the child's mind' about right and wrong and pushed sinister contraceptive propaganda. Sex education material, she argued, was sympathetic to pre-marital sex and homosexuality and evasive over the effects of contraception,abortion and promiscuity. Sex education, she concluded, had 'been a colossal failure' in terms of pregnancy,abortion and sexual disease yet it continued to be pursued because the sex education lobby was a vehicle for anti-family amoralism. The threat it posed needed an urgent counter-attack by those 'who believe in and support the family and the sanctity of life. It is a battle to be fought *now* by those who cherish the meaning of freedom.'[86]

For Valerie Riches, the changes achieved in the eighties were marginal. While a great deal of effort has been expended on seeking to influence Parliament, government and civil servants, she looks instead to the more long-term task of influencing values through educational work – talks, publications, videos presenting an alternative picture of teenage sexuality to that of the groups which she opposes.[87] Her pamphlet, and the other literature we have discussed, presents a general indictment of modern sex education and campaigners will continue in their efforts to change the way sexual mores are seen and children are socialised. In the most important of the battles we have examined in this chapter, the conflict over Haringey and Clause 28, opponents of 'positive images' focused on two important elements of the moral lobby's concerns. Firstly, as with Gillick or aspects of the Whitehouse campaign, they focused on childhood. Campaigners saw themselves as protecting the young against corruption. Thus PRG activist Katherine Stewart, speaking at a council meeting, declared that 'Our aim is to shield our children from any person or organisation who would exploit their innocence.'[88] The title 'Parents Rights Group' emphasises how members saw themselves defending parents' rights to decide their children's education and their sexuality. This, in turn, fitted in with the other concern – homosexuality. As we have seen, for PRG activists, as for other moral crusaders, certain forms of sex and of family life were normal and other forms deviant. Thus for Stephen Green, writing in the Conservative Family Campaign bulletin, homosexuality is a threat to the family, promiscuous, associated with sexually transmitted disease, 'utterly unmentionable' in its sexual practices, linked with paedophilia and, above all, abnormal. 'Never forget that the family is the norm', Green quoted from an address to a Family and Youth Concern meeting. Similarly, in a letter to the *Guardian* following his introduction of Clause 28, David Wilshire argued that his stance was based on 'the principle of supporting normality', a principle 'shared by the majority of the British public'. Homosexuality, he held, was 'not biologically normal' but was being promoted at the ratepayer's expense.[89] Opposition to homosexuality in recent years have been suffused with fears of disease and death, with Baroness Cox, for instance, announcing to the House of Lords: 'I cannot imagine how on earth in this age of AIDS we can be contemplating gay issues in the curriculum.' For Jill Knight too, homosexuality is extremely dangerous for both society and the children exposed to its teaching – 'some of that which is being taught to children in our schools would undoubtedly lead to a great spread of AIDS'.[90] But campaigners would oppose the 'promotion' of homosexuality, whether AIDS existed or not. Sex education, they argue, should promote 'pro-family' values, and forms of sexual relationship outside that realm should not be countenanced.

7 The Thatcher Government and the Policing of Sexuality

In enacting Section 28 of the 1988 Local Government Act, the Conservative government was clearly making a statement on the form of sexual relationship it favoured and the forms it did not. In its interventions into sex education, video censorship and broadcasting, it likewise made it clear that its insistence on individual freedom and a free market have important limits. But were these moves those of a government committed to a moral majority stance? To explore that question we will need to start with one of the most important issues the government has had to face – AIDS.

The discovery in the early eighties of a seemingly new virus and the destructive effect it had on the body's defences brought a terrible new dimension to sexual politics in Britain as elsewhere. That large numbers of people were and would be infected by the Human Immunodeficiency Virus (HIV) and many would go on to contract AIDS (Acquired Immune Deficiency Syndrome) has led to a vast amount of media attention and extensive activity by doctors, scientists and voluntary organisations, in Britain notably the Terrence Higgins Trust. A new and terrifying epidemic, linked in a significant number of cases with sexual intercourse, could not but reinfuse the age-old association of sex, disease and death. If, in the nineteenth and early twentieth centuries, venereal disease was often seen as nature's revenge on the impure, then in the late twentieth century the sexually active, particularly the homosexually active, could be represented as struck down by their own wrongdoings. In the popular press notion of the 'gay plague' or in Manchester Chief Constable James Anderton's attack on the 'degenerate' behaviour of 'people swirling around in a human cesspit of their own making', ancient fears of contamination and punishment were given new life.[1] But how would the government react? The virus was transmitted through the bloodstream: through transfusion, through injection, through sex. If the ways in which these took place could be modified, then the rate of spread could be curbed. But morality was inevitably to intercede at this point – was government to say that the injection of drugs could be done more safely by not sharing needles, that sexual intercourse could be made safer by the use of condoms? Or was it, as moral campaigners would argue, to say that drug use, homosexuality and heterosexual intercourse outside marriage was wrong and making them safer unacceptable? If this was the most obvious point of possible agreement, or tension, between government and moral campaigners, a second area was only to become evident as the government's education campaign unfolded – at whom should the campaign be aimed? In both cases, the government's AIDS campaign is crucial for understanding what role sexual morality played in Thatcherism.

From the beginning of 1986, the government was engaged in an education campaign aimed at 'informing the general public about the virus' and the precautions that could be taken to minimise its transmission.[2] This campaign reached a peak at the beginning of 1987, when somewhat obscure television adverts were joined by much more explicit television discussion programmes, newspaper advertising, hoardings and a leaflet delivered to every household in the country. Posters proclaimed 'AIDS is not prejudiced: It can kill Anyone.' 'Gay or Straight, Male or Female', they warned, 'Anyone Can Get AIDS from Sexual Intercourse. So the More partners, The Greater The Risk. Protect Yourself. Use a Condom.'[3]

Such an approach was not calculated to meet with the support of the moral lobby or any of its supporters on the backbenches. For some time, their response fell into two overlapping, but different, patterns. For some, AIDS was basically associated with 'deviant' minorities. For others, it reached far further and was a major threat to the heterosexually promiscuous. In the first grouping may be found, for instance, the MP who in early 1987 demanded that government material make it clear that the main dangers were 'posed by drug abusers and homosexuals' or his colleague who expressed concern that the campaign had been even-handed between heterosexuals and homosexuals and called for the banning of 'homosexual propaganda' in schools and TV.[4]

Similarly, the following year, a TV advertisement warning of the possibility of AIDS resulting from a heterosexual encounter came under fire, with, for instance, Conservative MP John Carlisle arguing that the campaign should be aimed at homosexuals.[5] When, shortly after, the government dropped the advertising agency it had been using, critics of government policy returned to the offensive. The campaign had taken 'the wrong line', Jill Knight declared, and because it had 'been afraid of offending the homosexual community', the Government had failed to focus upon high-risk groups.[6]

Such a view could take the form of calling for legal action. Tory MP Geoffrey Dickens suggested in a television programme that homosexuality should be made illegal again. There were signs, he later wrote, that 'the homosexual fraternity' was taking precautions against AIDS and this could make it less likely that the 1967 Sexual Offences Act would be repealed. But this would depend on the rate at which the disease spread – if it escalated and it could be proved that homosexuality was 'the root cause of the disaster inflicted upon a nation' then prison sentences for homosexuality could return.[7]

This view was particularly associated with the Conservative Family Campaign. As we have already seen in our discussion on sex education, the Campaign's intervention in the furore over the 1986 Education Bill included a fringe meeting at the Conservative conference on 'the teaching of homosexuality in schools'.[8] Much of the agitation against sex education at this time specifically focused on homosexuality and the launch of the government's campaign on AIDS later in the year gave the Campaign the opportunity to turn its attention to opposing not just sex education sympathetic to homosexuality but homosexuality as such. In November, in a letter to Lord Whitelaw, who chaired the Cabinet committee on AIDS, the Campaign called on the government to make AIDS a notifiable disease, introduce national testing of the population and put people with AIDS in isolation. Male homosexual acts, it argued, should be recriminalised by the repeal of the 1967 Sexual Offences Act, contraception should not be made available free, nor should needles be supplied to drug addicts. Instead official funding should be removed from the Family Planning Association and the Terrence Higgins Trust and the government should support bodies promoting family values and offering Christian counselling to persuade homosexuals to desist. In Graham Webster-Gardiner's view the government's advertising campaign was 'a *waste of taxpayers' money*, offensive and an encouragement to experiment with immoral sex and drugs'.[9] Shortly afterwards, he and Dr Adrian Rogers attacked the government campaign for failing to criticise homosexuality. It was necessary, Webster-Gardiner said, to take a moral stand yet the government was 'skirting round the issue'.[10] In early 1987, as arguments over the government's campaign intensified, the CFC launched a call for action which included urging that police action be stepped up to ensure that no gay activity occurred among under-21s.[11]

At the end of the following year, in a letter to *The Times*, Sir Alfred Sherman, now somewhat marginal on the New Right but in the seventies a co-founder with Thatcher and Joseph of the Centre for Policy Studies made an even sharper attack on government policy. AIDS, he argued, was predominantly associated with 'undesirable minorities...i.e. mainly sodomites and drug-abusers, together with numbers of women who voluntarily associate with this sexual underworld'. While, 'other things being equal', homosexuals should not be discriminated against, they should not be privileged and the Department of Health, BMA and other bodies should not seek to protect minorities by opposing such measures as compulsory testing and isolation.[12]

If homosexuality was a focus in some moralist arguments, it was subsumed into a more general attack on permissiveness in others. Even before the government's campaign was launched, criticisms of its response to the issue had already been voiced. In Parliament at the end of 1984, William Cash tabled an Early Day motion calling for a Health Education Council campaign on the dangers of sexual promiscuity. The motion linked sexually transmitted diseases, infertility and under-sixteen contraception, but in an article early the following year Cash also took up AIDS. It could be transmitted heterosexually, he declared, and without a campaign to change attitudes to sex there would be 'the death of so many of our young people'.[13]

When the government announced its national campaign, Mary Whitehouse claimed that advertisements about the dangers of AIDS would be contradicted by the permissive values of the programmes surrounding them. So-called 'girlie' magazines and books which described perversions, she declared, were part of a 'wave of permissiveness' that had resulted in AIDS and what was needed was for church figures to speak out and for parents to vet the nature of the sex education which would shape future attitudes.[14] Both Conservative MPs and moral groups were critical of government policy. Conservative MP Patrick Cormack suggested that every packet of condoms should carry a government health warning reading 'Promiscuity Kills' and accused the government of threatening 'the innocence of children' by its 'extremely explicit and frankly brutally worded literature and advertisements'.[15] Peter Bruinvels, meanwhile, was concerned that the government campaign could lead to children experimenting with sex when 'the whole thing might not have gone that far if they hadn't heard about the condom'.[16]

As for the moral groups, the chairman of the Order of Christian Unity urged the government not to flinch from making clear in its campaign that chastity was 'the main barrier against all sexually transmitted diseases' while CARE called for 'sexual chastity before marriage and monogamous exclusive faithfulness' after. This, it argued, should be the basis of any AIDS campaign.[17] Family and Youth Concern likewise proposed that the government's campaign should be based on the importance of family life and the 'explicit discouragement of promiscuous sexual relationships'. There was 'only one ultimate answer to Aids', it suggested, 'and that is lifelong faithful union. Let the Government have the courage to say so!' Instead, it subsequently complained, the government had subjected the country to amoral safe sex proposals and told young people that casual sex was acceptable if a condom was used.[18]

VALA too was involved, producing a report in early 1987, *Television Programmes and Aids*, which declared that many programmes featured extra-marital sexual relationships. Playwrights and producers, Whitehouse argued, should give a sense of 'the positive, joyful, challenging aspects of monogamy, fidelity and chastity'.[19] Speaking subsequently to VALA's annual convention, she called for a moral crusade. AIDS was not wholly negative, she declared, since it gave the chance to change priorities and end the situation where 'for the greatest part of the last three decades, television has propagated the idea that sleeping around...is the liberated thing to do'.[20] Later in the year, she attacked plans to advertise condoms on television and when this nonetheless went ahead lodged a complaint with the Independent Broadcasting Authority (IBA) that it was misleading when discussing condoms

to make no reference to their failure rates and give the impression
that they were a guarantee against cervical cancer and AIDS.
Condom advertisements, she urged, should be accompanied by
short films supporting chastity before marriage.[21] A hitherto
unknown group, Defence Against Media Manipulation, also
emerged, announcing plans for an injunction to stop any repeti-
tion of the advertisement. 'We are not against contraception',
declared its spokesman, 'but we are against conditioning the
younger generation into the belief that promiscuity is a good
thing.' The spokesman (and, according to one source, only
member), William Spring, was a veteran anti-abortion campaigner
of the seventies.[22]

A few months later, Family and Youth Concern released a video
as an 'antidote' to the government's AIDS campaign which, Valerie
Riches declared, promoted condoms instead of chastity. Because
the government did not want to 'upset powerful lobby groups',the
organisation claimed, it said little about which sexual practices
should be avoided. In an Early Day motion, sympathetic MPs
accused the Health Education Authority of encouraging attitudes
unconducive to marriage and the family and called upon the
Secretary of State for Social Services to examine his Department's encouragement of casual sex. The government, it was
urged, should condemn unnatural and unacceptable sexual practices.[23] Later in the same month, a New Right think-tank, the
Social Affairs Unit, published a pamphlet on government information policy. According to the *Daily Telegraph*, it argued that the
AIDS campaign had had little effect and might have encouraged
acceptance of extra-marital sex and thus contributed to AIDS.
(This, in fact, was somewhat milder than the pamphlet's actual
arguments. According to its author, Digby Anderson, the government campaign could have threatened values and institutions
needed for society's sustenance. By advocating condom use outside marriage, the campaign was encouraging 'the destruction of
the family' and it was also guilty of making 'perversions acceptable'. The government feared stigmatising social groups, he
commented, but if there had been more 'revulsion and stigma
toward certain "practices", several thousands now dead might be
alive.')[24]

For a considerable period, then, moral campaigners have seen
AIDS as a symptom of sexual permissiveness in general. But, as we

have seen, there has always been another strand of argument that only some groups are at risk and recently this has come to the fore. Thus Robert Whelan, writing in Family and Youth Concern's bulletin, argues that, contrary to the government's slogan, AIDS does discriminate. The overwhelming proportion of cases in the West are homosexual men and the remainder mainly drug-abusers and haemophiliacs. It is extremely difficult to contract through vaginal intercourse, he claims, and such transmission is so 'inefficient' that it poses no threat to the heterosexual population at large.[25]

This argument has not been confined to the *Family Bulletin* but also underpins its video. More importantly, as we have seen, similar views have been one of the strands of moralist argument from early on. In the recent period, they have achieved wide circulation through being espoused in the pages of papers such as the *Sun* and the *Daily Express*, particularly following a parliamentary question on the issue by Labour peer Lord Kilbracken.[26] Another figure who has argued along similar lines, former president of the Royal College of Surgeons (and a sponsor of Family and Youth Concern) Sir Reginald Murley, also attracted attention when he wrote in the *Daily Mail* that a young woman was unlikely to develop AIDS unless she became a drug addict or 'allows herself to be buggered'.[27]

Critics have attacked such claims as irresponsible, resting in part on a confusion between those with AIDS and the larger number, including a higher proportion of heterosexuals, who are HIV-positive but have not yet developed AIDS. There has also been some speculation whether Family and Youth Concern and other groups may be responsible for an apparent recent decline in government concern with AIDS, as evidenced in the dissolution of the Cabinet AIDS committee and the Health Education Authority AIDS unit, and the government's evident unhappiness over some proposed advertising. It seems more likely, however, that influence has been more indirect, with arguments from some experts that the spread of AIDS may be less than feared making the government less willing to accept the sexual diversity and blunt language that earlier advertising acknowledged.[28] What has received far less attention, however, is that the view of AIDS currently favoured by the moral lobby poses problems for its overall argument. Firstly, there is some confusion about whether

campaigners are arguing that AIDS *cannot* be transmitted heterosexually. While in its video, 'The Truth About AIDS', for instance,
Family and Youth Concern, as we have seen, talk about a lesser
chance of heterosexual transmission, it also promotes an American
study entitled *The Myth of Heterosexual AIDS*. Similarly, the
Conservative Family Campaign now argues that 'Normal heterosexual people have a non-existent risk of catching Aids.'[29] There is,
of course, somewhat of a difference between claiming a differential
risk and none at all. Secondly, if it is arguing that AIDS poses little
or no risk to heterosexuals, where does that leave the argument that
heterosexuals should adopt chastity before marriage and monogamy after in order to protect themselves? One book on the subject,
for instance, written by Dr Margaret White of the Order of
Christian Unity, had opened with the claim that 'AIDS is not a
disease of homosexuals ... it is a disease of the promiscuous.'[30] Yet
if it is now being said that vaginal intercourse is unlikely to
facilitate AIDS, what does this do to efforts to recruit AIDS to
police sexuality in general? Murley has been quoted since his
pronouncement on drugs and sodomy arguing that monogamy is
Family and Youth Concern's answer to AIDS.[31] What is unclear is
whether the two arguments can be held together with any
consistency.

While moral campaigners have attacked the government's
campaign as immoral and insisted it should be directed at homosexuals and drug users, the government remains persuaded that
heterosexual transmission is a real danger and continues to
recommend the use of condoms. Despite what we might expect,
then, it has not used AIDS in order to enforce a traditionalist
moral stance. But what of the occasions when leading ministers
have spoken out on morality? Can these be seen as heralding a
moral offensive?

As we have noted, moralist themes had played a part in the rise of
Thatcherism and the New Right in the seventies. Yet in the early
years of the Thatcher government they were almost completely
absent. The inner-city riots of 1981 led to Conservative concern
over order and some MPs argued that the permissive society had
contributed to a breakdown in discipline.[32] But it was not until early
1982 that morality moved to the fore of the government's argument.
Speaking to Conservatives in Loughborough in February, education minister Rhodes Boyson denounced 'The permissive age, which

blossomed in the late 1960s'. It had led, he declared, to the 'break-up of stable families ... debased morals and false values' and society had 'reaped dragons' teeth in the form of juvenile revolt'. Speaking again in Poole the following month, he argued that many of those who rioted, committed muggings or were football hooligans had been born in the 1960s, 'the heyday of the permissive society', when settled values had come under attack, pornography and sexual license had increased and family breakdown escalated. What was needed, he proclaimed, was a society where authority was once again respected. The following week, such views were echoed when the Prime Minister, addressing the Conservative Central Council, declared that 'permissive claptrap' had 'set the scene for a society in which the old values of discipline and self-restraint were denigrated'. We were now 'reaping', she declared, 'what was sown in the Sixties.' Over two decades standards had been attacked and there had been 'no riposte, no reply. The time for counter-attack', she announced, was 'long overdue'.[33]

The target for these strictures was not merely the urban disorders of the previous year or the continuing problem of violent crime. Where later attacks on the 'promotion' of homosexuality were aimed at the Labour Party, the 1982 speeches were, in part, aimed at the less obvious target of the Social Democratic Party. Following the Thatcher speech, the political correspondent of the *Daily Express* reported that Ministers had decided on a series of speeches calling for the restoration of discipline and attacking the changes in the sixties associated with the then Labour Home Secretary Roy Jenkins, now the recent victor for the SDP at the Glasgow Hillhead by-election. 'Top Tories', the *Express* reported, believed that 'the campaign for traditional values is a potential vote-winner'.[34]

A subsequent speech by the Prime Minister in July of the same year sought to link rising figures of illegitimacy, divorce and juvenile crime to 'the birth of the permissive society' and an obsession with rights rather than duties. On this occasion, there was no reference to Roy Jenkins. The following year, however, in the opening speech of the General Election campaign, an attack on the 'Marxist' Labour Party was accompanied by the accusation that former Labour SDP leaders had been responsible in the past for the destruction of grammar schools, the extension of nationalisation and the undermining of 'respect for the family in the name of a misleading permissiveness'.[35]

Yet in the election campaign itself the issue played no part.
Earlier in the year, the *Guardian* had speculated that a Conservative
team was already at work in an effort to present the party as the
party of the family. Revelations the following month that the
Cabinet had set up a Family Policy Group received a great deal of
publicity. 'Leaked' documents painted a picture of leading Ministers and advisers considering a wide array of possible proposals,
ranging from training children to manage their pocket money to
changes in the taxation system and government action on pornography. In part, this had been intended to produce proposals for
the election manifesto. Yet when it appeared, a mere three months
after the revelations, the question had been submerged beneath
other concerns. 'Of the infamous blueprints for sweeping new
approaches to "family" policy', Hugo Young noted in the *Sunday
Times* in late May, 'only a single anodyne paragraph remains.'[36]

In 1985 the issue re-emerged. Addressing the Rotary Club of
London in August 1985, Boyson returned to familiar themes. 'A
generation of muggers, football hooligans, drug takers and
couldn't-care-less individuals', he declared, were 'the dragon's
teeth sown by the permissive age of the 'sixties and early
'seventies'. That period had been responsible for the destruction
of values and the acceptance of under-age sex and easy abortion.
Total social breakdown was threatened and the answer lay in
morality and discipline.[37] While this received little attention, the
issues of family and morality moved to centre stage with Norman
Tebbit's much-publicised speeches in late 1985 and early 1986. In
November 1985, Tebbit used the occasion of the first Disraeli
Lecture to the St Stephen's Constitutional Club in London to argue
that collectivist policies were not the sole cause of the nation's ills:
'The effects of those policies have been dramatically worsened by
the onset of the politics of the permissive society.' Far from
encouraging self-discipline and responsibility, he continued, 'permissiveness compounded by the economic failure and personal
irresponsibility engendered by the socialist state leads inevitably to
the violent society'.[38] In describing the kind of country Britain
should become in the nineties, Tebbit concentrated on economic
questions – employment, taxation, the diffusion of property. But at
the end of his list of 'eight key objectives' came a restoration of the
conditions in which people could once again be safe in their streets
and homes. When he expanded on this towards the conclusion of

his speech, it was to argue that the 'trigger of today's outburst of crime and violence' lay in 'the era and attitudes of post-War funk which gave birth to the "Permissive Society" '. Permissiveness had rejected standards and derided family life while 'Violence and soft pornography became accepted in the media. Thus was sown the wind; and we are now reaping the whirlwind.'[39] The government, he went on, was already moving to improve education and deal with crime. But by the nineties we would see the results of revulsion against permissiveness. Sentences would be stiffer, education would be traditional and the public would 'demand that television producers think about the effects of what they broadcast upon impressionable people'. At the front of the 'campaign for a return to traditional values of decency and order', he declared, 'will be the Conservative Party: for we understand as does no other Party that the defence of freedom involves a defence of the values which make freedom possible without its degeneration into license'.[40]

It was an attack that was quickly taken up in pro-Conservative newspapers. The *Daily Mail* gave it front-page coverage (under the headline 'Tebbit Leads The Backlash'), editorialised in its support, published a strongly supportive article by Paul Johnson the following day and then launched a 'great debate' before announcing that readers had given their verdict: 'Bring Back the Good Old Values!'[41] For its part the *Daily Express* published an article by Tebbit reiterating his arguments and placed it on the same page as an editorial echoing his views and a cartoon in which previous decades were represented by Heath releasing hyper-inflation in the 1970s and Macmillan unleashing permissiveness in 'The Swinging Sixties'.[42]

But as a Channel 4 *Diverse Reports* programme showed at the beginning of the following year, Tebbit's views did not meet with support throughout the party. Interviewed by Christine Chapman, a reporter with libertarian Conservative views, Tebbit was at pains to argue that his views on morality were not in contradiction to his economic liberalism. He was, he declared, a liberal who favoured regulation in both spheres: just as the City needed regulation so did standards. The Obscene Publications Act needed to be strengthened but in general, he told Chapman, he was looking not towards legislation but to a change in public attitudes, taking care to point out that he did not agree entirely with Mary Whitehouse but accepted the importance of her stance. As Chapman made clear at the beginning of the programme, she believed Tebbit's views were incompatible with Conservatism, and Conservative MPs interviewed during the programme expressed their discontent with Tebbit's argument. For one, Tim Brinton, the possibility that the party might become the Mary Whitehouse of the nation would be to go in the wrong direction; personal responsibility, not government legislation, was needed in personal matters. For another, Matthew Parris, a Moral Majority strain had always existed in the party but it was not within the gift of government to make the kind of changes such people wanted nor should government try to do so.[43]

In April, however, Tebbit returned to the offensive with a speech at St James's Church, Piccadilly. Once again he stated that the Conservative Party would be at the forefront of the campaign for a return to decency and order, and towards the end of the speech he returned to the theme of permissiveness. There was a need, he declared, 'to overcome the poisoned legacy of the Permissive Society' and restore the centrality of standards. The 'debasement of the currency has run parallel to the debasement of standards', he told his audience, and the roots for this lay in the sixties. 'Legislation on capital punishment, homosexuality, abortion, censorship and divorce – some of it good, some of it bad' had followed in rapid succession, giving the impression of an end to restraints. In the same period trends in education, in the family, the media and the Churches all undermined the standards and beliefs of earlier times. Self-indulgence prospered. 'Tolerance of sexual deviation generated demands for deviance itself to be treated as the norm.' The broadcasting media scorned self-restraint and portrayed family life as a straitjacket. The number of reported rapes, he continued, had almost doubled since the mid-seventies, families had increasingly disintegrated, divorce and illegitimacy increased, the abortion rate among women under 20 more than trebled. 'And I do not see how anyone can doubt that the trends shown in those figures are deeply destructive of the cohesion and order of a free society.' The remedy, he concluded, was to restore traditional values and thus bring back responsibility and self-respect.[44]

In response to the speech, the *Daily Mail* editorialised that only in the Conservative Party could such a view flourish and predicted that 'when the General Election comes the Tebbit factor will certainly count'.[45] The second speech made it clear that for

Tebbit, more probably than any other leading Conservative, a 'pro-family' stance was politically important. For others in the Conservative Party (as well, of course, as outside it), this was a disturbing view. We have already noted the comments of critical MPs after the first speech. After the second, the *Daily Telegraph* carried an article by Julian Critchley, the maverick Conservative MP for Aldershot, disputing Tebbit's argument. Some Conservatives, he declared, saw religious 'revivalism as a vote-catcher'. But, in Critchley's view, a moral majority on this side of the Atlantic was not to be welcomed, while Tebbit's attack on the legislative reforms of the sixties and the social changes of 'the past 20 years' were nonsensical. On balance, he suggested, such changes had been to the good and, in any event, whatever politicians might say, 'the amount of sin tends to remain constant'.[46]

Yet if, for some Conservatives, Tebbit's speeches were worrying, what is perhaps more noteworthy is how they did not represent part of some calculated government moral offensive. Certainly, Tebbitt continued to put forward such views. Thus at Conservative Party Conference in October 1986, during the furore over *Jenny Lives with Eric and Martin*, he accused the Labour-run Inner London Education Authority of distributing 'explicit books which no decent parents would wish their children to see', while in an interview in the *New Statesman*, published the following month, he expressed sympathy for Mary Whitehouse's views and referred to public concern over pornography and violence.[47] But while Tebbit still held such views, they did not become a central part of Conservative policy. Indeed, that this might turn out to be the case was a fear expressed by some of his supporters at the time of the first speech. Two days after, Paul Johnson had praised Tebbit's views and described him as speaking for the 'silent majority'. His one criticism, he went on, was that the diagnosis did not 'go far enough'. It was not 'sufficient', he wrote, for Tebbit 'to predict a "final campaign to sweep away permissiveness" and to add that when the day comes "the Conservative Party will be at the forefront" '. The Conservatives were in office, with a massive majority, and instead of waiting until the nineties, Johnson called on them to lead 'a moral crusade' now. Apart from a few speeches, the government had so far done little. TV violence had increased; under 'successive Tory Ministers, the DHSS has used vast sums of taxpayers' money to defeat Mrs Gillick'; the welfare state continued to give greater priority to unmarried mothers than to 'normal families' and the government had done nothing to promote moral education in the schools. Ministers' words were not enough, Johnson insisted; 'What we want are effective deeds.'[48] Likewise, in its subsequent report on readers' responses to the first speech, the *Daily Mail* had warned that 'it was Mr Tebbit who chose to open the floodgates. And he and Mrs Thatcher were the ones who had asked for our votes to put them in Government'. They had better, then, start looking for the answers to the 'great pent-up tide of public emotion' the letters had revealed.[49] Both Johnson and the anonymous *Mail* writer had warned of the danger that the government would do nothing. But while government figures would return to the issues, the Tebbit speeches did not mark the beginning of a government moral offensive.

Again in the 1987 Election, the issue played relatively little part. The manifesto, in addition to its pledge on broadcasting standards, criticised 'sexual propaganda' in some schools and in mid-May the *Daily Mail* reported that Norman Tebbit would be using a special poster 'to go for Labour's throat in a ruthless attack on the hard Left and its corruption of Britain's schoolchildren'. The poster showed three booklets, one critical of the police, one on sex education for children and one for gay youth. 'Is This', the caption asked, 'Labour's Idea Of A Comprehensive Education?' Labour council support for 'gay studies in schools', the paper reported, was believed by Conservative Central Office to anger parents throughout the country.[50] Yet although John Moore raised the issue in an election broadcast and Kenneth Baker, during a press conference, attacked an Inner London Education Authority-funded booklet on heterosexism, the issue did not play a role of any significance in the national campaign.[51]

Recently, the attacks of the early eighties on the permissive society have reappeared, initially around urban disorder and then concerning the rising rate of single parenthood. Speaking to the Conservative Central Council in March 1989 the Prime Minister attacked 'the born-again prophets of the permissive society' who were responsible for the hooligans of the eighties.[52] The following year, she returned to the theme with an attack on 'the proponents of the permissive society' whose misleading of young people in the sixties had led to a generation of children at risk of 'seeing life without fathers not as the exception, but the rule'. Kenneth Baker too, in a speech later in the same month, declared that the family had been undermined by the permissive society.[53] In April the *Daily Mail* claimed that the Conservatives were 'planning a "family first" election manifesto to capitalise on the backlash against the permissive society'. The central policies, it suggested, would be aimed at easy divorce, fathers who deserted their families and child hooliganism. But while the pursuit of fathers for maintenance did, indeed, become part of government policy, how it would deal with other questions was far from certain. Different sections of the right offered advice. One particularly noteworthy development was the decision of the free-market No Turning Back Group of Conservative MPs to argue in its proposals for 'The Next Ten Years' that government should not be morally neutral towards the family. Divorce, it argued, was extremely costly to the state, while it was 'dismayed at the strain placed on the social services by the notion that voluntary single parenthood provides automatic entitlement to state support'. As we see in the next chapter, the Conservative Family Campaign has also been active but particularly prominent has been the Centre for Policy Studies. Lord Joseph, raising again some of the themes of his 1974 speech, argued in a Centre pamphlet that the family was 'at risk of falling apart' under such pressures as divorce, illegitimacy, 'adolescent mothers', 'almost universal contraception' and abortion. What was needed, he argued, was to foster the conditions of family stability through tax reform. David Willetts, the Centre's director of studies, argued for policies to strengthen 'the traditional family' by moving away from 'quick and easy divorce' and encouraging young mothers to stay at home. Kenneth Baker, speaking at a conference on crime organised by the Centre earlier the same month, argued that families needed two parents and boys a male role model. 'I know I am not alone', he declared, 'in my belief that the undermining of the family by the permissive Sixties and Seventies had a pernicious and damaging effect.' Concerned both at changes in family structure and the costs to public spending of single-parenthood, Mrs. Thatcher's enthusiasm for pursuing maintenance was unsurprising. But it remained unclear, given an economic situation in which the demand for female labour was rising, how far the government would go in discouraging women from entering the labour force or whether it would risk offending voters (or members of the party) who did not identify with a moral crusading stance.[54] This was strikingly demonstrated by contradictory reports of the speech by Home Office Minister Angela Rumbold when the Conservative Conference debated the family in early October. 'Mothers will be paid £400 to stay at home with their children', reported *Today*, quoting Rumbold on the need to help mothers who wanted to stay at home with small babies. *The Independent*, however, announced 'Rumbold rejects schemes to keep mothers at home', quoting her emphasis on the family's right to 'make its own choices' and the necessity to 'face up to the fact that family life has changed'. Some speakers at the conference, including the Conservative Family Campaign's Adrian Rogers, had denounced permissiveness or called for a 'moral crusade'. But what part such notions would play in electoral strategy remained unclear, as was even more the case with the replacement of Margaret Thatcher by John Major shortly after.[55]

A concern with the effects of the permissive society, then, has been a recurring theme of Conservative speeches over the last decade. It has been deployed against a variety of targets, ranging from criminals and rioters to single-parent families. It has had a divergent party-political target too, shifting from the electorally threatening SDP during the latter part of the first term to the more durable Labour Party in the second. But has it been more than rhetoric? Does it play some greater role in Thatcherism?

In recent years, a great deal has been written on Thatcherism and the New Right. While much of it has been concerned with economic policy or with its stance on welfare provision, a number of writers have posed questions concerning sexual politics. In their treatment of the Thatcher government and morality, they have sought to put forward one of two arguments – either that Thatcherism had a central concern with sexual and familial issues or that we can periodise the government to see a phase, variously dated from different points in the eighties, in which it launched a moralist offensive. In this section, I want to question both of these arguments.

The contention that Thatcherism was centrally about sexual counter-revolution and/or the restoration of patriarchy is particularly associated with writers arguing from a feminist perspective, notably Miriam David and Tessa ten Tusscher, but is also to be found in other accounts of Thatcherism and the New Right. For David, the New Right's novelty lies precisely in its focus on patriarchy and the family. It is anti-feminist, albeit more covertly in Britain than in the United States, and its moralist concerns can be seen in the Gillick campaign and in its orchestration of the campaign against the Warnock Report.[56] Tusscher, in a subsequent discussion of 'Patriarchy, capitalism and the New Right', has similarly suggested that an essential element of the New Right has been systematically marginalised or ignored. While left-wing commentators, she argues, had concentrated on the crisis of capitalism in the seventies, feminists have appreciated that moral and familial issues were central to Thatcherism and that the New Right was new for just that reason. What previous writers had missed, Tusscher suggested, was that there was a crisis of patriarchy which the New Right was seeking to solve through a reversal of feminism and a restoration of traditional relationships.[57]

A number of discussions of the New Right and Thatcherism have taken these arguments into their analysis. Tusscher's work is 'strongly recommended' by Jessop *et al.*, while Desmond King, in his discussion of the New Right, suggests that while moralism is less developed in the British New Right than in the American this may not remain the case and he draws attention to David's argument that there is a common core of anti-feminism and a traditionalist stance on the family.[58] To take a further example, we might cite Stuart Hall's suggestion that discourses on abortion, sex education and the position of women 'have always been key bastions of Thatcherite ideology' and that 'a continuous subterranean theme' of Thatcherism was 'the restoration of the family, the bulwark of respectable society and conventional sexualities with its fulcrum in the traditional roles for women'.[59]

To different degrees, these analyses of Thatcherism or the New Right share a common problem in the collapsing together of distinct elements. We discuss later the problems with characterising moral crusades as 'right-wing' or 'the moral right' but here we will be concerned with the overtly political right. Firstly, we need to disentangle the New Right and Thatcherism. Thatcherism as a particular combination of neo-conservative and neo-liberal themes was only one (albeit the major) element in the New Right. In addition, Thatcherism, whether in opposition or, even more, in power, operated under constraints and in unforeseen circumstances that make the consistent pursuit of an ideological project impossible. The government included non-Thatcherites, it had to negotiate its way through both the Civil Service and civil society, it was buffeted by public opinion, economic shifts, international tensions. It is distinctly unhelpful to amalgamate the New Right, Thatcherism and the Thatcher government into one identical object (let alone combine them with moral crusades as well).

Furthermore, as we discuss in the next chapter, the New Right does not speak with one voice on family or sexual issues but is divided, partly in its stance but even more in the importance it attributes to such questions. For some they are central; for others, they are far surpassed by economic or foreign policy questions. As for the government itself, as Andrew Gamble has emphasised, the government's handling of the AIDS crisis, like the fate of the Family Policy Group, suggests that moralist or patriarchal rhetoric does not easily transfer into policy.[60] As we have seen, while it met some moralist demands on sex education, on homosexuality and on censorship, on other issues – for instance, abortion, under-sixteen contraception and embryo research – it clashed with moralists within and without the party. Only on some issues did it take a moralist stance. Where medical health or scientific research was involved, then the Thatcher government was likely to harken to the advice of its civil servants, the British Medical Association or scientific bodies. But on other, more populist issues, where it believed expertise was a guise for sexual liberalism and where there was a chance to lambaste the Labour Party, then the government took up some of the hopes of the moral lobby.

Other elisions also occur in the argument we are discussing. For Tusscher, moralism is to be traced to a reaction against the crisis of patriarchy and the rise of feminism in the sixties. But to see moral backlash as a response to the shifts condensed in the terms 'the sixties' (or 'the permissive society') is not the same as saying they are about the rise of feminism. While the two overlap they also diverge, and on issues involving the commodification of sexuality can be seen as antagonistic rather than congruent. Similarly, recognising that Thatcherism had a gender dimension is distinct from the larger claim that the family was central to it. The family and gender are central to significant elements of the American New Right (and, as we will see, the Conservative Family Campaign in Britain) just as they are to moral crusades in both countries. But to much of the British New Right anti-feminism is not crucial, while issues of sexual morality, although more noticeable, are still overshadowed by economic and foreign policy issues. This is not to argue that the family and gender are not important in social policy or the labour market. But this needs to be distinguished from issues of 'family values' and sexual morality, so crucial to such figures as Jerry Falwell in the United States, so far less central in Britain.

If the general equation of the New Right, Thatcherism and moralism is to be challenged, there are also problems with attempts to periodise Thatcherism and identify a particular moment when an impulse to police sexuality came to the fore. David Edgar has argued that in the wake of the 1981 riots and the Falklands war, the social authoritarians in the New Right rose in importance at the expense of economic liberals. While his account was most concerned with race and with crime, it had clear implications for issues of sexuality. The Tory right, he suggested, would see no contradiction between 'getting the state out of the boardroom' and 'into the bedroom' and such a view might well 'find legislative expression'.[61] Miriam David has likewise suggested that the early eighties marked a shift to moralism and anti-feminism, as demonstrated by the Family Policy Group, while in a later discussion, Ian Taylor has contrasted the absence of sexual or familial concerns from the Conservative Party's 1979 election manifesto and its rhetoric during that period with a move from the 1981 riots onwards towards moralism, familialism and enthusiastic involvement in campaigns for video and television censorship.[62]

As we have suggested, however, a balance-sheet of the first two terms does not indicate any consistent adoption of a 'moral right' agenda. Other writers, however, have periodised the government rather differently and proposed that it was the third term that should be seen as heralding a turn towards moralism. This can be seen, for instance, in Weeks's suggestion that moral counter-revolution had always been close to the heart of Thatcherism but this had been tempered by political caution. In the late eighties, however, social issues came to the fore, as demonstrated by the government's change in stance on legislation against 'positive images' of homosexuality. The New Right, he argues, had launched an ideological offensive on moral issues. Similarly, Ruth Levitas, reviewing King's book on the New Right, cited the Alton Bill, Clause 28 and the Broadcasting Standards Council in arguing that an emphasis on the patriarchal family was a growing influence on government policy.[63]

Weeks distinguishes between the government and the different moral initiatives, some of which originated from outside the Conservative Party, and disavows any notion of a centralised moralist strategy. Nonetheless, we would need to nuance the argument still further, recognising an increase in concern with moralist issues in the late eighties, on the part of the government and sections of the New Right while at the same time emphasising the unevenness of that shift and the continuation of major areas in which government and moralists are in conflict rather than cahoots. In addition, we also need to untangle more morality in its sense of policing sexuality from its broader sense of how humans relate to each other, the latter encompassing such Thatcherite virtues as truth-telling, respecting authority and avoiding crime, litter and the excessive imbibing of alcohol. (This distinction overlaps strongly with the necessity to distinguish sexual politics from the broader rubric of 'social issues', in which to argue that the latter has come more to the fore need not mean the former has.)

Finally, to dissent from particular feminist readings of Thatcherism is not the same as rejecting feminist readings as such. An essay by socialist feminist Lynne Segal published in 1983 suggested that Thatcherism was not engaged in an anti-feminist or moralist offensive.[64] Writing subsequently, feminist and Communist Beatrix Campbell described Thatcherism's moral agenda as 'characterised as much by silences as by speeches' and proposed that the Tory right has failed to mount a 'coherent legislative counter-revolution' on moralist issues.[65] From a different stance within both feminism and Communism, Elizabeth Wilson has argued that the British New Right is not united on family issues and that while Thatcherism was anti-permissive this is not the same as anti-feminist. Nor is there a centralised moral offensive – Gillick failed, as did the Churchill bill.[66] Finally, Lucy Bland has noted that the British moral lobby is not politically aligned 'and thus cannot unproblematically be defined as part of the new Right, let alone of Thatcherism'. Even the term 'moral Right', she suggests, has its problems.[67] For all four writers, the equation of the Thatcher government and the moral lobby, their amalgamation into the notion of a British Moral Majority, is to misread the more complex development of Thatcherism in which moralism played a far from consistent or coherent role.

8 Morality and the Right

In the previous chapter we have examined whether Thatcherism and the Thatcher government were engaged in a moral offensive. While it was impossible not to make some reference to the New Right in that discussion, very little attention has been given so far in this study to the different political and ideological groupings which made up much of the Thatcher government's intellectual and practical support, and, on occasion, comprised some of its sharpest critics. The New Right is a term for a disparate array of organisations and individuals and it would not be feasible to comb through all its elements in search of discussion of moral issues. I have decided, therefore, to select four instances which, it is hoped, will illuminate how the modern British right sees issues of sexual morality. While the New Right is agreed it is against socialism, there is far less agreement about what it is for. In particular, as David Edgar has explored, there are major tensions over the relative merits of the freedom of the individual and the needs of discipline and order.[1] In this dispute between liberty and authority, if the ultimate prize is the state the penultimate is the Conservative party, and one valuable indicator of activists' views we will examine is the letters column of the party paper, *Conservative Newsline*. However, because of its role in the struggle for Thatcherism in the seventies and because of Edgar's important argument that its evolution on moral issues in the eighties is a benchmark of a major shift in the New Right, the first instance we will take will be the Freedom Association (FA), formerly the National Association for Freedom.[2] The Association, while supported by Jill Knight, Norman Tebbit and other figures of the Tory right in the seventies, is not part of the Conservative Party itself. We will also look, therefore, at two party groupings – the Conservative Family Campaign, standard-bearer of the moralist cause in the party, and the now dissolved Federation of Conservative Students which,

143

during its controversial final years in the early and mid-eighties, was a forceful voice for the libertarian New Right. These, it must be emphasised, make up only part of the variegated constellation of New Right groups and publications and, in the case of the official party paper, is considerably wider in its political brief. As we will see, however, these four cases will take us some considerable distance in suggesting that, rather than conducting a moral offensive, the New Right has no uniformity in its views and is subject to major tensions on sexual issues.

One of the most interesting examples of these tensions is to be found in the free market pressure group, the Freedom Association. In January 1983, the cover-article of its paper, the *Free Nation*, concerned itself with 'Freedom and Our Cultural Crisis'. The author, the paper's editor, Philip Vander Elst, began by noting that the paper had concentrated on exposing the political forces threatening freedom. Now, however, it was time to give attention to the cultural crisis which Britain (like other Western countries) was undergoing. A rising crime rate, sexual permissiveness and family breakdown, he argued, were as dangerous to society as socialism and nuclear pacifism. The article, which took up most of the first two pages of the issue, gave considerable attention to crime figures. But an early reference to 'offensive sex scenes' in Channel 4 programmes signalled another concern and, as the reader turned to the second page, the discussion of crime began to give way to a consideration of sexual disorder. A decline of self-restraint combined with, firstly, the rising expectations generated by post-war affluence and, secondly, the dominance of collectivist values, had resulted, it was argued, in marital breakdown and an increase in rape and pornography. People were increasingly unable to form lasting relationships and properly bring up their children, one-parent families were generating delinquency and, it was suggested, it was no coincidence that rape was rising in parallel with the sexual revolution and 'the flood of pornography'. Ultimately, Vander Elst declared, people were coming to equate freedom with an absence of restraint. Burke, he had noted at the beginning of the article, had held that society needed to exercise 'a controlling power' upon the appetites of the intemperate. The permissive society, on the contrary, subordinated reason to impulse and destroyed the very values of right and wrong that protected society from totalitarianism.[3]

This article, written as it was by the paper's editor, quickly attracted attention from the Freedom Association's critics. In the April issue of the anti-fascist magazine, *Searchlight*, which also keeps a watching brief on sections of the Tory right, the author of an article on Conservative family policy suggested that the article indicated that the once libertarian Freedom Association had now fallen to an authoritarian onslaught. An article later the same year by David Edgar in the *New Socialist* put forward a similar argument.[4] It appears unlikely, however, that the Vander Elst article indicates such a shift in Freedom Association concerns and, indeed, in its ideology. In the very next issue, the Association set down its priorities for the year, including trade union reform, privatisation, defence and parental choice in education but not the issues of family and morality raised by the *Free Nation*'s editor.[5] The freedom the Association defends is above all a freedom of the market supplemented, in recent years, by a fight to defend Britain's nuclear arsenal. Other issues are strictly secondary to this and, while some of its leaders hold moralist views on sexual and familial questions, this has not led the organisation itself to focus on such issues.

Furthermore, there are the disagreements between Association supporters about such issues. This was already evident in the response to Vander Elst's article in the letters column of following issues. In the February issue two correspondents agreed with the article, the second of them urging that the Association 'take the lead' in persuading the government of the necessity of fighting against immorality and crime. But a third letter accused such 'so-called defenders of freedom' of being in fact 'freedom's worst enemies'. Adults should be able to watch sex scenes on TV or in the cinema or buy pornography which did no harm and had no link with sexual violence.[6] While another letter in support of Vander Elst appeared in the next issue, it was evident that the editor's views did not please all the *Free Nation*'s readers.[7] This might not have been important if one dissenting letter had been the only sign of the contentious nature of Vander Elst's views among FA supporters. But, as we shall see, on other such issues too there was an evident strain of libertarian unrest with a moralist stance.

The *Free Nation* came back to such matters on a number of occasions. Later in the year the Association's Chairman, Norris McWhirter, praised Victoria Gillick for 'bravely' challenging the

DHSS over under-sixteen contraception and attacked the NHS for its 'usurpation of parental responsibility'. Unless the provision of under-sixteen contraception was expressly made legal, he argued, then bureaucrats should not be allowed to provide it.[8] This was supported in the next issue by a correspondent who clearly agreed with the argument that the provision of contraception to girls under sixteen aided in the commission of a criminal offence but, indeed, went further than Gillick by arguing that any parents who did consent to the provision of contraception would be guilty of condoning illegal sexual relations.[9] The following month, however, another correspondent expressed surprise at McWhirter's support for the Gillick campaign. While supporting parental responsibility, she wrote, children too had rights and responsibilities and if a girl had sexual intercourse she was right to decide whether or not to become a mother. The key issue, it was argued, was to stop unwanted pregnancy.[10]

In November, following McWhirter's piece, the *Free Nation* published an article by Rachel Tingle, another prominent figure in the Association, entitled 'Control Video Nasties'. Tingle began by referring to the shock she had felt at seeing extracts from 'nasties' shown at a Tory conference fringe meeting by Mary Whitehouse. Her husband, she remarked, had felt sick at seeing the extracts. (Her husband, in fact, being Philip Vander Elst.) Referring frequently to material produced by the Viewers' and Listeners' Association, Tingle suggested we could well be 'breeding a host of Yorkshire Rippers' and called for controls on the video industry. The Obscene Publications Acts, she went on, were inadequate in acting against such films and, while the Conservatives, in their manifesto, had promised to respond to public concern over obscenity and introduce legislation on 'video nasties', so far there was no indication of keeping that commitment except in supporting the Bright bill. This bill did not deal with children watching their parents' videos at home and what needed to be done was to make all excessively violent videos illegal. The Home Secretary, however, had written to Mrs. Whitehouse that there was no consensus about reforming the Obscene Publications Acts. Judging by his letter, Tingle commented, Mr. Brittan could 'not be bothered to do anything' about sadistic films. Perhaps, she suggested, he still accepted the sixties liberal belief that what people did in private was up to them. But rapes were committed as a result of such videos and what Brittan needed to do was introduce legislation that would be effective. For further information and advice, she concluded, people should contact VALA or CARE.[11]

In a subsequent issue a correspondent attacked 'hysteria' over 'video nasties' generated by 'misguided religious fanatics, self-appointed moral guardians and self-important MPs'. The government's position on videos, the letter went on, was fundamentally against its own principles. Not only were actions against victimless crimes a waste of money and resources but to enforce a moral code through government was reminiscent of Eastern Europe or pre-Reformation Catholicism.[12] The following issue gave space to a wide range of responses. The majority was strongly against any leniency towards 'video nasties'. One letter merely suggested that the previous correspondent had failed to understand that vicious films caused increasing crime. A second regretted that legislation was necessary but necessary it was. Two other letters were of greater interest, one because of the tone of its argument, the other because of its author. The first not only argued that decadence was 'deliberately fostered by political manipulators who have a vested interest' in reducing Britain to helplessness but suggested that the only reason the earlier correspondent could have had for defending 'nasties' was if he was making a fortune from selling them. The other letter concentrated on the weaknesses of the Bright bill, arguing that it would legalise obscene material for over-eighteens and that such material in turn would be seen by children. What was particularly interesting about this letter was its signatory: 'Miss A Whitaker, MA Secretary of the Community Standards Association'. The earlier letter had been wrong, Whitaker stated, in holding that the control of videos was contrary to Freedom Association principles. The late Ross McWhirter had been active in the campaign against obscenity and as for the Association itself, 'We are surely on the side of liberty, not licence.' Here, certainly, was a clear link between the right and moral crusades. But amidst the general chorus of criticism of the original letter, another reader expressed his support for it on clear right-wing libertarian grounds. The government should not legislate on personal matters, he argued, and 'video nasties' should no more be controlled than drugs or the right to discriminate on grounds of sex or race.[13] (The following month another letter appeared defending the view that the Freedom Association's protection of freedom was quite compatible with holding that 'video nasties' had an effect on the violent crime rate and had to be 'radically controlled'.)[14]

As the letters column of the *Free Nation* as well as debates elsewhere made clear, the right was divided on the question of morality and the law. Vander Elst did not abandon his stance. In his editorial in late 1985, 'Taking Stock', which reviewed the situation on the tenth anniversary of the Association's inception, he returned to the theme. There was, he argued, a moral and cultural crisis which had to be overcome if freedom was to be maintained. Crime was rising, marriages breaking up and a key cause was the change in values, particularly since the sixties. Affluence and changing intellectual currents had encouraged a preference for pleasure over duty and moral absolutes in sex were being denied. This threatened freedom because it undermined social solidarity and the successful socialisation of children – only if Conservatives fought against materialism as well as against socialism could the Judeo-Christian heritage be preserved and our country protected. But while Vander Elst plainly retained his views on the issue, the Association still did not adopt a moralist stance. While the same issue carried an article on 'Abortion and the Right to Life' it was clearly described as 'a personal view' of the author.[15]

There have, however, been some signs of the Association moving in this direction. We have already discussed the publication of Rachel Tingle's pamphlet on homosexuality and education. While it was not a Freedom Association publication, Tingle wrote a full-page article on the Haringey conflict in the *Free Nation* in February 1987 and her pamphlet was favourably reviewed in the previous December's issue. In May 1987, the government was criticised for not supporting Jill Knight's bill on the issue at a Freedom Association conference on education. More importantly, the Association decided to give tactical advice on the issue to the Haringey Parents Rights Group.[16] In June 1987, in a 'personal' editorial, Vander Elst suggested that the rise in divorce and in crime had discredited the consensus over permissiveness and necessitated the Conservative Party taking a pro-family stance.[17] The Association also published a pamphlet by Vander Elst after the 1987 election which, although described as a personal view, confirmed that his ability to raise moralist themes within Association literature continued unabated. In *The Future of Freedom:*

Agenda for the 1990s, Vander Elst discussed a number of themes but gave particular attention to the argument that, although the government had 'done a great deal to restore Britain's economy and international reputation', it had not concerned itself with the rebuilding of 'the traditional family' and stemming the soaring rate of divorce. As Paul Johnson had noted, Vander Elst observed, in the 'crucial area of the family' there was a great 'gap in current Tory philosophy and practice'. Criticising the government's failure to stem the flow of public funds to the FPA, the Brook Advisory Centres and the Health Education Council and the inadequacy of legislation on screen violence and pornography, Vander Elst urged it to apply 'its mind' to the conservation of Western moral values.[18]

Certainly a constituency exists for such views in the Association. In 1983, for instance, the Buckinghamshire branch heard a speech on 'The Family and Law and Order' by Valerie Riches of the Responsible Society. The two organisations, a subsequent report in the *Free Nation* declared, had 'a great deal in common'. Likewise, in June 1986, the East Surrey branch was addressed by the Conservative Family Campaign's Graham Webster-Gardiner, a member of the Association.[19] But while both its national publications and local branches often prove hospitable to moralist concerns, the Association itself has not taken up their standard.

The dispute in the columns of the *Free Nation* pitched libertarian against moralist over Victoria Gillick, 'video nasties' and the overall stance of the Freedom Association towards the concerns of the moral lobby. But such arguments are not confined to one perhaps untypical organisation, as a subsequent exchange in the pages of the Conservative Party's monthly, *Conservative Newsline*, makes clear.

In September 1985, *Conservative Newsline* published an article by Mary Whitehouse. The Director of Public Prosecutions, she reported, had refused to prosecute offensive material while 'successive governments, including the present one' had claimed that there was not enough support in Parliament to tighten up the obscenity laws. This, she suggested, was not true – the collapse of Labour MPs' opposition to the 1978 Child Protection Act had demonstrated that no MP would dare 'to face his constituents' having opposed necessary measures. The fault lay with the permanent civil servants at the Home Office and the 1959 Obscene Publications Act, originally a Private Members' Bill of Roy

Jenkins. The solution, she continued, lay in moving the argument from the freedom of adults to the protection of children; just as the government fought the drug traffic, so it should fight pornography. True, the government had made some effort to control indecent display, but it must go on to reform the Obscene Publications Act. If it did not, then it could well be argued that it had broken its 1983 Manifesto pledge to 'respond to the increasing public concern over obscenity'.[20]

A letter in a subsequent issue of the paper made it clear that Conservatives were not united about such views. Mrs. Whitehouse, the writer suggested, was guilty of 'moralising', which was both 'abhorrent and dangerous'. The party should certainly protect children from exploitation but a strengthening of the Obscene Publications Act was of no relevance to this end and represented a move to censorship. Indeed, obscenity laws as such denied adults free access to reading matter and the Conservative Party as 'the party of individual freedom' should have 'no truck' with enemies of freedom who had produced no evidence for a link between pornography and serious crime and used child abuse 'as a red herring'.[21]

The letters column in a subsequent issue carried three replies to this letter, all of them hostile. One writer, Charles Oxley, Vice-President of Whitehouse's organisation, argued that pornography was linked with sexual offences and insisted that obscenity, rather than a matter of taste, was 'a danger to be removed speedily'. A second writer, a psychiatrist, gave examples of the disturbing effect of certain material on vulnerable people. Tougher laws were necessary, he argued, and the BBC and ITV should be told 'clean up your act or the Government will take powers to do it for you'. The third letter, the shortest, protested at the attack on Whitehouse and suggested that the author of the offending letter should get out of the Conservative Party and take his vote to Labour instead.[22]

A further letter in the next issue took a similar line to the previous three letters, describing the issue as a choice between moralism and anarchism and settling for the former. There had once, the writer recalled, been a time 'before the mass circulation of pornography' when sex crime was far rarer than today and in order to change the present situation freedom needed to be curtailed.[23] Two months later, however, another correspondent criticised VALA's Charles Oxley for 'a near hysterical' response. Pornography, it was suggested, could only be defeated by public taste, not by driving it underground. As for any suggestion that certain Conservatives would be better to leave the party, this correspondent argued that Conservatism was 'a broad church' and that 'modern Conservatism' attracted voters by its commitment to freedom not authoritarianism.[24]

This entry of another critic of moralism into the fray brought a sharp counter-attack. A second letter appeared from the correspondent who had suggested opponents of Whitehouse should leave the party, while Graham Webster-Gardiner, the chairman of the Conservative Family Campaign, proposed that, while 'our Party cherishes freedom of thought', libertarianism needed to be tempered by responsibility to the vulnerable. Television, radio and other media were propagating and promoting violence, pornography and blasphemy and this needed to be opposed. 'We should', he declared, 'do everything we can to suppress it.' The most enthusiastic proponents of the availability of obscenity, he went on, were far left groups such as the Communist Party and the Humanist Association who 'clearly understood that the dismantlement of traditional Christian morality will lead to destabilisation of society and make their evil plans more easy to obtain'.[25]

These replies however did not silence the opponents of censorship. The following year the second of Whitehouse's critics replied to his antagonists. While accepting 'Mr Webster-Gardiner's comments about the Left's attack on family life' and the need to protect children, he wrote, this did not mean that adults had to be protected from pornography. 'Time and again', he declared, 'we have seen that the State does not know what is best for people in the economic sphere so why should it be any better equipped to lay down what is good or bad for people in the social or personal sphere'? Individuals increasingly wanted more control over their lives, he suggested, and they would not 'take kindly to being told what is best for them in their private lives'.[26] The sharpest of his critics was likewise not to be silenced, as the following month's letters page showed. He was 'astonished', he wrote, that the paper wasted valuable space on a view which was 'an insult to all good Conservatives'.[27]

Interestingly, none of the correspondents had taken up Whitehouse's criticism of the government's performance and defended a Conservative administration against her admonishments. Instead the debate (just as it had in the pages of the *Free Nation*) had quickly taken the form of an exchange between a minority of libertarians and a greater number of supporters of government action to restore traditional morality.

Some libertarians are organised in the Libertarian Alliance, a free market group which has, for instance, published material opposing the Obscene Publications Act and arguing that the state has no right to regulate marriage by law. In one of its publications, written by a Young Conservative activist, the government is criticised for combining economic liberalism with moral authoritarianism. It is fruitless and wrong, he argues, to attempt to ban sexual services, pornography or drugs.[28] Such uncompromising views were unlikely to meet with acclaim in the Conservative Party. They did, however, achieve some following among younger Conservatives, particularly in the Federation of Conservative Students (FCS), which in the early part of the eighties received a great deal of publicity as an alliance of the libertarian and traditionalist right took control and turned the Federation in the direction of an ultra-Thatcherite agenda of privatisation, trade union restriction and espousal of a combative foreign policy which included support for the South African government against the African National Congress (ANC) and advocacy of armed action against left-wing regimes in the Third World. Ultimately, controversy over the behaviour of some of its activists and, more importantly, criticism of the Conservative government for being insufficiently right-wing, led to the decision by Party chairman Norman Tebbit in 1986 to dissolve the FCS. Leading elements in the Federation did not agree on a number of issues, notably over whether to take a nationalist or a free market stance towards immigration.[29] While there was likewise disagreement over moral issues, there was a noticeable strand of hostility to moralism, as can be seen in the attacks in its publications on moral campaigners. Thus in a mock issue of *The Times* for 1996, Mary Whitehouse is portrayed contemplating voting Labour in the face of a Conservative government committed to social libertarianism and personal freedom. VALA, she is imagined saying, wants social conformity and the 'nationalisation of morality'. Similarly, in its London Region magazine, *New Agenda*, at the end of the previous year, an imaginary speaker for the 'National Union of Spinsters and Prudes' argues that freedom should not mean that adults can choose what they can read or watch and looks forward to 'a Britain in which television is just like Radio Two, except with pictures'.[30]

The *Diverse Reports* programme discussed earlier on Norman Tebbit and morality included interviews with FCS activists. Several of the interviewees, *New Agenda* subsequently noted, made the points 'that a belief in individual liberty is entirely in line with traditional Conservatism and that as long as the individual does not infringe the rights of others it is wrong for politicians to legislate to impose their particular brand of morality'.[31] But libertarianism was not the only strand in the Federation, as was evident in an article on 'The Role of Women' in the first issue of *New Agenda*. Conservatives, the author argued, should recognise that Man was made in God's image while 'woman was created out of his side as a companion for him'. Their roles were complementary, with woman as mother and housewife, but in our permissive age this was obscured, with women confused by feminism while 'sexually insecure' men were sucked into a homosexual 'vortex of criminality and vice, indisputably demonic in its destructive power' where AIDS 'slaughters at will'. Feminism and sodomy were the twin evils of our time, he concluded, and our only hope was to turn back to the 'God of our forefathers who alone is the architect of order, happiness and prosperity'. In a letter in the following issue, the article was described by a libertarian Conservative activist as more suited to a 'Reactionary Old Colonel's Newsletter' than a FCS publication.[32]

Such tensions were equally apparent in the Federation's 1986 'philosophy seminar' on sexual politics, where one speaker, Chris Tame of the Libertarian Alliance, had included in his defence of the legalisation of prostitution an attack on the 'whole Mary Whitehouse/Moral Majority brigade' for seeking to compel sexual morality. An earlier speaker, Nigel Ashford, discussing 'Morality and the Law', likewise opposed a 'moral right' stance, arguing that the state should restrain its desire to police morality. These were not the only views espoused at the event, however. The seminar had begun with Rachel Tingle addressing the issue of sex education, criticising the FPA, the Health Education Council and some local education authorities and teachers for failing to support traditional moral values. The Baker proposals on sex education, she suggested, represented a significant advance but more needed to be done. During discussion her emphasis on the unacceptability of 'promot-

ing' homosexuality met with support but there was some tension
over whether her views amounted to censorship and a denial of
pluralism. Conversely, Tame explicitly rejected Tingle's critique of
the 'promotion' of homosexuality, arguing that she was inconsis-
tent to oppose one group 'pushing' their values while favouring
pushing her own. If those present (some thirty for most of the day)
tended to be doubtful about censorship but hostile to homosexuality, they were divided on abortion, with Ashford's defence of
abortion on libertarian grounds coming under attack from anti-
abortionists. Abortion, he suggested, was a legitimate matter for
libertarians to disagree on, depending on the status they gave to the
foetus. But on other issues, he insisted, citing Mill on liberty (and
Thatcher on choice), libertarian Conservatives could not take a
moralist stance.[33]

If the strains between libertarian and moralist impulses were
highly visible at the 1986 seminar, they were equally evident earlier
in the year when the Scottish FCS produced a proposed 'Conservative Manifesto for Scotland'. Among the proposals were the
legalisation of incest over the age of 21, the decriminalisation of
prostitution and the establishment of a 'market for motherhood' in
the form of legal surrogate arrangements. Yet if these were
libertarian ideas, the same could not be said of the proposal that
the state should not facilitate immorality by allowing civil marriage
in a registry office. Marriage, it was claimed, was a religious
ceremony and 'Pagan and disrespectful' forms of marriage should
be ended. As well as suggesting that serious sex offenders should be
castrated, the manifesto also attacked 'the murder of thousands of
unborn babies by abortion... sanctioned by successive governments'.[34]

The manifesto presented a stance towards sexuality in which
libertarian and moralist impulses were strangely intertwined. But it
was the incest proposal, in particular, which attracted criticism,
with the Solicitor-General for Scotland referring to 'loopy libertarianism' and a proposal 'deeply offensive, corrosive of family
life'. Such views did not represent FCS opinion, it was claimed by
the Federation, and the incest section was quickly dropped
(although the rest of the document was retained).[35]

Libertarians have continued to work within the party since the
disappearance of the Federation. In 1989, for instance, the Libertarian Alliance published *A Conservative Manifesto for Scotland*

which, amidst arguments about privatisation, taxation and foreign policy, urged the ending of the legal regulation of marriage and of state interference concerning voluntary sexual acts in private and supported commercial surrogacy. The following year, a new group saw the light of day when Conservatives Against Sex Censorship leafleted and picketed a fringe meeting against pornography organised by Mary Whitehouse. Criticising Conservatives who favoured state censorship and the imposition of morality on the individual, the group's secretary, libertarian activist Sean Gabb, denounced 'the rising tide of sexual puritanism'. (While demonstrating outside Whitehouse's meeting brought attention to its arguments, the publicity which the group received the next day was at least equally concerned with 'Topless model Simone, 19', whom the group had hired to partially strip as part of the protest[36]).

But while libertarians have continued to argue for their interpretation of Conservatism,their opponents have been particularly vigorous in recent years. As we argued earlier, one of the noticeable differences between the situations in Britain and the United States is the absence in the former of a Moral Majority-type movement. In Britain moral crusades have steered clear of overt political identification and have functioned as a lobby on the Thatcher government rather than as part of the New Right. In 1986, however, a development occurred which did mark an American-style coming together of right-wing politics and 'pro-family' concerns with the launching of the Conservative Family Campaign, an organisation described by one of its founders as having 'similar' ideas to the American Moral Majority.[37]

Four Christian Conservatives active in the moral lobby – Graham Webster-Gardiner, Dr Adrian Rogers, Robert Whelan and Antonia Hopkins – had been meeting since the Spring of 1985 to plan such an initiative and the Campaign was eventually launched at a press conference held to coincide with a Conservative Central Council meeting in mid-March of the following year. Unlike other parties, declared Webster-Gardiner, the Campaign's chairman, the Conservative party had a unique record of supporting legislation to protect the family. Today, however, the family was under attack 'from too easy divorce, a social security and tax system which promotes unnatural arrangements, by the usurpation of parental rights in sex education, by a stream of immoral propaganda on TV, radio, in magazines and books and, fundamentally by the undermining of the role of the man, the father, in society today'. The Campaign, he announced, would work for the Conservative party to recognise the defence of the family as a central issue and for the upholding of Christianity.[38]

In a supporting message sent to the conference, the Conservative MP Peter Bruinvels declared that Conservatism would end the corruption of public morals by modern society and 'bring about the return of traditional Christian and moral values'. It was right, he announced, that the Campaign 'should be established now to help spread the message of the Gospels'.[39] But what is meant by the corruption of public morals is not always self-evident and possible strains in what it meant to be 'pro-family' came to the fore immediately upon the Campaign's launch by contradictory reactions to Clare Short's Page 3 bill. Bruinvels defended the *Sun* for its 'jolly attractive' girls and 'harmless fun' and later appeared in the tabloid in a series entitled 'Commons Crackers' in which photographs of topless models were accompanied by pictures of (fully-clothed) MPs quoted attacking the Short bill.[40] Bruinvels defended his support for Page 3 from criticisms of inconsistency by arguing that 'the Sun is tasteful and brightens up people's day, while girlie magazines intrude below the waist like a gynaecologist and shouldn't be encouraged'. Yet, while Bruinvels had defended Page 3, the Campaign itself had written to Short, declaring support for her proposal, an occurrence which Bruinvels dealt with by saying that the Campaign had no corporate view. If any strains were to develop, however, between the demands of male pleasure and those of social purity, they were not given chance to surface. Leading figures in the Campaign were unhappy about co-operating with Short and the organisation moved away from the issue to take up, as we have seen, interconnected issues of sex education and homosexuality.[41]

These remained, however, only part of the Campaign's agenda and in its literature and in articles written by Webster-Gardiner for both Christian and Conservative publications it is clear how wide-ranging its concerns are. Indeed, they were already set down in material published before the Campaign's inception. Much of its argument can be traced to a pamphlet published in 1985 by Adrian Rogers and Bill Clements. This publication, subsequently distributed by the Campaign, attributed liberal divorce laws, homosexuality and one-parent families to 'our sick society'. There was too much emphasis, it argued, on individual rights and the miners' strike was compared with 'irresponsible adulterers who create fatherless families' as industrial and social fronts of the same movement against authority and morality. Contraception, it declared, had released people from the 'natural consequences of intercourse' and weakened family life and society, while perhaps the greatest need of all was for legislation which recognised that marriage was for life. Law was for promoting national cohesion not pluralism, Rogers and Clements argued, and firm action was needed 'to roll back the incursions of the licentious society'.[42] Earlier still, we can also find key themes articulated in a report, introduced by Jill Knight, which was published in 1984 by the Western Area Conservative Political Centre. Publicised in the national press, the report, chaired by Adrian Rogers, criticised sex education and the rise of single-parent families and called for television censorship, stricter divorce laws, encouraging mothers to stay at home and a ban on under-sixteen contraception.[43]

In an article by Webster-Gardiner in the Bow Group journal, *Crossbow*, soon after the Campaign's inception, the main parties were contrasted. The Tory party, it was noted, provided the bulk of votes against abortion, embryo experimentation and obscenity. The Liberals, on the other hand, were led by David Steel, architect of the Abortion Act, while the Social Democratic Party (SDP) boasted Roy Jenkins, 'the author of the permissive society' and David Owen, supporter of abortion 'when Socialist Minister of Health'. As for the Labour Party, it had 'embraced the policies of social destruction and disease' through its stance on homosexuality, abortion and under-age contraception. Most of those active in support of 'sexual licence', it was argued, realised that the independence of families was a barrier to socialism. 'In practice', Webster-Gardiner wrote, 'the rising number of people dependent on welfare is fast replacing trades union power as a weapon of socialism. This has been conveniently aided by liberal legislation on issues such as abortion and divorce which has contributed to the destruction of... traditional values.'[44]

The Campaign claims the support of 30 MPs, including Jill Knight, Harry Greenway, James Pawsey, Ann Widdecombe and Ann Winterton (as well as Viscount Buckmaster and Baroness Cox in the Lords). It also has supporters, including councillors and constituency chairmen, in 170 constituencies and puts a strong emphasis on gaining access to ministers and Conservative Central Office in order to argue its views.[45] But while it is a specifically Conservative body, this does not mean it is uncritically so, as we have already seen. One article, by Campaign vice-chairman Robert Whelan in a 'Christian Tory' magazine, *Prag*, was particularly acerbic. The Conservative Party, he commented, had fought recent elections as the party of the family but this bore no relation to its policy in office. Abortion and divorce had become easier to obtain, a Conservative Secretary of State for Social Services had been responsible for the defeat of the Gillick campaign, and along with the Minister of State for Health had led the opposition to the Powell bill. Not only was the government not supporting the family, it was 'using its governmental prerogative to undermine it'.[46] Other activists too were critical of their party. At the Campaign's 1986 Conservative conference fringe meeting the Euro-MP Sir Frederick Catherwood criticised the government's 'neutralist stance on questions of morality' while in *Crossbow* Webster-Gardiner made a veiled reference to 'the Conservative Party, warts though it may have'.[47] In an article aimed at a non-party audience in the evangelical magazine *Prophecy Today*, Webster-Gardiner made his views clearer. 'Not all is wonderful within the Conservative Party, that is why our organisation was established.' In this article, he gave an account of his involvement in the party that he had not given in less sympathetic environments. During a service of healing for his two sons in May 1985, he revealed, a church elder had received a prophecy, the meaning of which had been initially unclear. 'Later that day I was able to explain to him that it was a word for me to re-enter party politics and raise up a standard for the nation on issues particularly affecting the family. I set about becoming a Conservative Party candidate...' The Lord, he wrote, had led the Campaign's founders to launch the organisation and 'also led me personally to seek election to Parliament, so that I am now adopted as prospective parliamentary candidate for Newport East'.[48]

Supporters of the Campaign subsequently received a letter urging prayer for a renewed mandate for the Prime Minister and 'for the destruction of the Labour Party, which is increasingly an agent for the promotion of homosexuality, feminism, and other anti-Christian attitudes and policies'. When it was suggested by a journalist that perhaps God did not take such a partisan view of the election Webster-Gardiner explained, 'He's involved in spiritual warfare' and 'would favour' a Conservative victory 'rather than any other. Which is not to say that He would endorse everything the Conservative government has done.'[49] In the event, while Webster-Gardiner was not himself elected, his party was indeed victorious and he suggested that doubters should 'reflect upon the result of the General Election in the light of the prayers of my own and other pro-family and Christian organisations'.[50]

Following the General Election, the Campaign reiterated its criticisms of the government, accusing it of permitting abortion, embryo experimentation and pornography and contributing to 'the decay of marriage' through divorce legislation and changes in the law concerning illegitimacy. The election manifesto, it was suggested, had omitted reference to the family because the 'government's own record in office' exposed it to 'charges of duplicity' in claiming to be pro-family while continuing 'to allow the creeping socialism of anti-family policies to be pursued since the 1979 landslide victory'.[51]

The Campaign has taken up issues ranging from religious education to embryo research, and the government, it reported, had thanked it for its role in the House of Lords in support of Clause 28. Increasingly, however, the Campaign turned its attention towards government policy on taxation and social security, which it proposed should be rethought in order 'to ensure that marriage and the family are supported and strengthened'. In early 1988 a CFC pamphlet on the subject was published by a 'non-political charitable foundation', Christians in Britain, while more recently it has called upon the government to use tax policy to encourage mothers to stay at home. Looking back over recent years, Webster-Gardiner has characterised the Campaign as only achieving marginal gains and is particularly critical of the eventual fate of Clause 28. On taxation and social security, however, and the Conservative hierarchy's recognition of the importance of a group supported by 30 MPs, he is hopeful.[52]

The Conservative Family Campaign is not alone in its arguments. Digby Anderson of the Social Affairs Unit has been particularly forceful in arguing for 'those traditional Christian moral standards so historically entwined with normal family structure'. The Conservative government, he argued in 1988, had 'consistently subverted the traditional family by tax laws which

have disadvantaged marriage, by Aids campaigns which condone
promiscuity and unnatural sex, by a massive £2,000 million-a-year
handout to encourage voluntary single parenthood, by the removal
of the stigma of illegitimacy and by divorce liberalisation'.[53]
Rhodes Boyson too, along with fellow-MP James Pawsey and the
Rev. David Samuel of the Church Society, organised fringe meetings on morality at the 1985 and 1986 Conservative Conferences, at
the latter attacking single-parent families as 'probably the most evil
product of our times'.[54] And one (but only one) of the themes of
the neo-conservative journal, *Salisbury Review*, and its editor
Roger Scruton, has likewise been the restoration of a traditional
sexual morality.[55] But much of the New Right has relatively little
interest in moral issues. The Adam Smith Institute and the Institute
of Economic Affairs, for instance, concentrate on economic issues
(although the latter body has recently become involved in the
argument about single parenthood)[56] while an array of smaller
groupings are concerned with defence and foreign policy. A
comprehensive account of the New Right would have to acknowledge that it does contain significant moralist strands. But this
remains fundamentally different from the situation in the United
States. Issues of family and morality were crucial to the rise of the
American New Right in the seventies and have remained central to
major components since. The British New Right is far less focused
and far more disparate on such issues.

9 Moral Crusades and the Right

We have discussed earlier the attitude of the Thatcher government and the New Right towards 'pro-family' and 'pro-life' issues. In this chapter I want to challenge the frequently made assumption that the moral lobby itself should be seen as part of the New Right, before going on to consider the more vexed question of whether a less frequently used term, 'the moral right', is more successful in capturing its political character. In exploring these questions I will examine four areas. Firstly, what role does the right play in moral crusading organisations? Secondly, what attitude did campaigners take towards the Thatcher government? Thirdly, to what extent do moral crusades resort to notions of a deliberate plan to destroy the family and morality and draw on, even without recognising it, right-wing conspiracy theory? And finally, can they be seen as sexually conservative, and what political connotations does such a stance have?

Even before the inception of the Thatcher government, a tradition of seeing moral crusades as part of a Thatcherite offensive had become an important part of critical writing on the rise of the New Right. In the seminal 1978 study, *Policing The Crisis*, Stuart Hall and his co-authors characterised the seventies as marked by a 'co-ordinated swing towards tougher *social discipline*, behind which a general turn to the right in civil and social life is being pioneered'. The economic recession, they argued, had enabled the profoundly Tory themes of nation, family, law and order and opposition to permissiveness to reappear in the public arena. This was as evident in Joseph's 1974 Birmingham speech (including his praise of Mary Whitehouse) as it was in 'the wide-ranging counter-offensive' led by her and others and 'cresting in the anti-abortion campaigns'. What was most important, *Policing The Crisis* contended, was the rise of the radical right within the Conservative leadership, aided not only by ideologues in the *Sunday Telegraph*, the *Spectator* and elsewhere but also by 'its more populist ventriloquists in the Clean-Up Television, Anti-Abortion, Festival of Light' and other lobbies which gave the authoritarian right a 'considerable popular depth of penetration in the aroused middle classes and petty-bourgeois sectors'.[1]

This account gave a powerful account of the relationship between the moral lobby and the New Right. As it suggested, the Whitehouse campaign and anti-abortion groups were reacting to some of the same developments that inflamed the political right. They were receiving support from sections of the right, shared some of the same vocabulary and even some of the same goals. But was the relationship between moral crusaders and political Conservatism as close as it suggested?

Despite its problems, this argument soon passed into common usage on the left. The influential collection, *The Politics of Thatcherism*, although published in 1983, brought together articles written from the late seventies onwards for the magazine *Marxism Today*, and one of the earliest, Martin Jacques's 'Thatcherism – Breaking Out of The Impasse', reiterated what was to become a familiar argument – that the sixties and seventies had seen the rise of a 'broad right trend' reaching beyond 'the organisational structures of the political right' and encompassing the Festival of Light, anti-abortionists and the National Viewers' and Listeners' Association.[2] In the same year as this volume appeared, David Edgar, writing in the *New Socialist*, took the argument a stage further and described VALA, SPUC and the Festival of Light as authoritarian 'pressure groups of the Conservative right'.[3]

In the period between Hall's initial work and 1983, of course, Thatcherism had turned from an emergent challenge into the dominant force in British politics, and already notions of the moral crusades' relationship to the resurgence of the right were being overlaid by the connection with a right now returned to power. This was particularly exemplified in work by Miriam David. The New Right, she suggested in 1984, has a moral strand, and this 'moral conservatism' was 'chiefly associated with the activities of right-wing political pressure groups and, to some extent, orchestrated by Mary Whitehouse'. A subsequent article likewise saw the 'moral right' as part of the New Right.[4] Other writers have echoed such views. Michelle Stanworth, for instance, describes the Gillick, anti-abortion and anti-sex education campaigns as 'waged by the new right' while Paul Gordon and Francesca Klug likewise appear to see VALA, the Festival of Light and the Responsible Society as part of the social authoritarian wing of the New Right.[5] Such views were put in perhaps their least mediated form by Bob Jessop and others in an exchange with Stuart Hall in the pages of *New Left Review*. Criticising the view that Thatcherism should be seen as hegemonic, they argued that it was organisationally weak, citing VALA, SPUC and the Festival of Light as instances.[6]

A particular orthodoxy, then, appears to have emerged on the left concerning the relationship between the moral crusades and the New Right. This need not have been the case. As we have already noted, *Policing The Crisis* had not argued that the two were one and the same. A lesser known article by Hall, based on a conference speech given in late 1978, was even more cautious. Its vivid account of Britain from the mid-sixties onwards portrayed a crisis of authority, a traditionalist backlash demanding 'the restoration of moral regulation' and the alignment of that traditionalism, including its moralist and anti-abortion elements, with the political right. Although arguably still making the connection too strong, this account avoided reducing the moral crusades to being part of or an instrument of the political right.[7] Some later studies maintained this sense of differentiation. Jeffrey Weeks, for instance, suggested in 1981 that Whitehouse's 'moral conservatism' should be seen as 'complicit' with the New Right despite its eschewal of 'overt political commitment'. But, he went on, moral conservatism was 'separate' from economic conservatism, as the 1979 Thatcher government had demonstrated by not endorsing abortion restrictions.[8] But in many accounts such distinctions are lost in the collapse of moralism into the New Right.

If the two are to be seen as distinct, what role does the right play in moral crusades? In America the Moral Majority and other conservative groups have played an active part in opposition to abortion. In Britain too Conservative MPs have been highly visible within 'pro-life' ranks and Conservative votes make up a high proportion of anti-abortion support within Parliament. The political views of crucial activists within SPUC also lend credibility to this argument, Antonia Hopkins, its parliamentary lobbyist, and

Robert Whelan, its Administrator, being founders of the 'moral right' Conservative Family Campaign.[9]

But while it is important to note the appeal of anti-abortion views to sections of the political right, this is not the same as drawing an equals sign between the two. Not only, as we discuss later, was the relationship between 'pro-lifers' and the Thatcher government far from happy but the movement itself is more politically diverse than the disproportionate support from Conservative MPs would suggest. In the seventies LIFE established groups within both the Conservative and Labour Parties but these were subsequently closed down. Later, however, independent groups were set up within the major parties. While the Conservative Pro-life Council existed only for a short period, the Labour Life Group argues that concern for the unborn is central to socialist principles. Another group, the Labour Pro-life Group, is active in the Scottish Labour Party. As for the Parliamentary Pro-Life Group itself, it is deliberately a non-party grouping including MPs from the Democrats, Labour and other parties.[10] As well as containing political party groups, the 'pro-life' movement also includes a small extra-parliamentary left. An anti-abortion feminist group, Women for Life, was set up in 1975 and another, Feminists Against Eugenics, originally Feminists Opposed to Eugenic Practices, in 1985. A peace movement group, Pro-Lifers for Survival, was established in 1984 and more recently Anarchists for Life has emerged.[11]

While left-wingers are visibly active in the anti-abortion movement, the situation is considerably different for other sections of the moral lobby. Here Conservatives are even more evident than in the opposition to abortion, with some of the same figures appearing in both. If we look at the Conservative Family Campaign, among its sponsors are Sir Bernard Braine, Peter Bruinvels, Jill Knight, Ann Winterton, Kenneth Hargreaves and Ann Widdecombe, all noted anti-abortionists, the last two, for instance, patrons of LIFE. Other CFC sponsors include Viscount Buckmaster and John Stokes, key figures (along with Knight and Bruinvels) in the sex education debate. There are also, as we have seen, points of contact between the moral lobby and the Freedom Association. Baroness Cox, for instance, is a sponsor of the CFC and on the management committee of the Association while in 1988 the *Free Nation*'s editor, Philip Vander Elst, joined the executive committee of the Order of Christian Unity.[12]

There are, then, significant overlaps between moral lobby activists and the political right. This is not surprising, given our earlier discussion of moralist strands on the New Right. But is the relationship closer? Does the moral lobby see Conservatism in power as an ally?

Contrary to a frequent assumption, the anti-abortion movement had a difficult and frustrating relationship with the Thatcher government. Over the Corrie bill, for instance, SPUC was strongly critical of the Secretary of State for Social Security, Patrick Jenkin, and the Health Minister, Dr Gerard Vaughan. Jenkin, it argued, was 'opposed to any substantial reforms' of the abortion law while Vaughan had sought to 'smash the Bill, clause by clause'.[13] Dr Peggy Norris of the World Federation of Doctors Who Respect Human Life likewise accused Vaughan of 'acting on behalf of the Department of Health to wreck the Corrie Bill in committee'. It was quite clear, she claimed, that the Department 'was determined that as many babies as possible will be aborted', not because of women's rights or their health but as part of a population control policy.[14]

Although in 1979 SPUC distinguished between the Prime Minister, whom it saw as 'pro-life', and her ministers, it was evident from early on that anti-abortionists had much to be dissatisfied with concerning the new government. As the Corrie bill headed towards defeat, the Society's feelings about Vaughan intensified. It was a grave mistake, it argued, to treat him as a 'fair-minded pro-life M.P.' Instead, an article in *Human Concern* claimed, he positively favoured abortion on demand up to the twelfth week.[15] Nor was the Corrie bill the only area in which the Society criticised Jenkin and Vaughan. It held them responsible, for instance, for the DHSS instruction to nurses concerning abortion which had led to the 1980 court case and SPUC's organiser for South East Scotland wrote to local MPs, calling for the ministers' resignation or sacking.[16]

This hostility has continued. Thus in 1989 *Human Concern* attacked the Thatcher government's 'appalling record' and the Prime Minister's support for 'the destroyers' of the Alton bill. The government, it declared, was not 'neutral or fair'. (When she was interviewed the following year, following the disastrous votes on embryo research and abortion, a strongly critical stance was very evident in the views of SPUC's Phyllis Bowman.) Other sections of the movement have been similarly condemnatory. LIFE, for instance, expressed the view in 1981 that 'Contrary to what some people may have hoped', the DHSS under a Conservative administration was even more sympathetic to the private abortion sector than Labour.[17] Perhaps the strongest indictment came from the Association of Lawyers for the Defence of the Unborn, which in 1981 accused the government of failing to fulfil its election pledge to defend the rule of law and fight against crime. When, it claimed, the Association had approached the Attorney General over a doctor who had admitted to offering abortion on request nothing had been done.[18] Two years later, arguing that the 'morning-after' pill was an abortificant, the Association attacked the Attorney General for refusing to prosecute those who supplied it. His refusal to prosecute under the 1861 Offences Against the Person Act, it went on, 'takes us back to the days where questions of law were determined by the fist of the executive, and in the political interests of the Government ... It is indeed a black day for our country when the appointees of the Government can manipulate the British constitution for political ends in this way.'[19]

The 'pro-life' movement's independence from Conservatism and dissatisfaction with the fruits of Thatcherism in power was already evident in the early eighties, when SPUC backed an independent Pro-Life candidate at the Croydon NW by-election in October 1981. (She gained 340 votes.)[20] LIFE the same year reportedly considered running independent candidates in local elections and in 1982 ran six candidates in Birmingham wards, including one of its leading figures, Keith Davies. Results ranged from 166 to 308 votes.[21] Where, elsewhere, it supported Conservative candidates, for instance in the Crosby by-election in November 1981, it did so because the Conservative was seen as the most acceptable candidate.[22] As we have seen, SPUC claimed credit for the survival of 'pro-life' Labour MPs in the 1983 General Election. More recently, SPUC has adopted techniques pioneered by the National Right to Life Committee in the United States and pursued a Voter Identification strategy of finding voters in localities willing to vote on the basis of where candidates stood on 'pro-life' issues.[23] In the party-political arena, then, neither LIFE nor SPUC support any candidate as such but judge them on the issues they are concerned with and are even willing to run independent candidates in certain circumstances.

If anti-abortionists, as we saw in detail in previous chapters, are often highly critical of the government, the situation is rather more complicated for 'pro-family' campaigners. For Mary Whitehouse, contact with Margaret Thatcher when she was still in opposition offered hope that a Conservative government would make a fundamental change to the state of the country's morals. Thus, addressing VALA activists shortly before the 1979 General Election, she attacked the Labour government's attitude towards pornography while declaring that 'There is no doubt that Mrs Thatcher is genuinely in support of our fight to protect the child and the family.'[24] In the early eighties, however, as we have seen, she expressed grave doubt about the new government's commitment to legislate against obscenity. While moments of doubt recurred on occasion, however, she frequently expressed support for Thatcher and clearly preferred a Conservative government either to Labour or, in the early eighties, to an SDP with Roy Jenkins in a prominent position. Thus, during the 1987 General Election campaign, for instance, she argued concerning the Howarth bill that the issue should be raised with candidates. 'The simple fact of the matter is that in spite of the amount of public concern over the pornography and violent material now available, Labour MPs have always fought against any tightening of control over obscenity... The truth is that the great bulk of support for such legislation has come from the Tories with Mrs Thatcher giving her personal support to Gerald Howarth's bill.'[25]

But if Whitehouse supported the government, other campaigners have been more critical. In the early eighties, when relationships between the moral lobby and the government were particularly difficult concerning obscenity, Raymond Johnston of the Festival of Light argued that the government had subordinated moral issues to economics and treated 'euthanasia, abortion, obscenity, homosexuality' as matters of conscience. On the contrary, he held, these were 'issues which most seriously affect the moral, and, sometimes physical, health of society' and, despite the Prime Minister's moral stance, her government had abdicated leadership and taken a 'craven' approach.[26] Subsequently, criticism was not so sharp but CARE continued to find that the Thatcher government fell short of the godly administration it hoped for. Thus, in 1989, Guy Hordern, the organisation's Regional Political Consultant, suggested that the government's stance on abortion and embryo research did not accord with the expressed Christian principles of its leading figures.[27]

Valerie Riches has also been highly critical of the government. Writing during the 1987 General Election campaign, she argued that all the parties had failed to make illegitimacy, divorce, sexual disease and other family issues central to politics. In a more extended discussion, published the same year, she held that governments of left and right since the war had presided over the state's assumption of power over the family, singled out the Department of Health and Social Security and the Home Office as particular foes and noted that 'under a government which professed concern for the welfare of the family', Victoria Gillick had been opposed, time had been refused to private members' bills against embryo research and the Buckmaster amendment on sex education and 'stable family life' had been mutilated. (Interviewed in 1990, her critical stance towards the government remained evident.)[28]

Victoria Gillick too, commenting on the 1980 guidelines on under-sixteen contraception, has described them as the 'abominably duplicitious trick' of 'the Tory government'. 'Traditional values ... Family stability ... Parental choice ...', she declares, were 'all electioneering humbug'. As for the later decision, following her Appeal Court victory, to take the case to the House of Lords: 'How Mrs Thatcher dared to do such a thing, having ridden into office on the back of "traditional family values", is a measure of just how hard-nosed politicians can be in defence of departmental policies and strategies of social planning.'[29]

As the previous chapters have made clear, the moral lobby has a strong parliamentary voice among sections of the Conservatives in the Commons. It also has had reason to be more grateful to the Thatcher government than any other since its inception. But for 'pro-life' campaigners the government was no friend, while even for the 'pro-family' cause, despite government rhetoric and occasional initiatives, the relationship was strained and far from easy.

It is far from true, then, that the moral lobby should be seen as an army of Thatcherites marching in step with the government. But the notion of the right is not confined to Thatcherism. Are there senses, despite their independence from the government, in which moral crusades can be seen as on the right? When we look at the theories put forward by moral campaigners as to the causes of 'moral decay', we find strong indications of conspiracy theory, often articulated to a right-wing political perspective. This takes two main forms: firstly, that sinister political forces, above all Communism, are behind Britain's moral decline and, secondly, a more recent variant, though with important antecedents, that secular humanists are engaged in an attack on God, family and nation.

In her fifth (and most recent) book, Mary Whitehouse suggests that when she started campaigning she had not realised the link between sexual and political anarchy. She had come to see, however, that a sexual 'free-for-all' led to the destruction of character, family life, democracy and the foundations of Christianity. A letter in 1970 in *The Sunday Times*, she notes, had illustrated this by citing an Italian Communist publication, *Cinema Documents*, which had declared that sex shows deserved support as they helped undermine bourgeois society. Perhaps even more important, Whitehouse continued, was the work of American FBI agent W. Cleon Skousen, who in his book *The Naked Communist* had set out Communism's objectives. These included the promotion of pornography and obscenity, infiltration of the media, the undermining of the family and encouragement of promiscuity, easy divorce and homosexuality.[30]

This argument has been put forward elsewhere in Whitehouse's writings. In a previous book, along with Skousen and the *Sunday Times* letter, she also cited a report from a moral crusader in Denmark. In 1919, he claimed, 'Communist Rules for Revolution' in Europe had been declared in the German city of Dusseldorf. These Rules had included instructions to '(a) Corrupt the young. Get them away from religion. Get them interested in sex' and '(b)...get people's minds off their government by focusing their attention on athletics, sexy books and plays and other trivialities'.[31]

Such claims have been made for a considerable period. In 1979 VALA was advertising a leaflet, 'Current Communist Goals', taken from Skousen's book, while the following year, in *Pornography...a matter of taste?*, the German 'Communist Rules for revolution' and the Italian publication, now described as 'a directive issued to members of the Italian Communist Party' appeared along with what were said to be 'words attributed to Stalin' that there should be 'continued propaganda abroad' to destroy patriotism by 'making readily available drugs of various kinds, by giving a teenager alcohol, by praising his wildness, by strangling him with sex literature'.[32]

Whitehouse has stated that 'the collapse of standards' is rooted in 'social, environmental and political conditions' and cannot be explained by a plot. Nonetheless, both she and VALA are deeply imbued with the notion of a Communist conspiracy behind permissiveness. Certainly, she has not attempted to explain everything by conspiracy, and one account of VALA's 1981 Conference describes her trying to discourage delegates from drawing such a conclusion.[33] But that it explains much of what has occurred has been part of her argument for a considerable period. Thus, in the mid-seventies, she was reported explaining to a local VALA conference that those who saw the destruction of Britain as crucial in the enslavement of the West encouraged pornography to weaken its people. Likewise, in that crucial year, 1968, she was arguing that 'the enemies of the West' had realised after the war that Britain was the 'kingpin of Western civilisation' and had to have its faith and character destroyed.[34]

When we look at writings of Whitehouse, as we have seen, the impression given is that the Communist conspiracy theory was only gradually understood as the campaign unfolded. It was, however, present within her material from early on. Whitehouse's 1971 book, *Who Does She Think She Is?*, used the Italian Communist document, as did the *Viewer and Listener* the following year.[35] Similarly, in 1969, VALA's newsletter included a document attacking an 'unremitting onslaught' on morality organised by 'a totally co-ordinated group' of humanists closely interlinked with a long-term Marxist attack on God and family.[36]

Such allegations, then, have long been part of VALA's argument. Equally importantly, they predate its creation, enjoying a currency in a Christian organisation with which Whitehouse had had a long connection, Moral Re-armament. Formed in the thirties as the Oxford Group, MRA argued that only through the spiritual regeneration of individuals could the world be remade. Acting on this, much of its energies in the post-war period was put into attempting to lessen industrial conflict by bringing together both sides of industry. Members' views made them fervent opponents of international Communism in the labour movement and elsewhere and Whitehouse, who had joined the Group in its early years, has described its deep influence on her thinking even though, by the early sixties, she had ceased to be active in it.[37] It is important, then, to realise that MRA had long argued that sexual liberalisation and Communism were closely intertwined. In *The New Morality*, published in 1964, two leading supporters of MRA had suggested that Communists deliberately encouraged sexual freedom in order to undermine 'the foundations of democracy', while the previous year MRA leader Peter Howard had claimed in his *Britain and the Beast* that Lenin had realised that morality in the West had to be sapped and perverted before the revolution could win.[38] As Tracey and Morrison have noted, MRA was particularly troubled by television during the period. In 1963, Howard argued that the BBC was corrupting the country and acting as 'a spiritual sewer' into the homes of Britain and in the same year the organisation's Secretary, Roly Wilson, had called for someone to take on the task of bringing the BBC back to righteousness. Whitehouse, they suggest, launched her movement in response to this challenge.[39]

It is not feasible here to explore in detail the evolution of Whitehouse's theory of the force behind immorality and her debt to MRA arguments. But it is important to raise the issue of the provenance of some of the remarkable documents and quotations used as evidence for such a theory. It has been suggested that MRA's use of quotations from Lenin and other Soviet leaders included some which appear to have been 'invented at "factories" of the kind maintained at various times by great powers for the production of convenient forgeries'.[40] Some of the material cited by VALA may well have originated in such quarters and it is intriguing to note that, according to one account, the German 'Rules for Revolution' first came to light in a MRA publication immediately after the Second World War. Other material, such as Skousen's 'Communist Objectives', express the political views of right-wing writers and are ill-suited for the status of documentary evidence that moral crusaders attribute to them. *The Naked Communist*, after all, draws in part on 'evidence' of the nationalisation of women during the Russian Civil War, one of the great classics of anti-Communist forgery. As for the Italian Communist document, it is unfortunate that Whitehouse does not say a little more about how she first learnt of it. If we turn to the letter in *The Sunday Times* to which she refers, it is somewhat surprising to find that its author is Lady Jane Birdwood, then organiser of VALA's

London branch and, untypically for moral crusades, subsequently an activist on the extreme right.[41]

Dallas Cliff, writing in the late seventies, has suggested that a tendency to conspiracy theory 'can be overstressed', noting that the more 'sophisticated' campaigners do not share such views and quoting Raymond Johnston of the Festival of Light as such a critic. Morrison and Tracey, she notes, see VALA's use of the term 'Communist' as really a 'summary statement', bringing together the 'disparate groups... individuals' and beliefs it opposes.[42] Certainly, there are important distinctions to be made within the moral crusades and it is noteworthy that Johnston's subsequent book, *Who Needs the Family?*, does not argue a Communist conspiracy view (although, as we shall see, it does believe in a deliberate attack on the family). As we saw in our reference to its 1981 Conference, within VALA itself there are differences on the role of political forces in the onslaught on morality. For many, as Morrison and Tracey suggest, it is likely that Communism functions as a symbol of all that VALA opposes, condensing disparate anxieties. Nonetheless, such campaigns are often influenced by overtly political arguments articulated to a long right-wing tradition. Thus in the late seventies the Community Standards Association circulated the Skousen document under the title 'Revolution by Stealth', while in the mid-seventies the Responsible Society published extracts from the German 'Communist Rules for Revolution'. Even the Festival of Light has given credence to such arguments, publishing Whitehouse on the Italian document in 1972 and arguing in 1975 that the Russians were 'keenly interested in the moral ruin' of the country.[43]

If for some, Marxism is the force behind immorality, for others it is only one aspect of the enemy. As can be seen in the document circulated by VALA at the end of the sixties, much of the fury of moral crusaders is aimed at humanists. This has been a constant thread of Whitehouse's argument against 'the permissive lobby', in which the launch in 1963 of the British Humanist Association (BHA), committed to the reform of moral legislation, is seen as crucial in explaining the subsequent legal changes, and the BHA, the Abortion Law Reform Association, the Campaign for Homosexual Equality and other bodies are described as engaged in 'ideological warfare' against society.[44] This has been represented in diagrammatic form by Valerie Riches, with some 36 organisations ranging from the British Humanist Association and the

National Secular Society to the DHSS, the Health Education Council and the Communist Party being portrayed as forming a 'British network'. Its 'ideology is absolutely devilish', she told a journalist in 1980, but 'I don't really know what it is. Communism, humanism, world domination, I don't know.' More recently, in her pamphlet *Sex and Social Engineering*, Riches has become more certain in her argument – the network is part of a world-wide attack on the family by the 'peddlers of secular humanism'.[45]

These are only two of the possible ways of interpreting the events and others have currency in moral campaign circles. As we have seen, in the anti-abortion movement, as with Victoria Gillick, notions of conspiracy are more concerned with population control and its implications, although there are important points of contact, particularly with Riches's argument. Among some campaigners there is a different idea again, in which the attack on the family comes not from enemies within but from the Enemy himself. Thus for Raymond Johnston, 'the attacks on the family ultimately come from... the father of lies', Satan.[46] But, amidst the different possible means of explaining the developments which they seek to reverse, leading moral campaigners have a decided bent towards a political conspiracy theory in which the moral fabric of the West is threatened by the machinations of an atheistic and collectivist foe.

Much of the moral lobby, then, is rather closer to elements of right-wing thought than it may even realise. Can it also be seen as sexually conservative? As we have already seen, particularly in discussing obscenity, campaigners are profoundly critical of recent developments in sexual values. Much of their argument is often implicit rather than explicit but both Mary Whitehouse and Raymond Johnston have developed their views at length.[47] For Johnston, both genders should live according to a scriptural ideal in which women are 'submissive to their husbands' and the husband is the ruler of the family as Christ is the husband and ruler of the Church. 'Man', he declares, 'will always gravitate towards the family of patriarchy or male headship.'

Whitehouse does not focus on the question of who leads the family but, like Johnston, does argue a natural division of labour. What Johnston calls the distinction between man 'performing tasks outside the home' and woman 'providing emotional support and comfort to the family' is described by Whitehouse as the distinction between husband and provider and child-bearer and home-maker.

'The woman', she suggests, 'is essentially the mate.' She, however, does link her opposition to feminism back to her argument against pornography. Feminists, she argues, are engaged in an 'attack on the family', a negation of feminity and masculinity which threatens human identity. Johnston had written of the rise of a 'cult of the aggressive female and . . . of the effeminate male'. For Whitehouse, 'If women deny men their instinctive role as father, husband and provider' then 'man's own deep sense of rejection and inadequacy may drive him to fantasies of sex and violence and even crime'.

Family and Youth Concern too has been critical of feminism and recently, Family Publications, from the same address, has produced a collection of essays on the subject, the authors of which include Valerie Riches, Robert Whelan and Joanna Bogle. A number of leading moral crusaders, then, have put forward anti-feminist arguments. So too, less surprisingly, has the Conservative Family Campaign. 'Years of militant feminism and harmful legislation, like the Equal Opportunities Act, [had] undermined the clear biblical concept of the father', Webster- Gardiner announced at the launch of the Campaign, and it would, he said, put 'Dad back at the head of the table'.[48] The situation is rather more complicated with the 'pro-life' movement. As we have already seen, anti-abortionists have used feminist language against the feminist movement's stance on abortion and sought to present it as playing into the hands of sexist males. LIFE, for instance, has produced a leaflet devoted to the idea that 'The Women's Liberation Movement has taken a Wrong Turning'. In it, LIFE argued that feminists' call for abortion on demand expressed a rejection of their sexual identity. Just as blacks, it claimed, were right to recognise that 'Black is Beautiful', so women needed to accept the womb. They should ensure society accommodated to their special needs rather than pander 'to a system devised and run by men' by treating pregnancy as incompatible with other activities. Furthermore, the leaflet argued, to defend abortion was to capitulate to male values and adopt 'the standards of the oppressor'. Finally, feminists who defended abortion were accused of displacing their anger onto scapegoats. Abortion, the leaflet claimed, was 'merely another way in which women are manipulated and degraded for male convenience and male profit' and to accept it was to delay the reforms (maternity and paternity leave, creche facilities, flexitime etc.) that could enable women to be truly equal.[49]

But a feminist presentation of anti-abortion arguments is not current throughout the movement. While SPUC too has utilised such arguments,[50] neither is feminist in its general stance. Instead, their use of feminist argument is part of an attempt to appeal as broadly as possible. The core arguments of the foetus's humanity and the societal consequences of legalised abortion can be argued in different ways, and a 'pro-life' feminist view is just one of the movement's different discourses. Certainly any attempt to overstate the significance of feminist input into the movement would flounder in the face of the very different argument used by some of its key activists. Thus Margaret White, SPUC's Vice President, argues in a recent book that the women's movement has been 'misguided' and in seeking 'to deliver women from the bondage of the kitchen and children' have devalued motherhood and children. 'Most women', she claims, 'find complete fulfilment' in being wife and mother, which is 'not surprising because that was the plan for them made by nature'. A stronger view still has been advanced by SPUC's Merseyside chairman, Chris Walsh. Interviewed in the local *Catholic Pictorial* in 1986, Walsh argued that contraception, abortion, in vitro fertilisation and experiments to enable men to bear children were parts of 'a concerted attack on Christian life' in which 'Some power, somewhere, is working to produce a unisex age where there is no difference between the sexes.' Despite the Biblical teaching on the role of men and women, he declared, 'The idea and ideal of woman in the home caring for her children has already largely disappeared.'[51]

In addition to the anti-feminism of some of its leading activists, SPUC has been noticeably sympathetic to arguments in favour of 'traditional' sexual morality. *Human Concern* has published articles against sex education and under-sixteen contraception, both outside its formal concerns, and SPUC, as we saw earlier, was active on the latter issue. According to Phyllis Bowman, while the society is a single-issue campaign, most members hold 'pro-family' views. Increased use of birth control among the young, she argues, leads to increased abortions, while sex education at present is effectively merely 'contraceptive merchandising'.[52] Writing in 1981, the Society's Chairman, Alan Rabjohns, held that such organisations as the International Planned Parenthood Federation were engaged in 'a world-wide, systematic attack on the traditional values of the family', encouraging birth control, abortion, promiscuity and the denial of the value of marriage while, later in the decade, Dr White connected the abortion rate with the 'tragic belief that everyone has a right to sexual gratification as and when they choose'. Virginity, she wrote, is being lost at an ever younger age but sex for pleasure 'bears little relationship with sexual intercourse between husband and wife, which is sex for commitment...Abortion goes hand in hand with second-class sex'.[53]

In part, these arguments are concerned with seeing abortion as an expression of sexual permissiveness, but they also involve a sense of common enemies. Both SPUC and Family and Youth Concern, for instance, have attacked the International Planned Parenthood Federation over population policy (as has Jill Knight as chairman of The Lords and Commons Family and Child Protection Group).[54] While we have insisted on the analytical separation of 'pro-life' and 'pro-family' campaigns, SPUC represents a partial breach in this separation, although not usually, it is important to emphasise, in its leaflets and other publicity material. Conversely, 'pro-family' organisations such as CARE and the Order of Christian Unity campaign on 'pro-life' issues too. This does not make the two movements the same or put campaigners on the political right. It does, however, suggest the powerful presence of a set of ideas which could fairly be termed sexually conservative.

To dub the anti-abortion movement 'right-wing' is to obscure its political independence and the diversity of its appeal. There may well be less problems in attaching the term to 'pro-family' campaigns, particularly in the light of their resort to conspiracy theories, but, even there, this threatens our efforts to understand moral crusades and resist a collapse of sexual conservatism into political Conservatism. Some writers, in discussing moral crusades, have utilised the term 'the moral right'. Is this a useful term?

Certainly the term did not please some moral campaigners. Ronald Butt, writing in *The Times* in early 1985, has claimed that the term was an attempt at 'intellectual annihilation' of those it purported to describe. While appearing to be objective, he claimed, it maligned parents concerned with the welfare of their children by its subliminal associations. Digby Anderson, writing in the same month, concurred with his rejection of 'the silly and offensive term "moral right"'.[55]

Victoria Gillick was similarly exercised by journalists' fondness for the term 'Moral Majority'. She was involved in a parents' revolt, she replied, and should not be equated with 'an Americanism'.[56] The National Council for Christian Standards in Society too was at pains to insist that it 'bore no resemblance and had no connection' with the American Moral Majority, while Raymond Johnston, for CARE, explicitly criticised the American organisation's involvement with 'propaganda against tighter gun laws, the signing of the Panama Canal Treaty and other purely political issues which cannot be judged on a biblical basis'. One could envy their influence, he suggested, but identification with a political stance was unacceptable.[57]

But such rejection was not universally the case. While Digby Anderson had rejected the term 'moral right', he did not feel the same about the Americanism. In 'Ripe for a British moral majority', which appeared in *The Times* in late 1985, he regretted that there was no large pro-family lobby in the country comparable to French Catholic parents' associations or the American Moral Majority. Neither the Conservative Party nor the Church had defended the family, he argued, and if they did not take up the role then 'an enterprising populist politician or...a British Moral Majority' would.[58] If Anderson seemed unsure whether Britain needed a moral majority, an article three months later in the *Telegraph* had no such doubts. In 'Free enterprise is not enough. ADRIAN ROGERS wants a Moral Majority', Rogers contrasted the situation in Britain and the United States. The American Moral Majority had achieved 'some success', whereas in Britain no force had been strong enough to repel permissiveness. What Britain needed was a real New Right which would recognise that the market economy needed the firm base of strong families and Judeo-Christian values.[59] It is not surprising, then, that, chairing a meeting of the Conservative Family Campaign, he should declare: 'We are the moral majority.'[60]

A pattern emerges in these different responses. For those recognisably on the political right, the term 'moral right' or 'moral majority' can be perfectly acceptable. For those concerned to build a non-aligned moral lobby or for those determined to avoid association with American televangelism, such characterisations could not be accepted. But, whatever their use for activists, are such terms helpful for understanding British moral crusades? While the notion of a moral right takes us away from getting to grips with the 'pro-life' movement, it does capture something

important about 'pro-family' organisations. But while it does draw
our attention to crusaders' views of Communism, their frequent
preference for a Conservative government and their relationship
with sections of the political right, it does so at the expense of
seeing the movement's diversity and above all its independence
from and criticism of the Thatcher government.

This problem takes us back to one of the earliest points in this
study, when we noted that, although there is no organisational
continuity with earlier moral campaigners, there is a connection in
terms of argument. Indeed, the nineteenth-century moral lobby
presents even greater problems in the central presence of feminist
campaigners alongside the Salvation Army and other crusading
organisations in the fight, for instance, to raise the age of consent
from 13 to 16. The questions of how we might understand these
alliances and whether terms such as 'conservatism' are appropriate
have been raised in a number of recent studies.[61] Even more than in
the present situation, such an approach runs major risks of
misunderstanding a social movement. The reasons for pursuing
any social reform can often diverge quite drastically and the
context of what we mean by feminism or what is expected of
marriage or of sex has substantially changed over a century.
Where, in the late nineteenth century, feminists could find strong
affinities with other campaigners against 'white slavery', for
instance, today the assumptions about sexuality and gender
relations make disagreement much more likely than co-operation.
Intriguingly, Victoria Gillick has suggested an affinity between her
campaign and that of the nineteenth-century feminist and moral
crusader Josephine Butler, both Christians attempting to protect
young girls against the state and depraved men.[62] Historians have
shown the problems Butler wrestled with in deciding whether or
not to rely on the state to secure an improved situation for women
and have cast doubt on whether we can usefully describe her
campaign as conservative. The term is more useful in discussing
many of her allies, as it is in considering Gillick herself. It remains
true, however, that terms with such strong resonances of political
alignment are likely to mislead when we consider arguments
around sexuality.

Conclusion

If the eighties were the decade of Margaret Thatcher, one of its many effects has been to popularise the term 'Victorian values'. A political project which was committed to privatisation, the restriction of trade union power and the restoration of Britain's standing on the world stage was also committed to a revival of discipline and standards. As part of that vision, the Prime Minister and other prominent Conservatives launched attacks on the sixties and 'the permissive society'.

Against this background, moral crusaders could well believe that the tide was turning in their favour. When sex education is placed in 'a moral framework', the 'promotion' of homosexuality by local government made illegal and government begins to show concern over single-parent families, then moral campaigners can believe their time has come. But on key issues the government proved to be a disappointment or even an antagonist rather than an ally, and many of the social indices which outrage campaigners – the abortion rate, the divorce rate, the illegitimacy rate – have risen and are continuing to rise. The replacement of Margaret Thatcher by John Major makes any moral offensive on the part of government even less likely, although defeat in a general election, should it occur, could well result in a reinvigoration of attacks not only upon Labour collectivism but also on permissiveness. But what we have not seen in the eighties, and are not likely to see in the nineties, is the coming together of the political right and the moral lobby and a shift from a rarely implemented government rhetoric to a sustained 'moral majority' stance.

Notes and References

1 The Permissive Society and the Moral Lobby

1. On the early moral lobby, see Edward J. Bristow, *Vice and Vigilance* (Gill and Macmillan, 1977); Frank Mort, *Dangerous Sexualities* (Routledge and Kegan Paul, 1987); Jeffrey Weeks, *Sex, Politics and Society* (Longman, 1981), pp. 84–95.
2. Weeks, *Sex, Politics*, p. 87; Mort, *Dangerous Sexualities*, p. 123.
3. More work is called for on this subject but see Bristow, *Vice and Vigilance*, pp. 225–32.
4. For excellent discussions of the general context, see Stuart Hall, 'Permissiveness and the Legislation of Consent' in National Deviancy Conference (ed.), *Permissiveness and Control* (Macmillan, 1980) and Weeks, *Sex, Politics*, chapter 13. On specific issues, see Peter G. Richards, *Parliament and Conscience* (Weidenfeld and Nicolson, 1979).
5. *Freedom* 15 July 1967.
6. For the early campaign, see Mary Whitehouse, *Cleaning Up TV* (Blandford Press, 1967) and *Who Does She Think She Is?* (New English Library, 1971). The quote is from *Cleaning Up*, p. 23. For VALA, see Michael Tracey and David Morrison, *Whitehouse* (Macmillan, 1979); David Morrison and Michael Tracey, 'American Theory and British Practice: The Case of Mrs Mary Whitehouse and the National Viewers and Listeners Association' in Rajeev Dhavan and Christie Davies (eds.), *Censorship and Obscenity* (Martin Robertson, 1978); Roy Wallis, *Salvation and Protest* (Frances Pinter, 1979), chapter VII.
7. For SPUC and early opposition to abortion, see Colin Francome, *Abortion Freedom* (Allen and Unwin, 1984), pp. 90–4; David Marsh and Joanna Chambers, *Abortion Politics* (Junction Books, 1981), pp. 56–7. For MRA and the Clean-Up TV Campaign, see Tracey and Morrison, *Whitehouse*, pp. 63–6; for the social characteristics of VALA's support, see David Morrison and Michael Tracey, *Opposition to the Age – A Study of the NVALA*, report to the SSRC, 1978, p. 103, cited in Dallas Cliff, 'Religion, morality and the middle class' in Roger King and Neill Nugent (eds.), *Respectable Rebels* (Hodder and Stoughton, 1979), p. 140.

8. See Weeks, *Sex, Politics*, pp. 273–82; Stuart Hall *et al., Policing the Crisis* (Macmillan, 1978), pp. 238–323.

9. On Powell, see Tom Nairn, *The Break-up of Britain* (NLB, 1977), chapter 6; John Wood (ed.), *Powell and the 1970 Election* (Elliot Right Way Books, 1970).

10. For Britain in the seventies, see Hall, *Policing the Crisis*, pp. 260–323; Phillip Whitehead, *The Writing On The Wall* (Michael Joseph, 1985).

11. For the different components of the moral lobby, see Cliff, 'Religion,morality and the middle class'.

12. Family and Child Protection Group, press release, 25 August 1976.

13. For LIFE, see Marsh and Chambers, *Abortion Politics*, pp. 59–60; Francome, *Abortion Freedom*, pp. 160–3. For the British section of the World Federation of Doctors Who Respect Human Life, see *Church Times* 9 October 1981; for the Association of Lawyers for the Defence of the Unborn, see Marsh and Chambers, *Abortion Politics*, pp. 62–3.

14. Tracey and Morrison, *Whitehouse*, pp. 143–5; Mary Whitehouse, *Whatever Happened to Sex?* (Hodder and Stoughton, 1977), p. 197.

15. *The Times* 21 October 1974.

16. *Sunday Times* 1 October 1978; Jean Coussins and Anna Coote, *The Family in the Firing Line* (NCCL/CPAG, 1981), p. 7; *Family Life* (NCH Occasional Papers, 1979), pp. 10–12.

17. See e.g. *Sunday Telegraph* 2 October 1977; *Times* 17 October 1977.

18. M.A. McCarthy and R.A. Moodie, 'Parliament and Pornography: the 1978 Child Protection Act', *Parliamentary Affairs, XXIV*.1, Winter 1981; Mary Whitehouse, *A Most Dangerous Woman* (Lion, 1982), chapter 13.

19. *Daily Telegraph* 15 May 1978.

2   The Battle Against Abortion

1. Both SPUC and LIFE have around 35,000 members. Interviews with Keith Davies, 24 August 1990; Phyllis Bowman, 4 September 1990. There are, as we have noted, other 'pro-life' organisations, the Association of Lawyers for the Defence of the Unborn, for instance, numbering in 1988 'well over 1,900 members', *News and Comment* 40 (Winter 1988).

2. For abortion before 1979, see Richards, *Parliament and Conscience*, chapter 5; Bridget Pym, *Pressure Groups and the Permissive Society* (David and Charles, 1974); Victoria Greenwood and Jock Young, *Abortion in Demand* (Pluto, 1976); Marsh and Chambers, *Abortion Politics*, chapter 1; Francome, *Abortion Freedom*, chapters 4 and 7.

3. *Catholic Herald* 14, 21, 28 August 1970.

4. *Catholic Herald* 28 October 1977, 21 April, 28 April 1978.

5. Marsh and Chambers, *Abortion Politics*, pp. 86–7.

6. *Human Concern* 3 (Summer 1979); *Catholic Herald* 12 January, 18 January 1979.

7. *Catholic Herald* 20 April 1979; Marsh and Chambers, *Abortion Politics*, pp. 87–9. Marsh and Chambers note that in each of the four seats the swing to the Conservatives was higher than the regional average and that SPUC and LIFE may indeed have had an effect on the result. However, they point out, in all the cases Labour would have lost even on the regional average swing.

8. On the Corrie Bill see Marsh and Chambers, *Abortion Politics*; Francome, *Abortion Freedom*, chapter 7; D. Marsh and J. Chambers, 'The Abortion Lobby: Pluralism at Work?' in David Marsh (ed.), *Pressure Politics* (Junction Books, 1983). See also David Marsh and Melvyn Read, *Private Members' Bills* (Cambridge University Press, 1988), chapter 6.

9. *Catholic Herald* 6 July 1979.

10. *Catholic Herald* 13 July 1979; *Guardian* 11 July 1979.

11. *Catholic Herald* 14 December 1979.

12. *Universe* 19 October 1979;*Church Times* 2 November 1979; Marsh and Chambers, *Abortion Politics*, p. 131; *Daily Telegraph* 31 January 1980.

13. *Universe* 7 March, 21 March 1980; *Church Times* 21 March 1980.

14. *Catholic Herald* 25 April 1980; *Human Concern* 5 (Summer 1980); Marsh and Chambers, *Abortion Politics*, p. 155.

15. *Church Times* 21 November 1980; *LIFE News* 8 (Spring/Summer 1981).

16. *Guardian* 28 November 1980.

17. *The Times* 14 January 1981; *Catholic Herald* 23 January 1981.

18. *Church Times* 29 January 1982; *Catholic Herald* 29 January 1982; *Human Concern* 9 (Spring 1982).

19. *Catholic Herald* 25 September 1981; *LIFE News* 9 (Summer–Autumn 1981).

20. *Observer* 21 November 1982; *Daily Telegraph* 22 November, 7 December 1982; *Human Concern* 12 (Spring 1983).

21. SPUC, 'A Matter of Life and Death' (leaflet); *LIFE News* 12 (Summer 1983).

22. *Guardian* 28 January 1984; *Universe* 27 January 1984; *Catholic Herald* 16 December 1983, 20 January, 3 February 1984.

23. *Guardian* 20 July, 30 July 1985; *Catholic Herald* 2 August 1985.

24. SPUC press release, 4 September 1986; *Church Times* 12 September 1986.

25. LIFE, 'Your Vote – Their Lives'(leaflet).

26. *Universe* 28 November 1986; *The Times* 11 December 1986.

27. *Independent* 26 January 1987; *Universe* 6 February 1987; *Daily Telegraph* 13 February 1987.

28. *Buzz* March 1987.

29. *Guardian* 24, 25 February 1987; *Daily Telegraph* 25, 26 February 1987; *Universe* 27 February 1987; *Human Concern* 23 (Early Summer [1987]).

30. *Independent* 4 March 1987; *Catholic Herald* 6 March 1987; *Universe* 27 March 1987.

31. *Guardian* 7 April 1987; *Universe* 10 April, 8 May 1987.
32. *Catholic Herald* 5 June 1987; *Universe* 22 May 1987.
33. (Birmingham) *Daily News* 10 June 1987; *Universe* 26 June 1987.
34. HC Debs 7 July 1987 c190.
35. *Catholic Herald* 14 August 1987; *Guardian* 27 October 1987.
36. *Observer* 30 August 1987; *Catholic Herald* 2 October 1987; *Guardian* 27 October 1987.
37. Interview with Phyllis Bowman, 4 September 1990; C. Whitehouse, 'The Embryo Bill – so what happened in Parliament?' (tape of 1990 SPUC Conference workshop, sold at Conference); *Mail on Sunday* 25 October 1987; *Today* 26 October 1987.
38. *Guardian* 17 December 1987.
39. *Universe* 18 December 1987, 1 January 1988.
40. *Universe* 15 January 1988; *Daily Express* 15 January 1988.
41. *Observer* 17 January 1988; *Sunday Telegraph* 17 January 1988; *Independent* 18 January 1988.
42. HC Debs 21 January 1988 c1090, 22 January 1988 c1271–3; *Guardian* 23 January 1988; *C21 Christian* March 1988; *Daily Mail* 23 January 1988.
43. *The Times* 3, 12 February 1988; *Catholic Herald* 11 March 1988; *Guardian* 30 April 1988.
44. *Guardian* 23, 25 March 1988; *Daily Telegraph* 31 March 1988.
45. *Daily Telegraph* 15 April 1988; *Universe* 22 April 1988.
46. *Independent* 22 April, 3 May 1988; *Guardian* 27 April, 5 May 1988.
47. *Guardian* 6 May 1988; *Times* 7 May 1988; *Independent* 7 May 1988; *Daily Telegraph* 7 May 1988.
48. *Guardian* 9 May 1988; *Catholic Herald* 13 May 1988; *Times* 13 May 1988.
49. *Daily Telegraph* 14 May 1988; *Guardian* 14, 17, 20 May 1988.
50. *Universe* 10 June 1988; *Guardian* 9 July 1988.
51. *Catholic Herald* 16 September 1988.
52. *Tablet* 3 September 1988; *Our Family* January–February 1990.
53. *Guardian* 6 December 1988; *Catholic Herald* 9 December 1988; *Times* 17 December 1988.
54. *Church of England Newspaper* 6 January 1989; *Guardian* 12 January 1989; *Universe* 15 January 1989.
55. *Guardian* 21 January 1989.
56. *Guardian* 18 February, 4 March 1989; *Universe* 26 February 1989.
57. *The Times* 3 February 1989; *Daily Telegraph* 16 February 1989; *Tablet* 25 February 1989.
58. *Universe* 23 April, 4 June 1989; *Times* 10 April 1989; *Human Concern* 27 (Summer 1989); *Sunday Express* 23 July 1989; *Tablet* 7 October 1989; *Guardian* 24 October 1989; Anne Widdecombe speech to 1989 LIFE Conference (personal attendance); interview with Phyllis Bowman, 4 September 1990.
59. *Sunday Express* 22 October 1989; *Sunday Times* 22 October 1989; *Guardian* 23 October 1989; *Independent* 23 October 1989.
60. *Guardian* 7 April 1990; *Observer* 22 April 1990.

61. *Guardian* 26 April 1990; *Catholic Herald* 27 April 1990; *Daily Telegraph* 26 April 1990; *Universe* 3 June 1990; *Independent* 22 June 1990; *Universe* 28 October, 4 November 1990.
62. Interview with Keith Davies, 24 August 1990; interview with Phyllis Bowman, 4 September 1990; C. Whitehouse, 1990 SPUC Conference workshop tape.
63. LIFE, 'Abortion. Why you can't believe in it' (leaflet); SPUC, 'A Baby – 6 1/2 weeks after conception' (leaflet).
64. Mother Teresa *et al.*, *Who is for Life?* (Crossway Books, USA, 1984).
65. *Birmingham Evening Mail* 1 October 1984; *Times* 29 November 1984; *Church of England Newspaper* 7 December 1984.
66. *Evangelical Times* July 1986.
67. *Catholic Herald* 1 July 1983; John Powell, *Abortion: The Silent Holocaust* (Argus, USA, 1981), pp. 103–7. See also Dr. and Mrs. J. C. Willke, *Handbook on Abortion* (Hayes, USA, 1979), pp. 162–4. For a British example, see Dr. Margaret White, *Two Million Silent Killings* (Marshall Pickering, 1987), pp. 44–5.
68. Personal attendance at SPUC rally, London, 25 June 1983; *Scottish Catholic Observer* 14 March 1980.
69. Personal attendance at LIFE rally, Manchester, 13 May 1989.
70. *Human Life Matters* 2 (January 1986).
71. An American speaker addressed a conference organised by the Human Life Council and others in Edinburgh in August 1987 and delegates protested outside a local hospital. *Proceedings of 'The Splintered Image' Pro-Life Conference* (Human Life Council, 1988), pp. 8–10, 140–8. See also *Human Life Matters* Spring 1988.
72. Humanae Vitae House mailing – A Pro-Life report 1988; Humanae Vitae House mailing, Easter 1989; Rescue leaflet distributed at Manchester LIFE rally, 13 May 1989.
73. *Mail on Sunday* 7 May 1989; *Catholic Herald* 12 May 1989; *Today* December 1989; interview with Keith Davies, 24 August 1990; interview with Phyllis Bowman, 4 September 1990; personal attendance at LIFE rally, Manchester, 13 May 1989.
74. *Guardian* 2 November 1989; *Today* December 1989; *Newsnight* (BBC), 15 December 1989; *Independent* Magazine 20 January 1990; *New Statesman* 2 February 1990; *Our Family* January–February 1990; Prolifers for Peace meeting, London, 21 October 1989, personal attendance.
75. Powell, *Abortion: The Silent Holocaust*, p. 40.
76. *Universe* 8 August 1980; *Human Concern* 8 (Summer 1981).
77. *Human Concern* 2 (Winter 1979).

3 Victoria Gillick and Under-Sixteen Contraception

1. Audrey Leathard, *The Fight for Family Planning* (Macmillan, 1980), pp. 135, 192–9; House of Commons, Standing Committee G, 17 April 1973, c253, 301–2.

2. 'Gillick v. West Norfolk and Wisbech Area Health Authority and another', *All England Law Reports*, 1984, pp. 367–8.
3. *Nationwide Festival of Light Broadsheet* June 1975; *Bulletin of the Responsible Society* 11 (Spring–Summer 1974).
4. *Daily Telegraph* 27 April 1978.
5. *Daily Mail* 15 May 1978.
6. *Spectator* 14 April 1979.
7. *Universe* 1 December 1978; *Nationwide Festival of Light Bulletin* 4 (n.d., 1978); 7(January 1980); *Bulletin of the Responsible Society* 26 (Spring 1979). Also see O.R. Johnston, *Who Needs The Family?* (Hodder and Stoughton 1979), pp. 134–5.
8. *Guardian* 26 April 1979; *Viewer and Listener* Summer 1979.
9. *Universe* 19 May 1978.
10. *Daily Telegraph* 21 July 1978; *CSA Newsletter* 7 (Winter 1978–9).
11. *County Express* 25 May 1979; *Wolverhampton Express and Star* 25 May 1979.
12. *Sunday Express* 23 December 1979.
13. *Sunday Telegraph* 4 May 1980; *Pulse* 9 June 1979; Victoria Gillick, *Dear Mrs. Gillick* (Marshalls, 1985), p. 74.
14. *Daily Mail* 28 January, 22 February 1980.
15. *Daily Mail* 5 May 1980; HC Debs 6 May 1980 c80–82w; *All England Law Reports* 1984, pp. 368–9.
16. *Daily Telegraph* 13 January 1981.
17. *Family Bulletin* 29(Summer 1980).
18. *Daily Mail* 18, 22 November 1980, 10, 15 January 1981.
19. *Family* January 1984.
20. *All England Law Reports*, 1984, p.369.
21. Ibid., pp. 369–70.
22. Ibid., pp. 365–75.
23. *Daily Express* 9, 10 November 1983; *Guardian* 15 November 1983; *Scottish Catholic Observer* 16 December 1983.
24. *Catholic Herald* 18 November 1983.
25. *Catholic Herald* 30 December 1983.
26. *Daily Mail* 22 June, 1 July 1983.
27. *Guardian* 17 February 1984.
28. *Pulse* 25 February 1984.
29. *Daily Telegraph* 21 December 1984; *All England Law Reports*, 8 March 1985, pp. 533–59.
30. *Guardian* 22, 24 December 1984.
31. *Western Morning News* 24 December 1984.
32. *Daily Telegraph* 5 July 1984.
33. *The Times* 15 November 1984.
34. *Guardian* 15 February 1985.
35. *Daily Telegraph* 4 May 1985.
36. *All England Law Reports*, 8 November 1985, pp. 402–37; *Daily Telegraph* 18 October 1985.
37. HC Debs 24 October 1985 c225w, 30 October 1985 c572w.
38. HC Debs 12 November 1985 c414–5.

39. *Daily Telegraph* 19 October 1985.
40. *Mail on Sunday* 20 October 1985.
41. *Catholic Herald* 25 October 1985; *Universe* 13 December 1985; *Daily Telegraph* 31 December 1985.
42. *Pulse* 26 October 1985; *Sunday Telegraph* 8 December 1985;*Catholic Herald* 21 February 1986; *Doctor* 27 February 1986; *Family Bulletin* 47 (Summer 1986). For the National Campaign in the press, see e.g. *The Times* 2 October 1987; *Sunday Times* 18 June 1989; *Independent* 29 June 1990.
43. *Guardian* 7 March 1986; *Catholic Herald* 14 March 1986.
44. *Guardian* 25 March 1986.
45. *Belfast Telegraph* 29 May 1986; *Guardian* 14 July 1986; *Daily Telegraph* 18 July 1986; *Catholic Herald* 8 August 1986.
46. *Proceedings of 'The Splintered Image' Conference*, p. 70.
47. *Guardian* 1 December 1986; *Independent* 2 December 1986.
48. *Guardian* 9 December 1986; *Independent* 2 December 1986; *Universe* 5 December 1986.
49. *Universe* 11 September 1987; *Guardian* 14 September, 6 October 1987.
50. *Guardian* 15 June 1989; *Universe* 25 June 1989; *Family Bulletin* 58 (spring 1990).
51. *Catholic Herald* 28 October 1983, 13 April 1984.
52. *Catholic Herald* 24 February 1984; *Universe* 6 April 1984; Order of Christian Unity, *Children and Contraception* (1985), p. 16.
53. Order of Christian Unity, *Children and Contraception*; Valerie Riches, *No Entry for Parents* (Family and Youth Concern,1984).
54. *Human Concern* 15 (Winter 1984).
55. *Daily Telegraph* 20 July 1983.
56. *Searchlight* February 1984; *Guardian* 31 January 1984.
57. *Guardian* 31 January 1984; *Caribbean Times* 18 May 1984.
58. *Guardian* 5 April 1984.
59. *Catholic Herald* 13 April 1984.
60. *Catholic Herald* 25 May 1984; *Universe* 11, 25 May 1984.
61. *Daily Express* 9 November 1983.
62. *Catholic Herald* 18 November 1983; *Daily Telegraph* 20 July 1983, 12 March 1984; *Guardian* 17 February 1984.
63. *Sunday Telegraph* 4 May 1980; *Catholic Herald* 24 February 1984.
64. *Catholic Herald* 8 November 1985.
65. *Nationwide Festival of Light Bulletin* 8 (September 1980).
66. *Guardian* 27 July 1983.
67. Gillick, *Dear Mrs. Gillick*, pp. 7, 8, 66, 101.
68. *Universe* 29 July 1983.
69. *Daily Mirror* 18 October 1985; Order of Christian Unity, *Children and Contraception*, pp. 8–15.
70. *Guardian* 12 March 1984; *Catholic Herald* 16 March 1984.
71. Victoria Gillick quoted in the *Daily Mirror* 27 July 1983.
72. *Liberal News* 15 November 1983.
73. *Guardian* 19 November 1984.
74. *Guardian* 1, 5, 6, 9, 16 March 1985.

75. Gillick, *Dear Mrs. Gillick*, pp. 137–8, 158–9, 194–5.
76. *Guardian* 27 July 1983; *Daily Mirror* 27 July 1983.
77. *City Limits* 14–20 June 1985.
78. *Catholic Herald* 23 December 1983; Victoria Gillick, *A Mother's Tale* (Hodder and Stoughton, 1989), pp. 27–8.
79. *Elle* June 1986.
80. *Searchlight* June 1985.
81. *Evening Chronicle* 2 May 1988; *News of the World* 14 May 1989.
82. *City Limits* 23–9 November 1984; *Outwrite* January 1985.
83. Personal attendance at British Housewives' League meeting, London 23 April 1985; see e.g. *Home* January, November 1982, May 1983, July 1985, January–February 1987, March 1988.
84. *Universe* 23 September 1990; *Love and Life* Winter 1984–1985.
85. *Catholic Herald* 28 December 1984.

4 Embryo Research: From the Warnock Report to Government Legislation

1. There is a wide range of material on the different issues raised by reproductive technology. See e.g. Mary Warnock, *A Question of Life. The Warnock Report on Human Fertilisation and Embryology* (Blackwell, 1985); Maureen McNeill, Ian Varcoe and Steven Yearley (eds.), *The New Reproductive Technologies* (Macmillan, 1990). On embryo research, see, in particular, Edward Yoxen, 'Conflicting Concerns: The Political Context of Recent Embryo Research Policy in Britain' in McNeill *et al.* Other material is cited elsewhere in the chapter.
2. *Human* Concern 3 (Summer 1979); *LIFE News* 11 (Autumn/Winter 1982).
3. *LIFE News* 12 (Summer 1983).
4. SPUC, *The Question of In Vitro Fertilisation* (1984), pp. 65, 62, 67; *LIFE News* 12 (Summer 1983).
5. *Times* 22 May 1984; *Daily Express* 22 May 1984; *Guardian* 22 May 1984; *Test-tube Babies – a Christian view* (OCU, 1984).
6. *Catholic Herald* 22 June 1984; *Church of England Newspaper* 15 June 1984.
7. *A Question of Life* pp. 60–6,59.
8. *Daily Telegraph* 20 July 1984; *Church of England Newspaper* 27 July 1984; *Church Times* 27 July 1984.
9. *Daily Telegraph* 21 July 1984; *Guardian* 21 July 1984.
10. *Catholic Herald* 21 September 1984; *Daily Telegraph* 28 September 1984.
11. *Love and Life* Winter 1984–1985.
12. *Daily Telegraph* 6 November 1984.
13. HL Debs 31 October 1984 c524–31, 535–93.
14. *Guardian* 24 November 1984.
15. *Catholic Herald* 7 December 1984.

16. *Guardian* 27 December 1984.
17. *Church Times* 25 January 1985; *Catholic Herald* 25 January 1985; (Birmingham) *Daily News* 29 January 1985; *Buzz* February 1985.
18. *Catholic Herald* 8 February 1985.
19. *Daily Telegraph* 12 February 1985.
20. *Guardian* 16 February 1985; HC Debs 15 February 1985 c655; *Catholic Herald* 22 February 1985; *Church of England Newspaper* 8 March 1985; *Catholic Herald,* 15 February, 1985.
21. *Church Times* 10 May 1985; *Catholic Herald* 3 May 1985.
22. *Church Times* 31 May 1985; *Catholic Herald* 31 May 1985.
23. *Guardian* 8 June 1985; *Daily Telegraph* 4, 7 June 1985.
24. *Catholic Herald* 17 May 1985.
25. *Guardian* 8 June, 16 July 1985; *Catholic Herald* 14,28 June 1985.
26. *Catholic Herald* 19 July 1985; *Human Concern* 19 (Summer 1985).
27. *Guardian* 30 August 1985.
28. *Guardian* 4 September 1985; *Catholic Herald* 6 September 1985.
29. *Guardian* 13,28 November 1985; *Daily Telegraph* 25 January 1986; *Catholic Herald* 17 January 1986.
30. *Catholic Herald* 31 January 1986; *Guardian* 4 March 1986.
31. *Universe* 28 March 1986; *Catholic Herald* 9 May, 18 April 1986; *Doctor* 13 February 1986.
32. *Universe* 11 July 1986; *Human Concern* 22 (Summer 1986).
33. *Church of England Newspaper* 2 January 1987; HC Debs 21 October 1986 c971; *Daily Telegraph* 22 October 1986; *Universe* 24 October 1986.
34. HC Debs 12 November 1986 c84; 25 November 1986 c190; *Universe* 5 December 1986; *Catholic Herald* 5 December 1986.
35. *Guardian* 11 December 1986; *Catholic Herald* 19 December 1986.
36. *Church of England Newspaper* 9 January 1987; *Catholic Herald* 15 May 1987; *Sunday Telegraph* 24 May 1987.
37. SPUC, 'The Time To Say No Is Now!',n.d.
38. *Human Concern* 24 (Midsummer 1987).
39. *Mail on Sunday* 28 June 1987.
40. *Times* 9, 10 July 1987.
41. *Mail on Sunday* 23 August 1987.
42. *Universe* 27 November 1987.
43. *Universe* 30 October, 4 December 1987; *Guardian* 27 October 1987;*Catholic Herald* 4 December 1987.
44. HC Debs 4 February 1988 c1239, 1225; *Guardian* 5 February 1988.
45. *Universe* 31 July 1988; *Pro-Life Parliamentary Monitor* June–July 1988; *Independent* 10 August 1988.
46. *Church of England Newspaper* 26 August 1988; *Universe* 18 September 1988.
47. *Christian Newsworld* January 1989.
48. *Universe* 11 December 1988; *Guardian* 17 December 1988; *Times* 17 December 1988.
49. *Catholic Herald* 17 March 1989.
50. *Catholic Herald* 14 April 1989; *Universe* 23 April 1989.

51. *Universe* 10 September 1989; *Catholic Herald* 6 October, 1 December 1989; *Daily Telegraph* 24 November 1989.
52. *Independent* 7 February 1990; *Guardian* 7, 9 February 1990; *Daily Telegraph* 9 February 1990; HL Debs 6 March 1990 c1053–5.
53. LIFE press release, 26 March 1990; *Universe* 18 March 1990.
54. *Guardian* 24 April 1990; *Catholic Herald* 27 April 1990.
55. LIFE, *Warnock Dissected* (1984), p. 7; SPUC, 'The Time To Say No'; CARE, *Warnock "weighed...and found wanting"*, n.d., pp. 6–8.
56. SPUC, *Question of In Vitro Fertilisation*, pp. 62–4.
57. CARE, *Warnock "weighed...and found wanting"*, pp. 4, 5, 8–11; LIFE, *Warnock Dissected*, p. 5.
58. OCU, *Test tube Babies*, back cover and pp. 3, 61, 48–51.
59. SPUC, *Question of In Vitro Fertilisation*, pp. 21, 31, 32.
60. *LIFE News* 15 (Winter–Spring 1986); *Human Concern* 24 (Midsummer 1987).
61. Rita Arditti, Renate Duelli Klein and Shelley Minden (eds.), *Testtube Women* (Pandora, 1984), p. 5.
62. Gena Corea *et al.* (eds.), *Man-Made Women* (Hutchinson, 1985), p. 70.
63. Ibid., p. 85.
64. Marge Berer, 'Breeding Conspiracies', *Trouble and Strife* 9 (Summer 1986), p. 33.
65. *Love and Life* Spring 1985.
66. Berer, 'Conspiracies', pp. 29–35.
67. *Women's Review* December 1985.
68. Michelle Stanworth (ed.), *Reproductive Technologies* (Polity Press, 1987) e.g. pp. 16–17, 72, 77, 145–6; Lynda Birke, Susan Himmelweit and Gail Vines, *Tomorrow's Child. Reproductive Technology in the 90s* (Virago, 1990), chapters 2 and 8. See also e.g. Rayah Feldman, 'The Politics of the New Reproductive Technologies', *Critical Social Policy* 19 (Summer 1987).
69. *Human Concern* 29 (Spring 1990); interview with Phyllis Bowman, 4 September 1990.

5 'Sex and Violence': The Whitehouse Campaign

1. On obscenity law, see Geoffrey Robinson, *Obscenity* (Weidenfeld and Nicolson, 1979). On recent parliamentary debates on the issue, see Marsh and Read, *Private Members' Bills*, chapter 7.
2. Moral lobby arguments on obscenity are discussed in more detail later but see e.g. Whitehouse, *Whatever Happened to Sex?* For VALA membership figures in the eighties, see e.g. (Birmingham) *Daily News* 6 February 1985. On other groups, see, for instance, the critical accounts of local activities of the Community Standards Association in *Freethinker* June 1980, September 1985.
3. *Viewer and Listener* June 1978.

4. *Viewer and Listener* Spring 1979; *Sun* 26 April 1979; *Wolverhampton Express and Star* 26 April 1979.
5. *Report of the Committee on Obscenity and Film Censorship* (HMSO, 1979), 159–66, 145. For a general discussion of the Williams Report and the response to it, see A. W. B. Simpson, *Pornography and Politics* (Waterlow, 1983).
6. *Report of Committee*, pp. 61–102; *Guardian* 29, 30 November 1979; *Church Times* 7 December 1979.
7. *Daily Telegraph* 26 November 1979.
8. *The Times* 17 January 1980.
9. *Universe* 29 February 1980.
10. *The Times* 25 April 1980; *Universe* 20 June 1980; Whitehouse, *Most Dangerous Woman*, pp. 202–3, 208–10; petition inserted in *Nationwide Festival of Light Bulletin* 8(September 1980).
11. *Daily Telegraph* 18 August 1980; *The Times* 18 August 1980.
12. *Catholic Herald* 1 August 1980; *The Times* 31 July 1980.
13. *Church Times* 31 October 1980.
14. HC Debs 30 January 1981 c1190; *Guardian* 27 June 1981; *Daily Telegraph* 27 June 1981.
15. *Viewer and Listener* Autumn 1981, Summer 1982.
16. *Guardian* 6 July 1979.
17. *Universe* 29 February 1980.
18. *Daily Telegraph* 14 January 1981; HC Debs 30 January 1981 c1186; *Daily Express* 31 January 1981. For a general discussion of the bill, see Robert Taylor, 'One man's Commons display', *New Society* 30 April 1981.
19. *Daily Telegraph* 2 February 1981.
20. *Universe* 27 February 1981. Joanna Bogle, previously Joanna Nash, was Youth Representative on the Responsible Society executive in the mid-seventies and early eighties. See e.g. 'The Responsible Society: An Invitation to Join' (n.d., mid- 1970s); 'The Responsible Society – Family and Youth Concern: An Invitation to Join' (n.d., c1981).
21. *Guardian* 16 April, 2 May 1981; *Sunday Telegraph* 25 October 1981.
22. *Walsall Observer* 14 August 1981; *Daily Telegraph* 7 July 1981. For a general discussion of the issue, see Colin Manchester, *Sex Shops and the Law* (Gower, 1986); Bill Thompson, 'Porn Wars: Moral Enterprise, Pornography, and Social Policy: The Local Government (Miscellaneous Provisions) Act 1982' (PhD, Essex, 1988).
23. *Daily Telegraph* 30 December 1980; *Observer* 4 January 1981.
24. Manchester, *Sex Shops*, p. 95.
25. *Sunday Telegraph* 25 October 1981.
26. Whitehouse, *Most Dangerous Woman*, pp. 215–16; *Daily Mail* 23 December 1981; *Daily Telegraph* 4 February 1982.
27. *Daily Telegraph* 16 March 1982; *Nationwide Festival of Light Bulletin* 13 (April 1982).
28. *Daily Telegraph* 1 February 1982; *Sunday Telegraph* 7 February 1982; *Viewer and Listener* Summer 1982; *Universe* 9 July 1982.

29. See e.g. *Viewer and Listener* Summer 1985; (Birmingham) *Daily News* 26 July 1989, 5 January 1990.
30. Manchester, *Sex Shops*, pp. 100–1.
31. *Daily Telegraph* 18 August 1980; *Universe* 29 August 1980.
32. Mary Whitehouse, *Mightier than the Sword* (Kingsway, 1985), p. 46.
33. For a discussion of these developments, see Julian Petley, 'A Nasty Story', *Screen* 25:2 (March–April 1984). For an overall view, see Martin Barker (ed.), *The Video Nasties* (Pluto, 1984); D. Marsh, P. Gowin and M. Read, 'Private Members Bills and Moral Panic: The Case of the Video Recordings Bill (1984)', *Parliamentary Affairs*, 39.2, April 1986.
34. *The Times* 31 May 1982.
35. *Sunday Times* 13 June 1982; *Times* 1 September 1982; *Guardian* 9 August 1982; *Daily Telegraph* 25 September 1982.
36. *Daily Telegraph* 24 September 1982.
37. *Daily Mail* 25 February 1983.
38. *Daily Telegraph* 2 March, 23 April 1983; *Christian Woman* May 1983.
39. *The Times* 11 April 1983; *Daily Telegraph* 8, 23 April 1983.
40. *The Conservative Manifesto 1983* (Conservative Central Office), p. 34; Marsh *et al.*, 'Private Members Bills and Moral Panic', p. 187.
41. HC Debs 30 June 1983 c698, 115w; *Guardian* 1 July 1983; Whitehouse, *Mightier than the Sword*, pp. 36–8; *Viewer and Listener* Summer 1983.
42. *Daily Mail* 8 July 1983; *Guardian* 15 July 1983.
43. *Church Times* 29 July 1983; *New Video Viewer* November 1983.
44. *Guardian* 12 October 1983; Whitehouse, *Mightier than the Sword*, pp. 43–4.
45. *Daily Mail* 2 November 1983; *Guardian* 11 November 1983.
46. *Times* 12 November 1983; *Guardian* 12 November 1983.
47. *Church of England Newspaper* 2 December 1983.
48. *Daily Mail* 21, 26 January 1984; *Times* 21 January 1984.
49. For accounts of the Video Enquiry see *Guardian* 13 December 1983; Barker, *Video Nasties*, chapter 5; Geoffrey Barlow and Alison Hill (eds.), *Video Violence and Children* (Hodder and Stoughton, 1985), chapter 3.
50. *Daily Telegraph* 2 February 1984.
51. *Guardian* 17 March 1984.
52. *Guardian* 2 December 1983.
53. *Daily Telegraph* 18 October 1985; *The Times* 17 October 1985; *Viewer and Listener* Autumn 1985.
54. *Daily Mail* 15 November 1985; *Guardian* 15, 22 November 1985.
55. *Viewer and Listener* Spring 1986; *Sunday Times* 1 December 1985; *Daily Telegraph* 2, 7 December 1985; *New Statesman* 13 December 1985. On the Churchill bill, see D. Marsh, M. Read and B. Myers, 'Don't Panic: The Obscene Publications (Protection of Children, Etc.) Amendment Bill (1985)', *Parliamentary Affairs* 40.1, January 1987.
56. *Daily Express* 18 December 1985; *Guardian* 2, 4 December 1985; *Daily Telegraph* 9 December 1985; *Times* 9 December 1985.

57. *Guardian* 30 December 1985; *Universe* 3 January 1986.
58. HC Debs 24 January 1986 c584, 591; *Daily Telegraph* 25 January 1986.
59. HC Debs 24 January 1986 c560–1, 593; *New Statesman* 13 December 1985; *Viewer and Listener* Spring 1986.
60. *Guardian* 7 February 1986.
61. *Daily Telegraph* 24 February 1986.
62. *Universe* 11 April 1986.
63. *Guardian* 26 April 1986; *Sunday Telegraph* 4 May 1986.
64. *The Times* 8 July 1986; *Guardian* 6 November 1986; *Independent* 28 October 1986.
65. *Independent* 4 November 1986.
66. *Independent* 21 November 1986; *Times* 11 December 1986, 18 February 1987; *Daily Telegraph* 12 February 1987; *Western Morning News* 5 March 1987.
67. *The Times* 4 April 1987; *Daily Mail* 4 April 1987.
68. *Independent* 8 May 1987; *Daily Telegraph* 20 May 1987; Conservative Central Office, *The Next Moves Forward* (1987), p. 70.
69. *Guardian* 14, 19 September, 8 October 1987; *Independent* 14 September 1987.
70. *The Times* 14 December 1987; *Guardian* 12 February 1988; *Mail on Sunday* 28 February 1988.
71. *Guardian* 14 March, 14 April 1988.
72. *Daily Telegraph* 23 April 1988.
73. *Independent* 5 May 1988; *Times* 17 May 1988.
74. *Daily Express* 9 June 1988.
75. *Guardian* 25 November 1988.
76. *Daily Telegraph* 23 February 1989; *Sunday Telegraph* 5, 12 March 1989; *Observer* 12 March 1989.
77. *Daily Telegraph* 11 April 1989.
78. *Daily Mail* 1 September 1989; *Daily Telegraph* 1 September 1989.
79. *Guardian* 1 September 1989; *The Times* 4 September, 1 November, 24 November 1989.
80. *Comments on Some Aspects of the Report of the Committee on Obscenity and Film Censorship* (n.d.), pp. 3, 6, 9.
81. D. Holbrook, *Pornography and Hate* (Responsible Society, 1972), pp. 2, 4–6, 10.
82. Whitehouse, *Whatever Happened to Sex?*, pp. 283, 176, 178, 211–22, 227, 241, 228.
83. Ibid., chapter 2, pp. 181, 254–5.
84. Ibid., pp. 246–53.
85. Ibid., p. 253.
86. Ibid., pp. 240–1.
87. *Pornography . . . a matter of taste?* (VALA, n.d., c1979), pp. 9, 7–8.
88. Leeds WAVAW statement, *Spare Rib* October 1982.
89. Laura Lederer (ed.), *Take Back the Night* (William Morrow, New York, 1980), pp. 19–20; *Guardian* 15 November 1989.
90. *Spare Rib* December 1977.
91. Whitehouse, *Whatever Happened to Sex?*, p. 254.

92. *Nationwide Festival of Light Bulletin* 6 (n.d., 1979), 11 (September 1981); *Third Way* March 1984.
93. *21st Century Christian* January 1989; *CARE Review* 1, 1989.
94. *Guardian* 15 November 1989; *CARE News* 25 (December–February 1989–90), 26 (March–May 1990).

6 The Politics of Sex Education

1. On developments in sex education, see Philip Meredith, *Sex Education. Political Issues in Britain and Europe* (Routledge, 1989). The total membership of Family and Youth Concern is approximately 25,000. Interview with Valerie Riches, 5 October 1990.
2. *Home* January–February 1987; *Daily Telegraph* 8 February 1980.
3. *Daily Telegraph* 15 March 1980; *Times* 15 March 1980; HL Debs 14 March 1980 c1390–2.
4. HL Debs 24 March 1980 c549–71.
5. *Daily Telegraph* 1 April 1980; HC Debs 1 April 1980 c162–3.
6. *Guardian* 15 May 1980.
7. HC Debs 4 August 1980 c196–215.
8. 'Saying No Isn't Always Easy' (Youth Concerned); *Guardian* 16 September 1980; *Times* 16 September 1980; *Universe* 19 September 1980.
9. *Universe* 29 August 1980.
10. HC Debs 25 November 1980 c64.
11. *Daily Telegraph* 28 April 1981; *Guardian* 28 April 1981; *Daily Mail* 28 April 1981; *Family Bulletin* 33 (Autumn 1981).
12. *New Society* 18 February 1982.
13. *Daily Telegraph* 3 June 1981.
14. *Daily Telegraph* 17 June 1981.
15. *Daily Telegraph* 23 June, 2 July 1981; *Times Educational Supplement* 31 July 1981.
16. *Daily Telegraph* 14 October 1981; *Times Educational Supplement* 16 October 1981.
17. *Family Bulletin* 35 (Summer 1982); HC Debs 16 March 1982 c191–2, 20 April 1982 c114; *Guardian* 21 April 1982.
18. *Daily Telegraph* 21 April 1982; *Family Bulletin* 36 (Autumn 1982).
19. *Daily Telegraph* 22 November, 18 December 1982.
20. *Daily Telegraph* 10 January 1983.
21. Rachel Tingle, *Gay Lessons* (Pickwick Books, 1986), p. 16; *Universe* 17 October 1986.
22. *New Statesman* 12 September 1986; HL Debs 15 April 1986 c646–52; *Daily Telegraph* 3, 4 June 1986.
23. *Daily Telegraph* 4 June 1986; *Daily Express* 4 June 1986.
24. *Christian Herald* 14 June 1986.
25. *Universe* 6 June 1986. For the National Council's formation, see e.g. *Church Times* 14 March 1986.
26. *Daily Telegraph* 4 June 1986.

27. *Daily Telegraph* 11 June 1986.
28. *Daily Mail* 1 July 1986; *Times* 1 July 1986.
29. *Guardian* 7 August 1986; *Daily Telegraph* 7 August 1986.
30. *The Times* 11 August 1986.
31. *The Times* 14 August 1986.
32. *The Times Educational Supplement* 15 August 1986.
33. *Guardian* 5 September 1986; *New Statesman* 12, 19 September 1986.
34. *The Times* 8 September 1986; Conservative Family Campaign, 'Sex Education and Your Child'.
35. *Guardian* 13, 16 September 1986.
36. *The Times Educational Supplement* 12 September 1986; *Church Times* 26 September 1986; *The Times* 23 September 1986.
37. *Universe* 19 September 1986; *Church of England Newspaper* 26 September 1986.
38. *The Times Educational Supplement* 10, 17 October 1986.
39. *Baptist Times* 25 January 1990.
40. (Birmingham) *Daily News* 8 October 1986; *Daily Mail* 14 October 1986.
41. *Independent* 20 October 1986.
42. *Guardian* 23 October 1986.
43. *Universe* 24 October 1986.
44. *Church of England Newspaper* 31 October 1986; *Evangelism Today* December 1986.
45. Family and Youth Concern AGM, 15 November 1986, personal attendance.
46. (Hornsey) *Journal* 9 May 1986; *Time Out* 22–9 October 1986; *Fight Back* number 24, Tottenham Conservative Association; *Lesbian and Gay Socialist* Winter 1987–88. For events in Haringey, see Davina Cooper, 'Positive Images in Haringey: A Struggle for Identity' in Carol Jones and Pat Mahony (eds.), *Learning our Lines. Sexuality and Social Control in Education* (Women's Press, 1989); Les Levidow, 'Witches and Seducers: moral panics for our time' in Barry Richards (ed.), *Crises of the Self* (Free Association Books, 1989).
47. *Daily Telegraph* 7 July 1986; Tottenham Conservative Association, 'Family Life under Grave Threat', press release, 2 July 1986.
48. (Hornsey) *Journal* 8, 29 August, 17 October 1986; *Daily Telegraph* 20 August 1986; *Guardian* 21 August 1986; *The Times Educational Supplement* 29 August 1986.
49. *Guardian* 10 September 1986.
50. (Hornsey) *Journal* 15 August 1986; *Daily Mail* 16 September 1986; (Haringey) *Independent* 21 August, 30 October 1986; *Fight Back* number 27.
51. *The Times Educational Supplement* 26 September 1986; (Hornsey) *Journal* 5 September 1986; *Daily Mail* 17 September 1986.
52. *Guardian* 14 October 1986; *Daily Mail* 15 October 1986; *Time Out* 22–9 October 1986.
53. Tingle, *Gay Lessons*; see e.g. *Daily Mail* 6 October 1986, *Daily Telegraph* 7 October 1986.

54. *Daily Telegraph* 6 October 1986.
55. *The Times Educational Supplement* 17 October 1986.
56. *Church of England Newspaper* 14 November 1986.
57. (Hornsey) *Journal* 31 October 1986; *Daily Telegraph* 1 November 1986; *Time Out* 26 November–3 December 1986.
58. *City Limits* 20–7 November 1986; *Time Out* 22–9 October 1986; (Hornsey) *Journal* 28 November 1986.
59. (Birmingham) *Choice* 11 March 1988; HL Debs 18 December 1986 c311, 320, 332–7. For the Halsbury bill and subsequent developments, see Sue Sanders and Gill Spraggs, 'Section 28 and Education' in Jones and Mahony, *Learning Our Lines.*
60. (Hornsey) *Journal* 30 January 1987; *Daily Mail* 24 January 1987.
61. *The Times* 28 January 1987. On Hart in the miners' strike, see e.g. Martin Adeney and John Lloyd, *The Miners' Strike 1984–5* (RKP, 1986), pp. 161–4.
62. *Daily Mail* 23 January 1987.
63. *City Limits* 29 January–5 February 1987.
64. *Time Out* 28 January–4 February, 4–11 February 1987; *City Limits* 5–12 February 1987.
65. (Hornsey) *Journal* 30 January, 6 February, 13 February, 13 March 1987.
66. HL Debs 11 February 1987 c706–9; *Independent* 18 February 1987.
67. *Christian Herald* 28 February 1987.
68. *Haringey Advertiser* 2, 30 April 1987; *Daily Express* 14 April 1987.
69. HC Debs 8 May 1987 c997–8, 1002, 1004–5; *Independent* 9 May 1987.
70. HC Debs 14 May 1987 c413.
71. *The Times* 10 June 1987; *Guardian* 23 June 1987; *Time Out* 30 December–6 January 1988; A Week In Politics (Channel 4) 9 December 1987.
72. *Towards a new Sexual Revolution* (Christians in Education and the Order of Christian Unity, sponsored by CARE, 1988), p. 5; Meredith, *Sex Education*, pp. 89–91.
73. *Daily Mail* 26 September 1987.
74. House of Commons Standing Committee A on Local Government Bill, 29th Sitting, 8 December 1987, c1199, 1202–14; *Guardian* 9, 15 December 1987.
75. HC Debs 15 December 1987 c988–9, 998, 995; *Guardian* 2 February 1988.
76. *Independent* 10 March 1988; *Times* 11 March 1988.
77. *Monthly News Bulletin* October 1988.
78. Conservative Family Campaign, 'The Family Needs Friends' (brochure); *Guardian* 8 April 1988.
79. (Hornsey) *Journal* 11, 31 December 1987; *New Statesman* 13 May 1988.
80. *Universe* 6 May 1988; *Independent* 26 May 1988.
81. *Sunday Times* 29 May 1988; *The Times Educational Supplement* 3 June 1988; *Gay Times* July 1988.
82. Conservative Family Campaign, 'Sex Education and Your Child'; *Towards a new Sexual Revolution.*

83. *Education or Manipulation?* (Responsible Society, 1975), pp.1–2, 9–10 and unnumbered page.
84. K. H. Kavanagh, *Sex Education. Its Uses and Abuses* (Responsible Society).
85. *Daily Telegraph* 13 March 1980.
86. V. Riches, *Sex and Social Engineering* (Family and Youth Concern, 1986).
87. Interview with Valerie Riches, 5 October 1990.
88. *Haringey Advertiser* 2 October 1986.
89. *Family Matters* September 1986; *Guardian* 12 December 1987.
90. HL Debs 21 May 1986 c230; HC Debs 8 May 1987 c997–8.

7   The Thatcher Government and the Policing of Sexuality

1. See Simon Watney, *Policing Desire* (Methuen, 1987); Pete Aggleton and Hilary Homans (eds.), *Social Aspects of AIDS*, Falmer Press 1988, Mort, *Dangerous Sexualities*; Erica Carter and Simon Watney (eds.), *Taking Liberties. AIDS and Cultural Politics* (Serpent's Tail, 1989). For Anderton, see *Daily Express* 12 December 1986.
2. HC Debs 30 April 1986 c992.
3. Watney, *Policing Desire*, pp. 136–9; John Street, 'British Government Policy on AIDS', *Parliamentary Affairs* 41.4, October 1988, pp. 492–3.
4. *Guardian* 11 March 1987.
5. *Daily Mail* 9 March 1988.
6. *Daily Express* 7 June 1988.
7. *Heart of the Matter* (BBC1), 8 March 1987; *Sunday Times Magazine* 21 June 1987.
8. *Guardian* 10 September 1986.
9. *Independent* 18 November 1986; *Family Matters* February 1987.
10. *Daily Express* 22 November 1986.
11. *Daily Mail* 21 March 1987.
12. *The Times* 14 December 1988. For Sherman in the seventies, see Morrison Halcrow, *Keith Joseph. A Single Mind* (Macmillan, 1989), pp. 61–7, 81–4.
13. *Guardian* 18 January 1985.
14. *Independent* 13 November 1986.
15. *Guardian* 22 November 1986; *Birmingham Evening Mail* 20 December 1986.
16. *Independent* 7 November 1986.
17. *Church Times* 2 January 1987; *Church of England Newspaper* 9 January 1987.
18. *The Times* 21 April 1987; *Family Bulletin* 50 (Summer 1987).
19. *Daily Telegraph* 12 March 1987.
20. *Church Times* 10 April 1987.
21. *Daily Telegraph* 14 July 1987; *Guardian* 3 August 1987.
22. *Guardian* 3, 15 August 1987; (Hornsey) *Journal* 21 August 1987.

23. *Universe* 13 May 1988; *Coventry Evening Telegraph* 9 May 1988; *Family Bulletin* 54 (Autumn 1988).
24. *Daily Telegraph* 23 May 1988; Digby Anderson, *The Megaphone Solution* (Social Affairs Unit, 1988), pp. 16–18.
25. *Family Bulletin* 55 (Winter 1989), 56 (Summer 1989).
26. *Sunday Times* 19 November 1989; *City Limits* 30 November–7 December 1989.
27. *Daily Mail* 7 November 1989; *Sunday Telegraph* 19 November 1989.
28. *Sunday Times* 19 November 1989; *Sunday Correspondent* 21 January 1990.
29. *Sunday Correspondent* 21 January 1990; *Family Bulletin* 56 (Summer 1989); *Sunday Times* 19 November 1989; 'The Truth About AIDS', Family and Youth Concern video.
30. Dr. Margaret White, *AIDS and the Positive Alternatives* (Marshall Pickering, 1987), p. vi; *Love and Life* Winter 1984–5.
31. *Sunday Times* 19 November 1989.
32. Martin Kettle and Lucy Hodges, *Uprising!* (Pan, 1982), pp. 183–4.
33. David Edgar, 'The Free or the Good' in Ruth Levitas (ed.), *The Ideology of the New Right* (Polity Press, 1986), pp. 55–6; *Daily Telegraph* 20 March 1982; *Sunday Times* 28 March 1982.
34. *Daily Express* 29 March 1982.
35. *Daily Telegraph* 27 July 1982; *Financial Times* 14 May 1983.
36. *Guardian* 31 January, 17, 18 February 1983; *Sunday Times* 22 May 1983.
37. *Daily Express* 2 August 1985.
38. Norman Tebbit, *Britain's Future – A Conservative Vision* (CPC, 1985), p. 6.
39. Ibid., pp. 7, 15.
40. Ibid., pp. 15–16.
41. *Daily Mail* 14, 15, 18, 20, 30 November 1985.
42. *Daily Express* 15 November 1985.
43. *Diverse Reports* (Channel 4), 15 January 1986.
44. Norman Tebbit, *The Values of Freedom* (CPC, 1986), pp. 3, 9–11.
45. *Daily Mail* 10 April 1986.
46. *Daily Telegraph* 21 August 1986.
47. *Times* 8 October 1986; *New Statesman* 14 November 1986.
48. *Daily Mail* 15 November 1985.
49. *Daily Mail* 30 November 1985.
50. *The Next Moves Forward*, pp. 70, 18; *Daily Mail* 15 May 1987.
51. *Daily Express* 28 May 1987; *Daily Mail* 28 May 1987.
52. *Daily Telegraph* 20 March 1989; *Guardian* 20 March 1989.
53. *Daily Mail* 18 January 1990; *Guardian* 18, 31 January 1990.
54. *Daily Mail* 16 April 1990; The 'No Turning Back' Group of Conservative MPs, *Choice and Responsibility. The Enabling State* (Conservative Political Centre, 1990), pp. 8, 12; Lord Joseph, *Rewards of Parenthood?* (Centre for Policy Studies, 1990), pp. 9–12; *Times* 21 May 1990; *Today* 10 May 1990; *Economist* 30 June 1990; *Sunday Telegraph* 8 July 1990.

55. *Today* 10 October 1990; *Independent* 10 October 1990; *Guardian* 10 October 1990.
56. Miriam David, 'Teaching and Preaching Sexual Morality', *Journal of Education*, 166 (1), March 1984; 'Moral and Maternal: The Family in the Right' in Levitas, *The Ideology of the New Right*, pp. 136, 152.
57. Tessa ten Tusscher, in Judith Evans *et al.* (eds.), *Feminism and Political Theory* (SAGE, 1986), pp. 67, 72, 73–6, 81.
58. Bob Jessop *et al.*, *Thatcherism* (Polity Press, 1988), p. 51; Desmond S. King, *The New Right* (Macmillan, 1987), pp. 20–1.
59. Stuart Hall, 'No Light At the End of the Tunnel', *Marxism Today* December 1986, p. 16.
60. Andrew Gamble, *The Free Economy and the Strong State* (Macmillan, 1988), pp. 198–201.
61. David Edgar, 'Bitter Harvest', *New Socialist* September–October 1983, pp. 19, 23–4.
62. David, 'Teaching and Preaching'; Ian Taylor, 'Law and Order, Moral Order', *Socialist Register 1987* (Merlin Press),pp. 315–16, 323.
63. Jeffrey Weeks, 'Clause for Concern', *Marxism Today* February 1988; Ruth Levitas, review, *Critical Social Policy* Autumn 1988.
64. Lynne Segal, 'The Heat in the Kitchen' in Stuart Hall and Martin Jacques (eds.), *The Politics of Thatcherism* (Lawrence and Wishart, 1983), pp. 213–14.
65. Beatrix Campbell, *The Iron Ladies* (Virago, 1987), pp. 173–5.
66. Elizabeth Wilson, 'Thatcherism and Women', *Socialist Register 1987*, pp. 200–5, 222–7.
67. Lucy Bland, 'Sex and Morals', *Marxism Today* September 1985.

8 Morality and the Right

1. Edgar, 'The Free or the Good'.
2. Edgar, 'Bitter Harvest', p. 23.
3. *Free Nation* January 1983.
4. 'Family Patrol Group?', *Searchlight* April 1983; Edgar, 'Bitter Harvest'.
5. *Free Nation* February 1983.
6. Ibid.
7. Ibid., March 1983.
8. Ibid., October 1983.
9. Ibid., November 1983.
10. Ibid., December 1983.
11. Ibid., November 1983.
12. Ibid., January 1984.
13. Ibid., February 1984.
14. Ibid., March–April 1984.
15. Ibid., October–November 1985.
16. Ibid., February 1987, December 1986; *Times Educational Supplement* 15 May 1987; *City Limits* 9–16 July 1987.

17. *Free Nation* June 1987.
18. Philip Vander Elst, *The Future of Freedom: Agenda for the 1990s* (Freedom Association), pp. 2, 4–7.
19. *Free Nation* June 1983, April 1986, August 1986.
20. *Conservative Newsline* September 1985.
21. Ibid., November 1985.
22. Ibid., January 1986.
23. Ibid., February 1986.
24. Ibid., April 1986.
25. Ibid., May 1986.
26. Ibid., February 1987.
27. Ibid., March 1987.
28. David Botsford, *Against Censorship* (Libertarian Alliance, Political Notes 20, n.d.); Mathew O'Keefe, *Marriage and the State* (Libertarian Alliance, Political Notes 31, 1988); Simon Mcllwaine, *Freedom, Law and Morality: A Libertarian–Conservative View* (Libertarian Alliance, Political Notes 29, 1986).
29. See e.g. *Guardian* 4 April 1985; Richard N. Kelly, *Conservative Party Conferences* (Manchester University Press, 1989), chapter 6.
30. Mock copy of *The Times* 12 October 1996, circulated at FCS seminar, 1986; *New Agenda* Winter 1985–6.
31. *New Agenda* Winter 1985–6.
32. *New Agenda* Winter 1985–6, Autumn 1985.
33. Personal attendance at FCS Seminar, 25 October 1986; Nigel Ashford, 'Morality and Conservatism', hand-out at FCS seminar.
34. Scottish Federation of Conservative Students, *A Conservative Manifesto for Scotland*, May 1986, pp. 22–4.
35. *Scotsman* 16 May 1986; *New Society* 23 May 1986; *Times Higher Education Supplement* 23 May 1986.
36. Tim Evans and Antoine Clarke, *A Conservative Manifesto for Scotland* (Libertarian Alliance, Political Notes 42, 1989); *Guardian* 11 October 1990; *Independent* 11 October 1990; *Sun* 11 October 1990; telephone interview with Sean Gabb, 27 October 1990.
37. *City Limits* 1–8 January 1987.
38. *Crossbow* Summer 1986; *Church of England Newspaper* 21 March 1986; *Family Matters* May 1986; *Prophecy Today* January–February 1987; interview with Graham Webster-Gardiner, 16 August 1990.
39. *Church of England Newspaper* 21 March 1986.
40. *Guardian* 26 March 1986; *Sun* 9 April 1986. See e.g *Sun* 10 April 1986.
41. *Guardian* 26 March, 10 April 1986; *Buzz* May 1986; interview with Graham Webster-Gardiner, 16 August 1990.
42. Dr. Adrian Rogers and Bill Clements, *The Moral Basis of Freedom* (Victoria Books, 1985), pp. ii, 12, 11, 29, 56–7.
43. *Daily Telegraph* 14 March 1984; *Daily Mail* 14 March 1984; 'A Political Outlook for the Family'(Western Area CPC Advisory Committee).
44. *Crossbow* Summer 1986.

45. *Family Matters* April 1990; interview with Graham Webster- Gardiner, 16 August 1990.
46. *Prag* 34, Easter 1986.
47. *Crossbow* Summer 1986; *City Limits* 16–23 October 1986.
48. *Prophecy Today* January–February 1987.
49. *Independent* 28 May 1987.
50. *Private Eye* 24 July 1987.
51. *Family Matters* August 1987.
52. *Family Matters* May 1988; Stephen Green and Graham Webster-Gardiner, *A Tax on Marriage* (Christians in Britain, 1988); *Daily Telegraph* 16 February 1990; *Wolverhampton Express and Star* 15 March 1990; interview with Graham Webster-Gardiner, 16 August 1990.
53. Digby Anderson and Graham Dawson, (eds.), *Family Portraits* (Social Affairs Unit, 1986), p. 10; *Sunday Telegraph* 31 July 1988. On recent developments concerning the New Right and morality, see Joan Isaac, 'The New Right and the Moral Society', *Parliamentary Affairs* 43.2, April 1990.
54. *Back from the Brink* (Church Society, 1986); *The Defence of the Family* (Church Society, 1987).
55. See e.g. Angela Ellis-Jones, 'The Politics of Economics',*Salisbury Review* April 1985; *Times* 15 February, 13 September, 13 December 1983.
56. *Daily Mail* 14 May 1990.

9 Moral Crusades and the Right

1. Hall *et al.*, *Policing The Crisis*, pp. 314–15.
2. Hall and Jacques, *The Politics of Thatcherism*, p. 51. The article was originally published in late 1979.
3. Edgar, 'Bitter Harvest', p. 19.
4. David, 'Teaching and Preaching'; 'Morality and Maternity', *Critical Social Policy* 16 (Summer 1986), p. 40.
5. Stanworth, *Reproductive Technologies*, p. 23; Paul Gordon and Francesca Klug, *New Right, New Racism* (Searchlight, 1986), pp. 8, 11.
6. Jessop *et al.*, *Thatcherism*, p. 79.
7. Alan Hunt, (ed.), *Marxism and Democracy* (Lawrence and Wishart, 1980), pp. 172–3, 176–81.
8. Weeks, *Sex, Politics*, p. 278.
9. *The Times* 5 January 1987.
10. Marsh and Chambers, *Abortion Politics*, pp. 62, 83; *Catholic Herald* 16 December 1983, 22 June 1984, 2 May 1986; *Human Concern* 18 (Spring 1985); conversation with Paul Lennon, SPUC Conference, 15 September 1990; Ann E. Farmer, 'The Right to Choose' (Labour Life Group); Labour Life Group executive meeting, Coventry, 24 February 1990, personal attendance.

11. *Catholic Herald* 10 January 1975, 28 September 1984; letter from Pauline M. Connor, Feminists Against Eugenics, 16 October 1989 *Freedom* June, July 1988.
12. *Family Matters* October 1989; *OCU Journal* Autumn–Winter 1988; LIFE headed paper for press releases, 1989; *Freedom Today* June 1989.
13. *Human Concern* 3 (Summer 1979).
14. *Scottish Catholic Observer* 28 December 1979.
15. *Human Concern* 5 (Summer 1980).
16. *Universe* 14 November 1980; *Scottish Catholic Observer* 28 November 1980.
17. *Human Concern* 27 (Spring 1989); interview with Phyllis Bowman, 4 September 1990; *LIFE News* 8 (Spring–Summer 1981).
18. *Universe* 12 June 1981.
19. *Catholic Herald* 7 October 1983.
20. *Catholic Herald* 16 October 1981; *Catholic Pictorial* 5 July 1981.
21. *Birmingham Evening Mail* 4 June 1981, 7 May 1982. For LIFE support for a local election candidate in London more recently, see *Universe* 30 October 1988.
22. *Guardian* 12 November 1981; *Catholic Herald* 20 November 1981.
23. *Human Concern* 22 (Summer 1986), 24 (Midsummer 1987).
24. *Wolverhampton Express and Star* 28 April 1979; see also e.g. *Daily Mirror* 27 October 1978.
25. (Hornsey) *Journal* 22 May 1987.
26. *Crusade* January 1982.
27. *CARE Review* 1, 1989.
28. (Bournemouth) *Evening Echo* 3 June 1987; Valerie Riches, 'The Politics of Responsible Parenthood' in Richard Whitfield (ed.), *Families Matter* (Marshall Pickering, 1987), pp. 21–30; interview with Valerie Riches, 5 October 1990.
29. Gillick, *Mother's Tale*, pp. 210, 250–1.
30. Whitehouse, *Mightier than the Sword*, pp. 103–5.
31. Whitehouse, *Whatever Happened to Sex?*, pp. 241–2, 103, 106.
32. *Viewer and Listener* Summer 1979, Autumn 1980; 'Current Communist Goals'; *Pornography ... A Matter of Taste?*, p. 9.
33. Whitehouse, *Whatever Happened to Sex?*, p. 227; *Sunday Times* 26 April 1981.
34. *Sunday Times* 19 October 1975; *Observer* Magazine 10 November 1968.
35. Whitehouse, *Who Does*, p. 112; *Viewer and Listener* January 1972.
36. *Viewer and Listener* Autumn 1969; Dillon McCarthy, *Atheist Agenda*.
37. See e.g. Tracey and Morrison, *Whitehouse*, pp. 57–69.
38. Arnold Lunn and Garth Lean, *The New Morality* (Blandford Press, 1964), pp. 38–9; Peter Howard, *Britain and the Beast* (Heinemann, 1963), pp. 96–7.
39. Tracey and Morrison, *Whitehouse*, pp. 61–9.
40. Tom Driberg, *The Mystery of Moral Re-armament* (Secker and Warburg, 1964), p. 239.

41. A. Ralph Epperson, *The Unseen Hand. An Introduction to the Conspiratorial View of History* (Publius Press, Tucson, 1985), pp. 399–400; *Sunday Times* 9 August 1970; W. Cleon Skousen, *The Naked Communist* (Ensign Publishing Co., Salt Lake City, 1961), pp. 72–3. On Lady Birdwood see e.g. *Spearhead* November 1972; *Searchlight* April 1985.

42. Cliff, in King and Nugent, *Respectable Rebels*, p. 136, citing Morrison and Tracey, *Opposition to the Age. A Study of the NVALA*, p. 31.

43. *CSA Newsletter* 7 (Winter 1978-9); Responsible Society press release 23 October 1976; *Bulletin of the Responsible Society* 17 (Summer 1976); *Why a Petition for Decency?* (New Life Press, 1972); *Nationwide Festival of Light Broadsheet* Autumn 1975.

44. Whitehouse, *Whatever Happened to Sex?*, pp. 70–72.

45. *Now!* 20 June 1980; Riches, *Sex and Social Engineering*, p. 6. When recently interviewed, she put a strong emphasis on the existence of an international network while saying that it was more a matter of power rather than whether it was left or right. Interview with Valerie Riches, 5 October 1990.

46. Johnston, *Who Needs the Family?*, p. 144.

47. Ibid., pp. 52–3, 71, 86–7, 112–13; Whitehouse, *Whatever Happened to Sex?*, pp. 88–9, 124–5.

48. *Family Bulletin* 52 (Winter 1988); *Feminism v. Mankind* (Family Publications, Wicken, 1990); *Church of England Newspaper* 21 March 1986.

49. LIFE, 'Abortion:The Feminist Sell Out' (leaflet).

50. See e.g. the leaflet cited in Chapter 2, reference 63.

51. White,*Two Million Silent Killings*, pp. 124–5; *Catholic Pictorial* 15 June 1986.

52. *Human Concern* 19 (Summer 1985); 22 (Summer 1986); interview with Phyllis Bowman, 4 September 1990.

53. *Human Concern* 7 (Spring 1981); White, *Two Million Silent Killings*, pp. 119–21.

54. *The Times* 28 October 1985; *Human Concern* 17 (Summer 1984); *Universe* 20 July 1984; Riches, *Sex and Social Engineering*, pp. 11–19.

55. *The Times* 7, 26 March 1985.

56. Gillick, *Dear Mrs. Gillick*, pp. 8, 216.

57. *Buzz* May 1986; *Crusade* January 1982.

58. *The Times* 15 October 1985.

59. *Daily Telegraph* 27 January 1986.

60. *The Times* 5 January 1987.

61. See e.g. Judith R. Walkowitz, 'Male Vice and Feminist Virtue: Feminism and the Politics of Prostitution in Nineteenth Century Britain', *History Workshop* Spring 1982; Mort, *Dangerous Sexualities*; Lucy Bland, *Banishing The Beast: Feminism, Sex and Morality, 1885–1918*, forthcoming.

62. *Sunday Times Magazine* 17 March 1985; *Sunday Times* 2 June 1985.

Index